Prayers Upon The Chosen Prophet Muhammad ﷺ

"with Arabic Text and Transliteration"

Published by Fercan Corporation

Waterloo, Ontario, Canada

www.fercan.ca

ISBN: 978-1-7776080-6-4

First Edition 2025

Printed in Canada

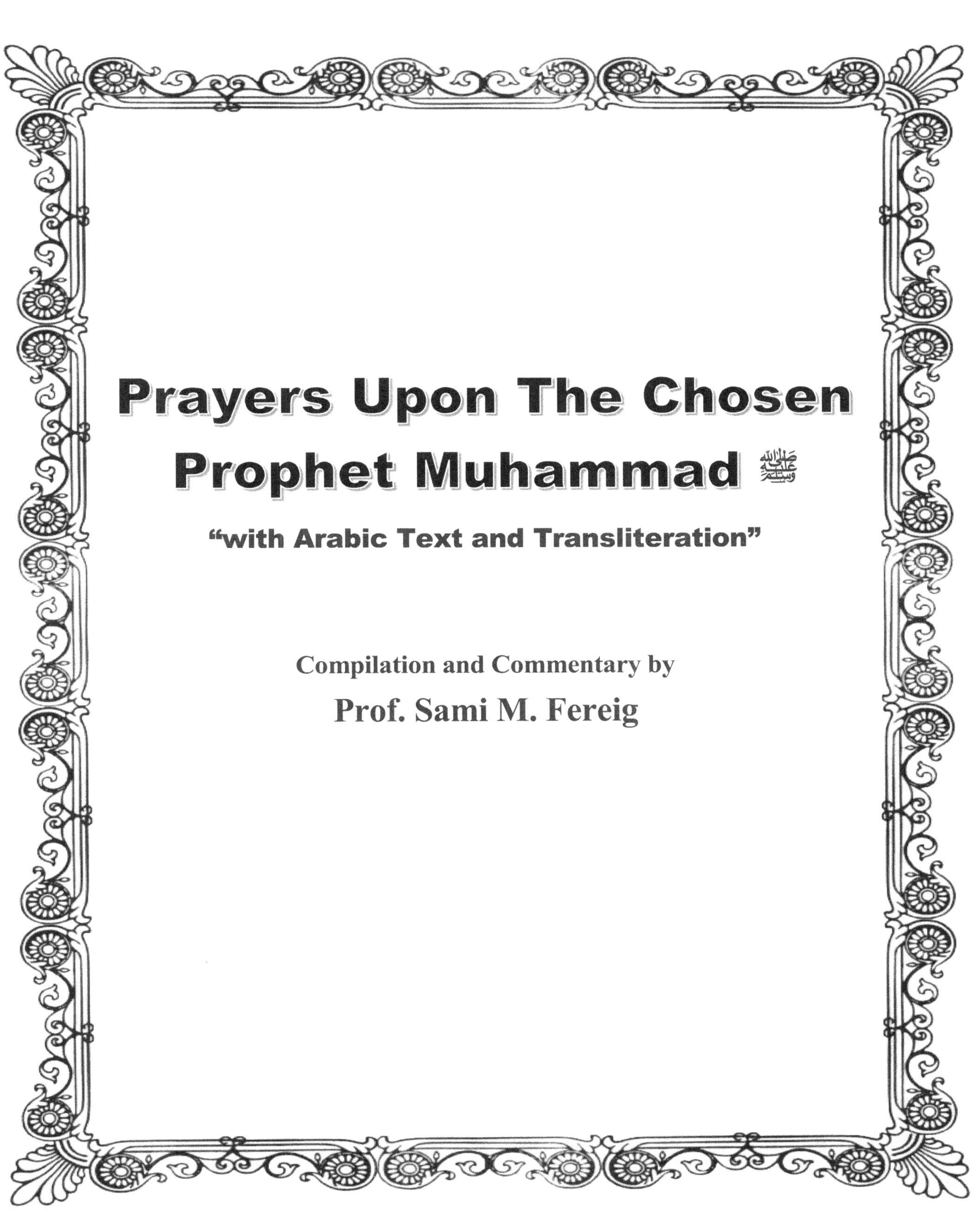

Prayers Upon The Chosen Prophet Muhammad ﷺ

"with Arabic Text and Transliteration"

Compilation and Commentary by

Prof. Sami M. Fereig

Contents

❋ *... say, "Verily, unto God do we belong and, verily, unto Him we shall return."* ❋ *[Q 2:156]*

Praise be to God for His Compassion and Mercy, and for what He has ordained and willed.

On the evening of 8th July 2008 (5th Rajab 1429 AH), our son Omer was reading a book while sitting under a maple tree in Christie Pits Park, Toronto. At about 7:30 pm, this tree was struck by lightning, and Omer departed this life. He was 28 years old.

He was a graduate of Civil Engineering at the University of Waterloo and had recently married. All his family and friends greatly miss him, and we pray that he is now in paradise.

This book has been compiled in Omer's memory, hoping that others might benefit from its contents, especially those who have gone through similar experiences and difficult circumstances. We hope that they will keep Omer and us in their prayers.

❋ *... call upon Him in reverence and hope. Surely the Mercy of God is ever near to the virtuous.* ❋ *[Q 7:56]*

❋ *Their supplication therein shall be, "Glory be to Thee, O God!" And therein their greeting shall be, "Peace." And the conclusion of their supplication shall be, "Praise be to God, Lord of the worlds!"* ❋ *[Q 10:10]*

إهـــداء

الحمد لله وإنا لله وإنا إليه راجعون

الحمد لله على قضاء الله وقدره وهو الرحمن الرحيم، ماضٍ فيَّ حكمه عدلٌ فيَّ قضاؤه، موقنٌ بأن رحمة الله أَجَّلُ من حبنا لفلذات أكبادنا وألطف. ولعل تقديم هذا العمل يمثل إضاءة في طريق الواصلين إلى الرضا والنور الإلهي وسبيلاً لرحمة الله على روح المرحوم نجلي بإذن الله تعالى

المهندس/ عمـر سامي محمد فـريـج

((ونسأل القارئ الدعاء له ولنا ولسائر المسلمين بالرحمة والمغفرة))

قال تعالى ﴿إِنَّ رَحْمَتَ اللَّهِ قَرِيبٌ مِّنَ الْمُحْسِنِينَ﴾

[الأعراف: ٥٦]

وآخر دعوانا أن الحمد لله رب العالمين

Acknowledgements

I wish to express my gratitude to my wife, Catherine (Um Omer), for her help in editing this book. I also give my sincere thanks to Dr. Mohammad Rustom, Professor of Islamic Studies and Global Philosophy and Director of the Carleton Centre for the Study of Islam at Carleton University in Ottawa, Ontario, and Dr. Atif Khalil, Associate Professor in the Department of Religious Studies at the University of Lethbridge, Alberta, and Dr. Hany Talat at the University of Calgary, Alberta for their helpful comments on the text and title of this book.

I also acknowledge the efforts of Mr. Ahmed Radwan and Mr. Mohamed El-Nshrtawy at Dar Al-Rida Corporation in Cairo, Egypt, for their help in gathering the Quranic verses and Prophetic Hadith used in this book and for preparing and formatting the manuscript. My special thanks go to Mr. Radwan for designing the book's front and back covers.

From the visit of the book's compiler, Dr. Sami Muhammad Farij, to the Jazuli Zawiya in Marrakesh, Morocco.

Dr. Sami with Hajj ʿAbd al-Rahman al-Talmudi exchanging books.

Dr. Sami in front of the door of the mausoleum of Sidi Muhammad ibn Sulayman al-Jazuli.

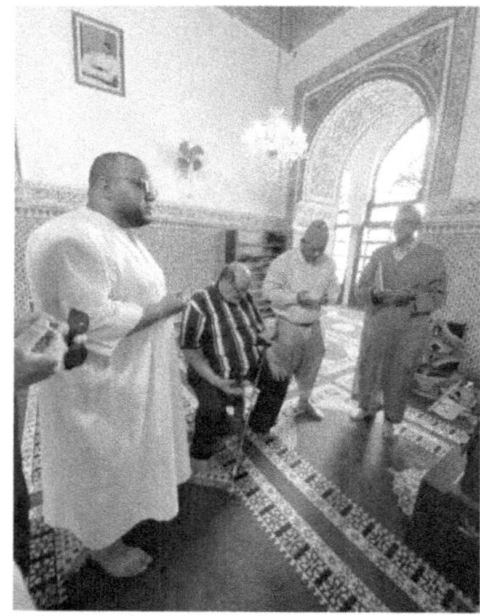

Dr. Sami with Mr. Ahmad Muhammad al-Mir beside him.

Dr. Sami with Hajj Ahmad Baltaqi "al-Qarmudi," presenting him with the book Dala'il al-Khayrat.

Introduction

The meaning of the Arabic words 'dhikr Allah' is to engage in remembering and praising God, exalting and glorifying Him, and sanctifying and thanking Him for everything He has bestowed upon us.

حيث قال الله -تعالى-: (وَمَا خَلَقْتُ الْجِنَّ وَالْإِنْسَ إِلَّا لِيَعْبُدُونِ). [51 الذاريات: 56]

{ And I have not created the invisible beings (jinn) and mankind to any other end than that they worship Me } *[Q 51:56]*

ويقول الله -سبحانه وتعالى-: ﴿ الَّذِينَ ءَامَنُوا وَتَطْمَئِنُّ قُلُوبُهُم بِذِكْرِ اللَّهِ أَلَا بِذِكْرِ اللَّهِ تَطْمَئِنُّ الْقُلُوبُ ۝ ﴾[الرعد: 28]،

{ … those who believe and whose hearts find peace in the remembrance of God. Truly in the remembrance of God, hearts do find peace. } *[Q 13:28]*

The tranquillity of one's heart is linked to the remembrance of God, the Most High. Remembering God is the key to peace of mind and reassurance and is a secret between the believer and his Lord. In it, believers feel close to God, thereby increasing their spirituality and tenderness of heart.

وعن جويرية بنت الحارث أم المؤمنين رضي الله عنها قالت أنَّ النَّبِيَّ صَلَّى اللهُ عليه وَسَلَّمَ خَرَجَ مِن عِندِهَا بُكْرَةً حِينَ صَلَّى الصُّبْحَ وَهِي في مَسْجِدِهَا، ثُمَّ رَجَعَ بَعْدَ أَنْ أَضْحَى وَهِي جَالِسَةٌ، فَقَالَ: ما زِلْتِ عَلى الحَالِ الَّتِي فَارَقْتُكِ عَلَيْهَا؟ قَالَتْ: نَعَمْ، قالَ النَّبِيُّ صَلَّى اللهُ عليه وَسَلَّمَ: لَقَدْ قُلْتُ بَعْدَكِ أَرْبَعَ كَلِمَاتٍ ثَلَاثَ مَرَّاتٍ، لو وُزِنَتْ بما قُلْتِ مُنْذُ اليَومِ لَوَزَنَتْهُنَّ: سُبْحَانَ الله وَبِحَمْدِهِ، عَدَدَ خَلْقِهِ، وَرِضَا نَفْسِهِ، وَزِنَةَ عَرْشِهِ، وَمِدَادَ كَلِمَاتِهِ.

Juwairiya, a wife of the Prophet (ﷺ) (may God be pleased with her), reported that God's Messenger (ﷺ) came out from her apartment one morning as she was busy observing the dawn prayer in her place of worship. He (ﷺ) returned in the forenoon while she was still sitting there. He (ﷺ) said: "Have you been in the same seat since I left you." She replied, 'Yes.' Thereupon, God's Apostle (ﷺ) said, "I recited four words three times after I left you, and if these are weighed against those you have recited since the morning, these will outweigh them. They are: 'Glory (be to) God' (subhaan Allah), 'Praise (is due to) God' (alhamdu lillah) according to the number of His creation, the contentment of His Self, the weight of His Throne, and the ink used to record the words for His Praise." [1]

وفي الحديث عن أبي هريرة رضي الله عنه قال: كانَ رَسولُ الله ﷺ يَسِيرُ في طَرِيقِ مَكَّةَ، فَمَرَّ عَلى جَبَلٍ يُقَالُ له: جُمْدَانُ، فقَالَ: سِيرُوا، هذا جُمْدَانُ، سَبَقَ المُفَرِّدُونَ، قالوا: وَما المُفَرِّدُونَ يا رَسولَ الله؟ قالَ: الذَّاكِرُونَ الله كَثِيرًا وَالذَّاكِرَاتُ. ".

Abu Huraira (may God be content with him) reported that God's Messenger (ﷺ) was travelling on the path leading to Mecca when he happened to pass by a mountain called Jumdan. He said, "Proceed on, it is Jumdan, and the 'Mufradun' have gone ahead."

---

(1) The speaker: **Muslim** – Source: Sahih Muslim – page or number: 2726. Conclusion of the speaker: sound.

They (the Companions of the Prophet, pbuh) asked, 'God's Messenger, who are the 'Mufradun?' He replied, "They are those (males and females) who remember God much." [1]

There are many types of remembrance, including the following:

- The best remembrance and the highest in rank is the Noble Quran. Reciting it, reading it and reflecting on it are among the best ways the believer can remember his Lord. Glory be to Him, the Most High. It is a Book of Remembrance described by God, the Most High, in His saying, "And the Qur'an is remembrance."
- Mentioning the names of God, Glory be to Him, the Most High, and His attributes, and praising Him for them. And venerating and sanctifying Him for what is worthy of Him, Glory be to Him, the Most High, such as saying: "Glory be to God, all praise is due to God, there is no deity but God, and God is the greatest."

وذلك لما ورد في الحديث الصَّحيح عَنْ أَبِي هُرَيْرَةَ، قَالَ: قَالَ رَسُولُ الله صَلَّى اللهُ عَلَيْهِ وَسَلَّمَ: لأَنْ أَقُولَ: سُبْحَانَ الله، وَالْحَمْدُ لله، وَلَا إِلَهَ إِلَّا اللهُ، وَاللهُ أَكْبَرُ؛ أَحَبُّ إِلَيَّ مِمَّا طَلَعَتْ عليه الشَّمْسُ.

Abu Hurairah (may God be content with him) reported God's Messenger (ﷺ) as saying, "The uttering of these words: 'Glory (be to) God' (subhaan Allah), 'Praise (be to) God (alhamdu lillah), (There is) no deity but God (la illaha il Allah), and 'God (is) Great' (Allahu akbar), is dearer to me than anything the sun rises over." [2]

- Among the highest levels of remembrance is the prayer upon the Prophet (ﷺ), one's keenness and concern to continuously pray for the Prophet (ﷺ) and ask for God's blessings on and support of the Prophet (ﷺ), as much as one can.

قال تعالى: ﴿ إِنَّ ٱللَّهَ وَمَلَٰٓئِكَتَهُۥ يُصَلُّونَ عَلَى ٱلنَّبِيِّ يَٰٓأَيُّهَا ٱلَّذِينَ ءَامَنُواْ صَلُّواْ عَلَيْهِ وَسَلِّمُواْ تَسْلِيمًا ٥٦ ﴾ [33 الأحزاب [56:

﴿ Truly, God confers blessings upon the Prophet, and His angels (ask Him to do so). O you who believe, ask (God to confer) blessing upon him and ask (God to grant him) peace. ﴾ [Q 33:56]

God Almighty informs His servants of the status of His Prophet (ﷺ), that the angels pray for him, then God Almighty commands the believers to pray for him.

The Messenger of God (ﷺ) is the most deserving of all people on the Day of Resurrection. And entry into Paradise with him (ﷺ) will be for those who remembered him (ﷺ) the most. The reward for sending prayers upon the Prophet (ﷺ) will be gaining his company on the Day of Judgement. And prayers be upon God's Messenger, may God bless him and grant him peace.

فعن عبد الله بن مسعود رضي الله عنه قال: قال الرسول ﷺ: (إِنَّ أَوْلَى النَّاسِ بي يومَ القيامةِ أَكْثَرُهم عليَّ صلاةً).

---

(1) The speaker: Muslim – Source: Sahih Muslim – page or number: 2676. Conclusion of the speaker: sound.

(2) The speaker: Muslim – Source: Sahih Muslim – page or number: 2695. Conclusion of the speaker: sound.

Abdullah bin Mas'ud (may God be contented with him) narrated that God's Messenger (ﷺ) said, "On the Day of Judgement, the person nearest to me will be the one who sent the most prayers upon me." [1]

وعن أبي هريرة رضي الله عنه قال: قال الرسول ﷺ: (ما من أحدٍ يسلِّمُ عليَّ إلَّا ردَّ اللهُ عليَّ روحي حتَّى أردَّ عليهِ السلامَ).

Abu Hurairah (may God be contented with him) narrated that the Prophet (ﷺ) said: "No one says prayers of peace upon me but God returns my soul to me so that I can return his greetings." [2]

وعن أبي هريرة رضي الله عنه قال: قال الرسول ﷺ: لا تجعلوا بيوتَكُم قبورًا، ولا تجعلوا قَبري عيدًا، وصلُّوا عليَّ فإنَّ صلاتَكُم تبلُغُني حَيثُ كنتُمْ

Abu Hurairah (may God be contented with him) reported that the Prophet (ﷺ) said: "Do not make my grave a place of celebration, but pray for God's blessings upon me, for your blessings reach me from wherever you are. [3]

وعن أوس بن أوس رضي الله عنه قال: قال الرسول ﷺ: (إنَّ من أفضل أَيَّامِكُم يوم الجمعةِ فيه خُلِقَ آدمُ وفيه قُبِضَ وفيهِ النَّفخةُ وفيهِ الصَّعقةُ فأَكْثِروا عليَّ منَ الصَّلاةِ فيهِ فإنَّ صلاتَكُم معروضةٌ عليَّ قالَ قالوا يا رسولَ اللهَ وَكَيفَ تُعرَضُ صلاتُنا عليكَ وقد أَرِمتَ – يقولونَ بليتَ – فقالَ إنَّ اللهَ عزَّ وجلَّ حرَّمَ على الأرضِ أجسادَ الأنبياءِ).

Aws ibn Aws (may God be pleased with him) narrated that the Prophet (ﷺ) said, "Among the most excellent of your days is Friday. On it, Adam was created, and died on it. The last trumpet will be blown on it. And the Call will be made on it. So, on that day, invoke more blessings on me, for your blessings will be submitted to me." The people asked, 'O Messenger of God, how can our blessings be submitted to you when your body is decayed?' He replied, "God, the Exalted, has prohibited the earth from consuming the bodies of Prophets." [4]

The Prophet (ﷺ) likened the one who remembers God to the living and the one who does not remember God to the dead.

فعن أبو موسى الأشعري رضي الله عنه قَالَ: قَالَ رَسُولُ الله صَلَّى اللهُ عَلَيْهِ وَسَلَّمَ: مَثَلُ الذي يَذْكُرُ رَبَّهُ والذي لا يَذْكُرُ رَبَّهُ، مَثَلُ الحَيِّ والمَيِّتِ.

Abu Musa (may God be contented with him) narrated that the Prophet (ﷺ) said, "The example of one who praises his Lord compared to one who does not, is like that of a living creature and one who is dead." [5]

---

(1) The speaker: Tirmidhi – Source: Sunan Al Tirmidhi – page or number: 484. Conclusion of the speaker: fair but strange.
(2) The speaker: Abu Dawood – Source: Sunan Abu Dawood – page or number: 2041. Conclusion of the speaker: Did not comment [He wrote in his letter to the people of Mecca that whenever he did not comment, it is accepted].
(3) The speaker: Al-Albani – Source: Sunan Abu Dawood – page or number: 2042. Conclusion of the speaker: sound.
(4) The speaker: Al-Albani – Source: Sunan Abu Dawood – page or number: 1047. Conclusion of the speaker: sound.
(5) The speaker: Al-Bukhari – Source: Sahih Al-Bukhari – page or number: 6407. Conclusion of the speaker: sound.

Regarding the virtue of sending blessings upon the Prophet (ﷺ), it is a way of elevating one's rank. It is a feature that God, the Glorified and Exalted, has singled out and restricted to the best of people, our master Muhammad (ﷺ), as he is the spreader and carrier of the Islamic Call and is the Seal of the Prophets.

It is a phrase considered to be one of the obligatory acts of worship and carries a great reward from God Almighty. Its meaning is: "O God, bless and support our noble master Muhammad;" that is, ask God Almighty to bless our noble master Muhammad in the Highest of the Heavens, meaning: 'repeat his praise among the angels,' and this prayer is only upon the Prophet (ﷺ) and his family.

Praying for the Prophet (ﷺ) rewards the worshiper with ten good deeds, raises his rank by ten degrees, removes ten bad deeds from him, and is a reason for the Messenger (ﷺ) to intercede for him on the Day of Resurrection. Another reason for offering blessings is to make the worshipper's feet firm on the straight path on the Day of Resurrection. And it is a way of drawing closer to God Almighty and attaining what one hopes for in this world and the hereafter. It is also a reason for opening the Gates of Mercy and definitive proof of one's love for the Messenger of God (ﷺ), and a reason to increase one's sustenance.

عَنْ أُبَيِّ بْنِ كَعْبٍ رضي الله عنه قَالَ: «كان رسولُ الله ﷺ إذا ذهب ثُلُثَا الليل قام فقال يا أَيُّها الناسُ اذكُروا اللهَ اذكُروا اللهَ جاءتِ الراجفةُ تَتْبَعُها الرادِفَةُ جاء الموتُ بما فيه جاء الموتُ بما فيه قال أُبَيٌّ قلتُ يا رسولَ الله إنِّي أُكْثِرُ الصلاةَ عليْكَ فكم أَجعَلُ لكَ من صلاتِي فقال ما شِئْتَ قال قلتُ الربعَ قال ما شِئْتَ فإنْ زِدتَّ فهو خيرٌ لكَ قلتُ النصفَ قال ما شِئتَ فإنْ زِدتَّ فهو خيرٌ لكَ قال قلتُ فالثلثينِ قال ما شِئْتَ فإنْ زِدتَّ فهو خيرٌ لكَ قلتُ أَجعَلُ لكَ صلاتي كلَّها قال : إذًا تُكْفَى همَّكَ ويغفرُ لكَ ذنْبُكَ

At-Tufail bin Ubayy bin Ka'b reported from his father (may God be pleased with them), narrated, "After a third of the night had passed, God's Messenger (ﷺ) stood and declared, 'O you people! Remember God! Remember God! ... on the Day when the quaker quakes and the successor follows upon it. [Q 79:6-7] Death and what it brings is coming, death and what it brings is coming!'" Ubayy said, 'O Messenger of God! Indeed, I say many prayers for you. How much of my prayer should I make for you?' He (ﷺ) said: 'As you wish.' I asked, 'A fourth?' The Prophet replied: 'As you wish, but if you add more, it will be better for you.' I said: 'Then half?' He said: 'As you wish. And if you add more, it will be better [for you].' "I asked: 'Then two-thirds? 'He said: 'As you wish, but if you add more, it will be better [for you].' I asked: 'Should I make all my prayers for you?' He (ﷺ) said: 'Then your problems will be solved, and your sins will be forgiven'''. [1]

وعن أبي هريرة رضي الله عنه قال: قال الرسول ﷺ: ما مِن أحدٍ يسلِّمُ عليَّ إلَّا ردَّ اللهُ عليَّ روحي حتَّى أردَّ عليهِ السَّلامَ

Abu Hurayrah (may God be pleased with him) narrated that the Prophet (ﷺ) said: "If any of you greets me, God returns my soul to me, and I respond to the greeting. [2]

عن أبي هريرة رضي الله عنه قال. قال النبي:(ما جلَس قومٌ يذكُرونَ الله إلَّا حفَّتْهم الملائكةُ وغشِيَتْهم الرَّحمةُ ونزَلَتْ عليهم السَّكينةُ وذكَرهم الله فيمَن عندَه).

---

(1) The speaker: Tirmidhi – Source: Sunan Al Tirmidhi – page or number: 2457. Conclusion of the speaker: fair and sound.
(2) The speaker: Al-Albani – Source: Sunan Abu Dawood – page or number: 2041. Conclusion of the speaker: fair.

Abu Hurairah and Abu Sa'eed (may God be pleased with them) reported that the Prophet (ﷺ) said, "When people sit in a gathering (for the purpose of) remembering God, they are surrounded by angels, mercy covers them, tranquillity descends upon them, and God remembers them before those who are with Him". [1]

The above hadiths show that continuous prayer upon the Prophet (ﷺ) has blessings and benefits for the righteous believers of this world.

Believing in this, we have compiled these prayers for the Prophet (ﷺ), as Muslims throughout the ages have been keen to pray for the Prophet (ﷺ) and remember God, which helps them to spend their days and nights in the protection of God, the Most High, the Great. Four forms of prayer have been selected - the first is the Prayer of Al-Ibrahimiya (used in the five daily prayers), the second is the Prayer of Ibn Mashish, the third is the Prayer of at-Tijani, and the fourth is the Prayer of al-Jazuli, known as 'Dala'il al-Khayrat' – the Guide to Righteousness.

We pray to God that this work will be accepted, and I address everyone who reads this book with a request to pray that God will be contented with this work. Praise be to God, the Lord of all the Worlds.

﴿ وَمَا تَوْفِيقِي إِلَّا بِاللَّهِ عَلَيْهِ تَوَكَّلْتُ وَإِلَيْهِ أُنِيبُ ﴾.

❨ *... but the achievement of my aim depends on God alone. In Him have I placed my trust, and to Him do I always turn!* ❩ *[Q 11:88]*

Prof. Sami M. Fereig

---

(1) The speaker: Ibn Hibban – Source: Sahih Ibn Hibban – page or number: 768. Conclusion of the speaker: He included in Sahih Ibn Hibban.

الصلاة الإبراهيمية

As-salat al-Ibrahimiyya

الصلاة الإبراهيمية

عن أبي مسعود عقبة بن عمرو رضي الله عنه قال أَتَانَا رَسُولُ اللهِ صَلَّى اللهُ عليه وسلَّمَ ونَحْنُ في مَجْلِسِ سَعْدِ بنِ عُبَادَةَ، فَقَالَ له بَشِيرُ بنُ سَعْدٍ: أَمَرَنَا اللهُ تَعَالَى أَنْ نُصَلِّيَ عَلَيْكَ يا رَسُولَ اللهِ، فَكيفَ نُصَلِّي عَلَيْكَ؟ قالَ: فَسَكَتَ رَسُولُ اللهِ صَلَّى اللهُ عليه وسلَّمَ، حتَّى تَمَنَّيْنَا أَنَّه لَمْ يَسْأَلْهُ، ثُمَّ قالَ رَسُولُ اللهِ صَلَّى اللهُ عليه وسلَّمَ: قُولوا اللَّهُمَّ صَلِّ على سيدنا محمدٍ وعلى آلِ مُحَمَّدٍ، كما صَلَّيْتَ عَلَى آلِ إِبْرَاهِيمَ وبَارِكْ على سيدنا محمدٍ وعلى آلِ مُحَمَّدٍ كما بَارَكْتَ على آلِ إِبْرَاهِيمَ في العَالَمِينَ، إِنَّكَ حَمِيدٌ مَجِيدٌ، والسَّلاَمُ كما قدْ عَلِمْتُمْ. (1)

Allāhumma ṣalli āla Muḥammadinwa `aalā ’āli Muḥammadin, kamā ṣallayta `aalā 'Ibrāhīma wa `aalā ’āli 'Ibrāhīma, 'innaka ḥamīdum-majīd. Allāhumma bārik āla Muḥammadin wa āala ’āli Muḥammadin, kamā bārakta `aalā 'Ibrāhīma wa `aalā āali 'Ibrāhīma, 'innaka ḥamīdum- majidu.

As-Salat al-Ibrahimiyya

Bashir bin Sa'd (may God be pleased with him) narrated that he said to the Prophet (ﷺ), "God has commanded us to invoke blessings on you, O Messenger of God! But how should we bless you?" God's Messenger (ﷺ) kept quiet (for a while) and then said, "Say, 'O God, bless Muhammad and the members of his family as You have blessed Abraham, and sanctify Muhammad and the members of his family as You have sanctified Abraham and his family in all the worlds. You are indeed Praiseworthy and Glorious.' And the 'Taslim' (Peace be upon you) is as you know." [Reported by Muslim]

---

(1) The speaker: Muslim – Source: Sahih Muslim – page or number: 405. Conclusion of the speaker: sound.

الصلاة المشيشية

As-Salat al-Mashishiyya

Abd as-Salam ibn Mashish al-Alami

Lineage and Early Life

Abd as-Salam, son of Suleiman, son of Abu, son of Ali, son of Bu Harmah, son of Issa, son of Salam al-Arous, son of Ahmad Mazwar, son of Ali Haidara, son of Muhammad, son of Idris II, son of Idris I, son of Abdullah al-Kamil, son of al-Hassan al-Muthanna, son of al-Hassan, son of Ali, son of Abu Talib al-Hashimi is better known as ibn Mashish. He was born in 559 AH (1163 AD) in Morocco's north-eastern region of the Atlas Mountains range.

Contributions to Sufism

Imam Abd as-Salam ibn Mishish became a Sufi scholar who lived at the time of the al-Moad Caliphate. He was the mentor of Sufi Imam Abu al-Hassan al-Shadhili, founder of the Shadhili Order. Imam ibn Mashish was a very private man, and one of his prayers included the words, "O God! I ask You for protection from the perverseness of creation so that my refuge is only to You."

His contributions to Sufism include the wisdom received through his student Sidi Abu al-Hassan al-Shadhili. His narrations are characterized by their purity, clarity and compatibility with the Holy Quran and Sunnah. Sidi Abu al-Hassan said, "My Sheikh gave me this advice, 'Do not move your feet except when you hope for the reward of God. Do not sit except when you are most likely to be safe from disobedience to God. And do not accompany anyone except those from whom you seek help in obedience to God.'

End of Life

Sidi ibn Mashish confronted ibn Abu al-Tawajn al-Katami, who claimed to be a prophet, and Al-Katami and his followers plotted against him, resulting in his murder in 626 AH (1228 AD) at the age of sixty-five.

<h1 dir="rtl" align="center">الصلاة المشيشية</h1>

اللهمَّ صلِّ على مَنْ منهُ انشقتِ الأسرارُ، وانفلقتِ الأنوارُ، وفيهِ ارتقتِ الحقائقُ، وتنزلتْ علومُ آدمَ عليهِ السلامُ فأعجزَ الخلائقَ، ولهُ تضاءلتِ الفهومُ فلمْ يدركهُ منا سابقٌ ولا لاحقٌ، فرياضُ الملكوتِ بزهرِ جمالهِ مونقةٌ، وحياضُ الجبروتِ بفيضِ أنوارهِ متدفقةٌ ولا شيءَ إلا وهو بهِ منوطٌ، إذْ لولا الواسطةُ لذهبَ كما قيلَ الموسوطَ، صلاةً تليقُ بكَ منكَ إليهِ كما هو أهلهُ، اللهمَّ إنهُ سِرُّكَ الجامعُ الدالُّ عليكَ، وحجابكَ الأعظمُ القائمُ لكَ بينَ يديكَ، اللهمَّ ألحقني بنسبهِ وحققني بحسبهِ، وعَرِّفْني إياهُ معرفةً أسلمُ بها مِنْ مواردِ الجهلِ، وأكرعُ بها مِنْ مواردِ الفضلِ. واحملني على سبيلهِ إلى حضرتكَ حملا محفوفا بنُصرتك واقذف بي على الباطلِ فأدمغهُ وزجَّ بي في بحارِ الأحديةِ وانشلني من أوحالِ التوحيد وأغرقني في عينِ بحرِ الوحدةِ حتى لا أرى ولا أسمع ولا أجِدَ ولا أحسَّ إلا بها. واجعلِ الحجابَ الأعظمَ حياةَ روحي وروحَهُ سِرَّ حقيقتي وحقيقَتَهُ جامعَ عوالمي بتحقيقِ الحقِّ الأولِ يا أولُ يا آخرُ يا ظاهرُ يا باطنُ اسمع ندائي بما سمعتَ به نداءَ عبدِك زكريا

Allahumma salli āla man minhu-n-shaqqati-l-asrar wa-n falaqati-l-anwar wa fihi-rtaqati-l-haqa'iq wa tanazalat 'ulum Adama fa-a'jaza-l-khala'iq wa lahu tada'alati-l-fuhum fa-lam yudrik-hu minna sabiqun wa la lahiqa fa-riyadu-l-malakuti bi-zahri jamālihi muniqa wa hiyadu-l-jabaruti bi-faydi anwarihi mutadafiqah wa la shay'a 'illa wa huwa bihi manuta idh lawla-l-wasitatu la-dhhaba kama qila mawsut salatan taliqu bika minka ilayhi kama huwa āhluhu Allahumma innahu sirruka-l-jami'u-d-dallu bika ālayk wa hijabuka-l-a'azamu-l-qa'im u laka bayna yadayk Allahumma alhiqni bi-nasabihi wa haqqiqni bi-hasabihi wa 'arifni iyyahu ma'rifatan aslamu biha min mawaridi-l-jahl wa akra'u biha min mawaridi-l-fadl wa-hmilni āla sabilihi ila Hadratik hamlan mahfufam bi-nusratik wa aqadhif bi āla-l-batil fa-admaghuhu wa zujja bi fi bihari-l-Ahadiyya wa-nshulni min ahwali-tawhid wa-ghriqni fi 'ayni bahri-l-Wahda hatta la ara wa la asma'a wa la ajida wa la uhissa 'illa biha wa-j'ali Allahumma-l-hijaba-l-a'zama hayata ruhi wa ruhahu sirra haqiqati wa haqiqatahu jami'a 'awalimi bi-tahqiqi-l-Haqqi-l-Awwal Ya Awwal Ya Akhir Ya Zahir Ya Batin Isma' nida'iy bima sami'ta bihi nida'a abdika Zakariyya

As-Salat al-Mashishiyya

Dear God! Give Your support and blessing to him from whom burst open the secrets, from whom stream forth the lights, in whom the realities rise up, and upon whom the knowledge of Adam descended, which is impossible for all other creatures. Our knowledge is limited, and no one can fully comprehend all his knowledge from before or to come. The gardens of the spiritual kingdom blossom resplendently with his loveliness. And the reservoirs of God's Dominion overflow with the outpouring of his light. There is nothing that is not connected to him because if there were no intercessor, everything to be interceded for would vanish, as it is said. So bless him with a prayer worthy of You, from You, as befits his stature.

Dear God! Indeed he is the all-encompassing secret that leads to You and is Your Supreme Veil raised before You, between Your Hands. Dear God, join me with his descendants, establish me through his account, and let me know him with a deep understanding that keeps me safe from the sources of ignorance so that I might drink fully from the sources of excellence.

Bring me, by his path, to Your Presence, surrounded by Your Victory. And throw me at the false so that I may devastate it. Plunge me into the Sea of Oneness, pull me out of the swamp of metaphorical Unity, and drown me in the Ocean of Unicity Essence until I neither see, hear, nor sense except through it. Dear God! Make Your Supreme Veil the life of my spirit, his soul the mystery of my reality, and his reality the merging of my worlds through the comprehension of the First Truth. The First! The Last! The Manifest! The Unmanifest! Hear my call as You heard the call of your servant Zachariah.

وانصرني بكَ لكَ وأيِّدني بكَ لكَ واجْمعْ بيني وبينِك وحُلْ بيْني وبينَ غيْرِك. الله، الله، الله، إنَّ الذي فرَض عليكَ القرآنَ لرادُّكَ إلى معادٍ. ربَّنا آتنا من لدُنْكَ رحمةً وهيِّءْ لنا من أمرِنا رشَدا (ثلاثاً)، إنَّ اللَّهَ وَمَلَائِكَتَهُ يُصَلُّونَ عَلَى النَّبِيِّ يَا أَيُّهَا الَّذِينَ آمَنُوا صَلُّوا عَلَيْهِ وَسَلِّمُوا تَسْلِيمًا. صَلَوَاتُ اللهِ وَسَلَامُهُ وَتَحِيَّاتُهُ وَرَحْمَتُهُ وَبَرَكَاتُهُ عَلَى سَيِّدِنَا مُحَمَّدٍ عَبْدِكَ وَرَسُولِكَ النَّبِيِّ الأُمِّيِّ وَعَلَى آلِهِ وَصَحْبِهِ عَدَدَ الشَّفْعِ وَالْوَتْرِ. وَعَدَدَ كَلِمَاتِ ربنا التَّامَّاتِ الْمُبَارَكَاتِ. سُبْحَانَ رَبِّكَ رَبِّ الْعِزَّةِ عَمَّا يَصِفُونَ وَسَلَامٌ عَلَى الْمُرْسَلِينَ وَالْحَمْدُ لِلَّهِ رَبِّ الْعَالَمِينَ. ألف سلام، ألف سلام، ألف ألف سلام في قلوبنا ولا حول ولا قوة إلا بالله العلي العظيم.

wa-nsurni bika laka wa ayyidni bika Laka wa ajma' bayni wa Baynak wa hul bayni wa bayna ghayrik Allaaah! Allaaah! Allaaah! Inna-l-ladhi farada ālayka-l-qur'ana la-radduka 'ila ma'ad [Holy Qur'an 28.85] Rabbana 'atina min ladunka Rahmatan wa haiy' lana min 'amrina Rashada [Holy Qur'an 18.10] Inna-Llaha wa malai'katahu yusalluna āla-n-nabi ya ayyuha-lladhina 'amanu sallu ālayhi wa sallimu taslima [Holy Qur'an 33.65] Salawatu-Llahi wa sallamuhu wa tahiyyatuhu wa Rahmatuhu wa barakatuhu āla sayyidina Muhammadin 'abdika wa nabiyyika wa rasulika an-Nabiyyi-l-Ummi wa āla ālihi wa sahbihi wa sallim 'adada-sh-shaf'i wa-l-watri wa 'adada kalimati Rabbina-t-tammati-l-mubarakat Subhana rabbika rabbil izzati 'ammaa yasifoon wasalamun ālal mursaleen waal-hamdu l'illahi rabbil ālameena [Qur'an 37:180-183] Alfu salaam - Alfu salaam - Alfu Alfi sallaamin fi qulubina wala hawla wala quwwata ''illa b'illahil 'aliyyil 'adheem

And grant me triumph through You, for You. And sustain me through You, for You. And connect me to You and come between me and anything other than You (Allah, Allah, Allah). "Surely, He Who ordained the Qur'an for you will surely bring you back to the place of return." [Q 28:85].

"Dear Lord! Grant us mercy from Your Presence, and make us incline to sound judgment concerning our affair." [Q 18:10] (three times). "Truly, God and His angels give their support and blessings to the Prophet. O you who believe, give your support and blessings to him and greet him abundantly." [Q 33:56]. May the sublime blessings of God, His Peace, Greetings, Mercy, and Grace be upon our noble master Muhammad, His Servant, Prophet and Messenger, the Prophet sent to all nations — and his family and companions. Upon him be peace multiplied, and also multiplied by the inconceivable number of the perfect and blessed words of our Lord.

Glorified is your Sustainer, the Lord of Glory and Mercy, beyond all they attribute, and peace be on the Messengers, and Praise be to God, the Lord of all the Worlds.

A thousand-fold Peace, a thousand-fold Peace, a thousand thousand-fold Peace in our hearts. There is no power nor strength except from God, The Most High, The Exalted.

الصلاة التجانية

Salat al-Tijaniyya

Abu al-Abbas Ahmad al-Tijani

Lineage and Early Life

Ahmad, son of Muhammad, son of al-Mukhtar, son of Ahmad, son of Muhammad Salem al-Tijani, is better known as Al-Tijani. His mother was Aisha, daughter of Muhammad, son of al-Senussi al-Madawi al-Tijani.

He was born in 1150 AH (1737 AD) in the Algerian village of Ain Madi, the seat of his ancestors. He had memorized the Holy Qur'an by the time he was seven years old. His teacher at that time was Imam Warsh, a student of Imam Nafi' bin Abu Naim and reciter Muhammad bin Hamou al-Tijani al-Madawi who, in turn, studied memorization and recitation of the Holy Quran from his Sheikh, Issa Boukaz Al-Madawi Al-Tijani.

Contributions to Sufism

After memorizing the Holy Quran, Al-Tijani engaged in the application of fundamentalist, secondary and literary sciences. He continued seeking knowledge in his home country until he reached the rank of eligibility to teach and issue fatwas. He gave his first fatwa and taught when he was not yet sixteen years old.

Al-Tijani's parents died in 1166 AH (1753 AD) during an outbreak of the plague in the region. Therefore, the residents of Ain Madi appointed him to replace his father as the President of the Zawiya (literal translation: corner of a room) despite his young age – he was sixteen years old at the time.

Al-Tijani taught the Holy Quran, Sunnah and other Islamic sciences in Ain Madi for five years, then emigrated to Fez. He is recognized as a sheikh, cleric and mystic who devoted his life to spiritual education. He founded the Tijaniyya Sufi Order and the Tijaniyya Zawiya, whose Maqam (station) and Zawiya are still visited in Ain Madi to this day. He began his life in Algeria but also travelled to Mauritania, Sudan, Hejaz, Tunisia and Egypt before settling in Fez, Morocco.

End of Life

Al-Tijani died in Fez on Thursday, 17th Shawwal, 1230 AH (1815 AD) when he was eighty years old and is buried there.

<h1 align="center" dir="rtl">صلاة الفاتح</h1>

اللَّهُمَّ صَلِّ عَلَىٰ سَيِّدِنَا مُحَمَّدٍ ❊ الْفَاتِحِ لِمَا أُغْلِقَ ❊ وَالْخَاتِمِ لِمَا سَبَقَ ❊ نَاصِرِ الْحَقِّ بِالْحَقِّ ❊ وَالْهَادِي إِلَىٰ صِرَاطِكَ الْمُسْتَقِيمِ ❊ وَعَلَىٰ آلِهِ حَقَّ قَدْرِهِ وَمِقْدَارِهِ الْعَظِيمِ.

Allahumma salli āla sayidina muhamadin alfatihi lima aughliqa walkhatimi lima sabaqa nasiri alhaqi bialhaqi walhadi ila siratika almustaqimi wa āla ālihi haqa qadrihi wamiqdarihi alāzimi.

Salat al-Fatih

Dear God! Give Your support and blessings to our noble master Muhammad, the opener of what was closed, the seal of what had preceded him, the triumph of truth by the Truth, and the guide to Your straight path. May God send prayers upon his family according to his greatness and great rank.

الصلاة النورانية

Salawat Nuraniyyah

Sayyid Ahmad al-Badawi

Lineage and Early Life

Ahmad, son of Ali, son of Yahya, famously known as al-Badawi, was one of the most revered saints in Egypt and the Islamic world. He was born in 596 AH (1200 CE) in the city of Fez, Morocco, into a noble family tracing its lineage back to Hussein ibn Ali ibn Abi Talib (may Allah be pleased with them).

From an early age, he memorized the Qur'an and studied Islamic sciences under prominent scholars in Fez. Drawn to spirituality, he immersed himself in worship and asceticism, displaying remarkable piety even in his youth.

Journey to the East and Settlement in Egypt

In his early adulthood, al-Badawi traveled to the Hijaz to perform Hajj and later visited Iraq, where he met several Sufi masters and scholars. Eventually, he settled in Tanta, Egypt, where he devoted himself to teaching and guiding people toward Tasawwuf (Islamic mysticism).

His deep spirituality, miracles (karamat), and unwavering devotion attracted countless followers. He became renowned for his extreme asceticism, often spending long periods in seclusion, fasting, and prolonged prayer.

Founding the Badawiyya Sufi Order

Ahmad al-Badawi established the Badawiyya Tariqa, a Sufi order emphasizing strict adherence to the Sunnah, remembrance of Allah (dhikr), and serving the poor. His teachings spread rapidly across Egypt, Sudan, the Levant, and beyond, making him one of the most influential Sufi saints in Islamic history.

Despite his humble lifestyle, he wielded significant spiritual influence, even advising rulers and standing against injustice. His zawiya (lodge) in Tanta became a center for seekers of knowledge and spirituality.

Death and Legacy

Ahmad al-Badawi passed away in 675 AH (1276 CE) in Tanta, where he was buried. His shrine remains one of Egypt's most visited religious sites, drawing millions of devotees annually, particularly during his mawlid (birth anniversary) celebrations.

The Badawiyya Order continues to thrive, preserving his teachings of piety, charity, and divine love. He is remembered as "al-Sayyid al-Badawi"—a title of honor—and remains a symbol of spiritual guidance in the Islamic world.

May Allah have mercy upon him and grant him the highest ranks in Paradise.

اَللَّهُمَّ صَلِّ وَسَلِّمْ وَبَارِكْ عَلَى سَيِّدِناَ وَمَوْلَانَا مُحَمَّدٍ شَجَرَةِ ٱلْأَصْلِ النُّورَانِيَّةِ، وَلَمْعَةِ الْقَبْضَةِ الرَّحْمَانِيَّةِ، وَأَفْضَلِ الْخَلِيقَةِ ٱلْإِنْسَانِيَّةِ،

وَأَشْرَفِ الصُّوَرَةِ الْجِسْمَانِيَّةِ، وَمَعْدِنِ ٱلْأَسْرَارِ الرَّبَّانِيَّةِ، وَخَزَائِنِ الْعُلُومِ ٱلِاصْطِفَائِيَّةِ، صَاحِبِ الْقَبْضَةِ ٱلْأَصْلِيَّةِ، وَالْبَهْجَةِ السَّنِيَّةِ،

وَالرُّتْبَةِ الْعَلِيَّةِ، مَنِ انْدَرَجَتِ النَّبِيُّوْنَ تَحْتَ لِوَائِهِ، فَهُمْ مِنْهُ وَاِلَيْهِ، وَصَلِّ وَسَلِّمْ وَبَارِكْ عَلَيْهِ وَعَلَى آلِهِ وَصَحْبِهِ عَدَدَ مَاخَلَقْتَ،

وَرَزَقْتَ وَأَمَتَّ وَأَحْيَيْتَ اِلَى يَوْمِ تَبْعَثُ مَنْ أَفْنَيْتَ، وَسَلِّمْ تَسْلِيمًا كَثِيرًا وَالْحَمْدُ لِلهِ رَبِّ الْعَالَمِيْنَ.

Allahumma salli wa sallim wa baarik `ala Sayyidina wa Mawlana Muhammadin shajarati 'l-asli 'n-nooraaniyyati wa lam`atil qabdati 'r-rahmaaniyyati wa afdali 'l-khaleeqati 'l-insaaniyyati wa ashrafi 's-soorati 'l-jismaaniyyati wa m`adini 'l-asraari 'r-rabbaniyyati wa khazaaini 'l-`uloomi 'l-istifaaiyyati, saahibi 'l-qabdati 'l-asliyya wa 'l-bahjati 's-saniyya wa 'r-rutbati 'l-`aliyya, man indarajati 'n-nabiyyoona tahta liwaa'ihi, fahum minhu wa ilayhi, wa salli wa sallim wa baarik `alayhi wa `ala aalihi wa sahbihi `adada maa khalaqta wa razaqta wa amatta wa ahyayta ilaa yawmi tab`athu man afnayta wa sallim tasleeman katheera wa 'l-hamdulillahi rabbi 'l-`alameen.

Salawat Nuraniyyah

O Allah! Exalt, greet and bless our master and liege lord Muhammad, the Tree of Original Light, the Sparkle of the Handful of Divine Mercy, the Best of All Humankind, the Noblest of Physical Frames, the Vessel of the Lord's Secrets and Storehouse of the Sciences of the Elect, the Possessor of the Original Divine Grasp, Resplendent Grace, and Uppermost Rank, under whose flag line up all the prophets, so that they are from him and point to him. Bless, greet and sanctify him and his Family and Companions, to the number of all that You have ever created, sustained, caused to die, and caused to live again, to the Day You resurrect those You reduced to dust, and greet him with an abundant and endless greeting. Glory and praise belong to Allah, the Lord of the Worlds!

الصلاة الذاتية

Salawat aldhaatia

Sayyid Ibrahim al-Dasuqi

Lineage and Early Life

Ibrahim ibn Abd al-Aziz Abu al-Majd al-Dasuqi, known as Burhan al-Din (Proof of the Faith) and Qutb al-Aqtab (Pole of Poles), was born in 653 AH (1255 CE) in the city of Desouk, Egypt. He was a descendant of the Prophet's family (ﷺ) through Imam Hussein ibn Ali (may Allah be pleased with them).

From a young age, he memorized the Qur'an and studied Islamic sciences under prominent scholars of his time. Renowned for his sharp intellect and deep piety, he quickly distinguished himself as a gifted student destined for spiritual greatness.

Spiritual Journey and Founding of the Dasuqiyya Order

After mastering exoteric knowledge, Ibrahim al-Dasuqi devoted himself to Sufism, engaging in intense worship and divine remembrance. He became famous for his spiritual miracles (karamat) and saintly status, eventually establishing the Dasuqiyya Sufi Order.

His teachings emphasized inner purification (tazkiya), strict adherence to Islamic law (Sharia), and selfless service to humanity. Known for his asceticism and generosity, he divided his time between guiding disciples and aiding the poor. His fearless stance in advising rulers and upholding justice earned him widespread respect.

Death and Legacy

Sayyid Ibrahim al-Dasuqi passed away in 676 AH (1277 CE) in Desouk, where he was buried. His shrine remains a major pilgrimage site, attracting visitors from across the Muslim world.

The Dasuqiyya Order continues to thrive, preserving his legacy of Sunni Sufism and social welfare. He is celebrated annually during his mawlid (birth anniversary), one of Egypt's most vibrant religious festivals.

Regarded as one of the Four Spiritual Poles (al-Aqtab al-Arba'a) of Sufism—alongside Ahmad al-Badawi, Ahmad al-Rifa'i, and Abd al-Qadir al-Jilani—his influence endures as a beacon of mystical Islam.

الصلاة الذاتية

اللَّهُمَّ صَلِّ عَلَى الذَّاتِ الْمُحَمَّدِيَّةِ، اللَّطِيفَةِ الْأَحَدِيَّةِ، شَمْسِ سَمَاءِ الْأَسْرَارِ، وَمَظْهَرِ الْأَنْوَارِ، وَمَرْكَزِ مَدَارِ الْجَلَالِ، وَقُطْبِ فَلَكِ

الْجَمَالِ، اللَّهُمَّ بِسِرِّهِ لَدَيْكَ وَبِسَيْرِهِ إِلَيْكَ، آمِنْ خَوْفِي وَأَقِلْ عَثْرَتِي وَأَذْهِبْ حُزْنِي وَحِرْصِي، وَكُنْ لِي وَخُذْنِي إِلَيْكَ مِنِّي وَارْزُقْنِي

الْفَنَاءَ عَنِّي، وَلَا تَجْعَلْنِي مَفْتُونَاً بِنَفْسِي مَحْجُوباً بِحِسِّي، وَاكْشِفْ لِي عَنْ كُلِّ سِرٍّ مَكْتُومٍ يَا حَيُّ يَا قَيُّومُ.

Allahumma salli aladh-dhaatil-muhammadiyyah. al-Lateefa-til-ahadiyyah. Shamsi samaa'il-asrar. wa mazharil-anwar wa markazi madaaril-jalal wa qutbi falakil-jamaal.

Allahumma bi-sirrihi ladayka wa bi-sayrihi ilayk. aamin khawfi wa aqal 'athrati wa adh-hib huzni wa hirsi wa kunli wa khudhni ilayka minni warzuqnil-fanaa'a 'anni wala taj'alni maftunan bi-nafsi mahjuban bi-hissi wakshif li 'an kulli sirrin maktumin Ya Hayyu Ya Qayyum.

Salawat aldhaatia

O Allah, send blessings upon the Muhammadian essence, which is both subtle and unique, sun of the sky of secrets, the made visible of the luminescence, the majestic centre around which all revolves, the beautiful Pivot-(Qutb) of Spheres-(Falak).

O Allah, by his secret with You, quieten my fears-Khawf decrease my faults, remove my afflictions and miserliness. Exist for me and take me to You from me. Grant me annihilation from myself-(Nafs). Do not make me lead astray by my nafs, nor make me veiled by my senses. Reveal to me all of the hidden-(Maktum) secrets-(Sirr.) Ya Hayy, Ya Qayyum.

الصلاة العظيمية

Salat al- al-Azeemiyya

IMAM AHMAD IBN IDRIS

Name and Lineage

Imam Ahmad ibn Idris was one of the seminal figures of Islam in the nineteenth century. He came from the noble family of al-Adarisah, who were well-known in North Africa. He was a descendant of the Prophet (peace be upon him), through Sayyiduna Hassan ibn Ali ibn Abu Talib.

Even though Imam Ahmad ibn Idris was blessed with a noble family lineage, it was never his nature to boast about it. This is clearly illustrated in the writings of Imam Sayyid Muhammad ibn Ali al-Sanusi, a prominent student of Imam Ahmad Ibn Idris, who wrote about the lineage of his teacher. In it, Imam Ahmad ibn Idris stated:

"My lineage is the Book and the Sunnah. Look at me. If you find me on the path of the Book and the Sunnah, then say, "Ahmad ibn Idris is on the path of the Book and the Sunnah." This is my lineage. Allah, glory be to Him, states: "On this day, I have made your lineage irrelevant and raised My lineage, which is piety (God-consciousness)."

Imam Ahmed ibn Idris was born on the 21st of Rajab 1163 AH (1750 AD) in a small village in Mzoura, near the coastal town of Larache in northern Morocco.

Knowledge

Even as a child, Imam Ahmad ibn Idris was nurtured with the teachings of Islam and showed signs of his future scholarly pursuits.

During the early stages of his schooling, he memorized the Quran and other disciplines of sacred knowledge. He acquired a basic understanding of Islam by studying with a teacher while, at the same time, in the care of his two brothers, Sayyid Muhammad and Sayyid Abdullah ibn Idris.

In Fez, he studied in the Great Mosque of al-Qarawiyyin with various scholars who taught there.

Looking back at his educational background, he had attained chains of transmissions covering all fields, including hadith, commentary (tafsir), Shariya law (fiqh), the esoteric aspects of Islam (sufism), and others.

Imam Ahmad ibn Idris also narrated many 'Musalsal' Hadith (those that have a clear chain of narrators), some of which have the status of 'Aali' (the highest authentication). Shaykh Muhammad ibn Ali al Shyaukani, writer of the famous book 'Nail al Autar,' acknowledged these narrations from Imam Ahmad ibn Idris.

His Passing

Between Maghrib and Isha, on Saturday, the 21st of Rajab 1253 AH (1837 AD – at the age of 87), Imam Ahmad ibn Idris was invited to meet his Lord.

الصلاة العظيمية

اَللّٰهُمَّ إِنِّي أَسْأَلُكَ بِنُورِ وَجْهِ اللهِ الْعَظِيمِ ❀ الَّذِي مَلَأَ أَرْكَانَ عَرْشِ اللهِ الْعَظِيمِ ❀ وَقَامَتْ بِهِ عَوَالِمُ اللهِ الْعَظِيمِ ❀ أَنْ تُصَلِّيَ عَلىٰ مَوْلَانَا مُحَمَّدٍ ذِي الْقَدْرِ الْعَظِيمِ ❀ وَعَلىٰ آلِ نَبِيِّ اللهِ الْعَظِيمِ ❀ بِقَدْرِ عَظَمَةِ ذَاتِ اللهِ الْعَظِيمِ ❀ فِي كُلِّ لَحْظَةٍ وَنَفَسٍ عَدَدَ مَا فِي عِلْمِ اللهِ الْعَظِيمِ ❀ صَلَاةً دَائِمَةً بِدَوَامِ اللهِ الْعَظِيمِ ❀ تَعْظِيمًا لِحَقِّكَ يَا مَوْلَانَا يَا مُحَمَّدُ يَا ذَا الْخُلُقِ الْعَظِيمِ ❀ وَسَلِّمْ عَلَيْهِ وَعَلىٰ آلِهِ مِثْلَ ذَلِكَ ❀ وَاجْمَعْ بَيْنِي وَبَيْنَهُ كَمَا جَمَعْتَ بَيْنَ الرُّوحِ وَالنَّفْسِ ❀ ظَاهِرًا وَبَاطِنًا ❀ يَقْظَةً وَمَنَامًا ❀ وَاجْعَلْهُ يَا رَبِّ رُوحًا لِذَاتِي مِنْ جَمِيعِ الْوُجُوهِ فِي الدُّنْيَا قَبْلَ الْآخِرَةِ يَا عَظِيمُ ❀

Allāhumma innī asaluka bi nūri wajhi Llāhi l-ʿaẓīmi(i), (a)lladhī mala'a arkāna ʿarshi Llāhi l-ʿaẓīm(i), wa qāmat bihi ʿawālimu Llāhi l-ʿaẓīm(i), an tuṣalliya ʿalā mawlānā Muḥammadin dhi l-qadri l-ʿaẓīm(i), wa ʿalā āli Nabiyyi Llāhi l-ʿaẓīm(i), bi qadri ʿaẓamati dhāti Llāhi l-ʿaẓīm(i), fī kulli lamḥatin wa nafasin ʿadada mā fī ʿilmi Llāhi l-ʿaẓīm(i), ṣalātan dā'imatan bi dawami Llāhi l-ʿaẓīm(i), taʿẓīman li ḥaqqika yā mawlānā yā Muḥammadu yā dha l-khuluqi l-ʿaẓīm(i), wa sallim ʿalayhi wa ʿalā ālihi mithla dhalik(a), wajmaʿ baynī wa baynahu kamā jamaʿta bayna r-rūḥi wa n-nafsi, ẓāhiran wa bāṭinan, yaqẓatan wa manāman, wa jʿalhu yā Rabbi rūḥan li dhātī min jamīʿi l-wujūhi fi d-dunyā qabla l-ākhirati yā ʿaẓīm(u).

Prayer of the Greatest

O Allah, truly I ask You by the Light of Your tremendous Countenance, that illuminates the pillars of Your magnificent Throne, and by which Your worlds are established—that You send prayers upon our liege-lord Muhammad, the possessor of immense rank, and the family of the Prophet of Allah, as great in magnitude as Your tremendous Essence; with every glance and breath, and as many times as the number of what is contained within Your knowledge, O Allah, the Tremendous, with a prayer that is perpetual by Your perpetuity. [This I ask] out of reverence for your right, O liege-lord, Muhammad, the possessor of tremendous character. Send peace upon him and his family with the like thereof. Join us together just as You have joined the soul with the self - outwardly and inwardly - in wakefulness and sleep, and make him, O Lord, a soul for my essence in every aspect, in the lower world before the Hereafter, O Allah the Tremendous.

دلائل الخيرات وشوارق الأنوار في ذكر الصلاة على النبي المختار ﷺ

Dala'il al-Khayrat wa Shawariq al-Anwar fi Dhikri as-Salat ala an-Nabiyyi l-Mukhtar

Muhammad al-Jazuli

Lineage and Early Life

Abu Abdullah Muhammad bin Suleiman bin Abu Bakr al-Jazuli al-Samalali al-Hassani is better known as al-Jazuli. He was born in 807AH (1405 AD) and spent his early years in the historical Souss region of Morocco, located between the Atlantic Ocean and the southern Atlas Mountains.

Contributions to Sufism

He studied locally, then moved to Fez, where he continued his studies in the sciences of interpretation, hadith, jurisprudence and principles. His room in Fez is still open to visitors to this day. In Fez, he focused on the principles of jurisprudence and Maliki laws. He also met the famous mystic and jurist Ahmad Zarrouk. After settling a tribal dispute, he left the region and spent the next forty years in Mecca, Medina, and Jerusalem. He then returned to Fez, where he compiled a book of prayers entitled 'Dala'il al-Khayraat wa Shawaraq al-Anwar' in remembrance of the Prophet Muhammad (ﷺ). His book is divided into seven sections, for every day of the week. Al-Jazuli is also known as one of the Seven Scholars of Marrakesh.

End of Life

Imam al-Jazuli passed away in the Souss region of Morocco in 870 AH (1466 AD) at the age of sixty-one. Some believe he died as a result of being poisoned.

Introduction

Praying for the Messenger of God (ﷺ) is one of God's commands. He urges us to do this and explains its merits. God Almighty says in His Holy Book, "Truly, God and His angels bless the Prophet. (Hence,) O you who have attained to faith! Request blessings upon him and greetings of peace!" [Q 33:56].

God singles out Prophet Muhammad (ﷺ) to receive our prayers as he (ﷺ) is God's Chosen One, the Seal of the Prophets, and the Beloved of God.

The one who intends to pray for the Messenger of God (ﷺ) should comply with the command of God: to believe in His Prophet, love him and yearn for him, glorify his destiny, and be worthy of all that.

Dala'il al-Khayrat is a very well-known prayer for the Prophet Muhammad (ﷺ) .

Juwairiya (one of the Prophet's wives – may God be pleased with her) reported that God's Messenger (ﷺ) came out (from her apartment) in the morning as she was busy observing the dawn prayer in her place of worship. He (ﷺ) came back later that morning, and she was still sitting there. He (ﷺ) asked her, "Have you been in the same seat since I left you?" She replied, "Yes." Thereupon, God's Apostle (ﷺ) said, "I recited four words three times after I left you, and if these are weighed against what you have recited since the morning, these would outweigh them. These words are: 'Glory (be to) God' (Subhaan Allah) and 'Praise (be to) God' (Alhamdu lillah) according to the number of His creation, the contentment of His Self, and according to the weight of His Throne, and the volume of ink used in writing the words for His Praise." [1]

The Messenger of God (ﷺ) shows us, in this hadith, that believers can increase or magnify their prayers by referring to large numbers as a way of increasing the reward for their prayers. Imam al-Jazuli adopted this in writing his prayers for the Prophet.

Fudalah ibn Ubayd (may God be pleased with him) narrated that the Messenger of God (ﷺ) heard a man supplicating during prayer, but the man did not mention the greatness of God, nor did he invoke blessings upon the Prophet (ﷺ) . The Messenger of God (ﷺ) said, "He has prayed in haste." He (ﷺ) then called the man and said (either to him or to another man), "When any of you pray, he should exalt his Lord and praise Him at the beginning, then invoke blessings upon the Prophet (ﷺ). After that, he should supplicate to God for anything he wishes, and end with again invoking blessings upon the Prophet (ﷺ) .

Abu Suleiman Ad-Darani (may God be pleased with him) reported that the Prophet (ﷺ) said, "Whoever wishes to request something from God, let him first ask for blessings upon the Prophet (ﷺ) . And then he may ask God about his affair, and seal his request by once more asking for blessings upon the Prophet (ﷺ) . God will then

---

(1) The speaker: Muslim – Source: Sahih Muslim – page or number: 2726. Conclusion of the speaker: sound.

accept the two requests for blessings upon the Prophet (ﷺ) and, as God is the Most Noble and Generous, He will also accept whatever he has asked for in between." [1]

Thus, Imam Jazuli – the author of Dalai'l Al-Khayrat - followed this approach, beginning first with the praise of God, glorifying and thanking Him, then praying for the Prophet (ﷺ) , and then praying for himself and all Muslims. He concludes by again praying for the Prophet (ﷺ) . He also magnifies the number of his prayers by referring to vast numbers of things in nature, the creation, the earth and the Heavens, as the Prophet (ﷺ) did when describing his morning prayer to his wife, Juwairiya.

Dala'il al-Khayrat is divided into daily parts that can be read or recited in any of the following ways. The first way is to read or recite a part of it every day, divided into each day of the week. The second way is to read or recite it in four quarters, one-quarter a day, completing it in four days. The third way is to read or recite it in thirds, one-third a day, completing it in three days. The fourth way is to read or recite it in its entirety over the duration of a twenty-four hour period, dividing it into seven daily prayer times: beginning with the Fajr (dawn) prayer, then the Duha (sunnah) prayer, then the Zuhr, Asr, Maghrib and Isha prayers, and finally the night (sunnah) prayer. The fifth way is to read or recite it in its entirety once every day, in one sitting.

Some religious orders recommend that you start by reading or reciting the Beginning Dua, then the Ninety-Nine Most Beautiful Names of God, followed by the Two Hundred and One Names of the Prophet (ﷺ) . Then the prayer itself (Dala'il al-Khayrat), and end with the Final Dua.

---

(1) The speaker: Al-Albani – Source: Sunan Abu Dawood – page or number: 1481. Conclusion of the speaker: sound.

في فضائل الصلاة على النبي صلى الله عليه وسلم:

The Benefits of Asking for Blessings and Peace upon the Prophet, may God's blessings and abundant peace be upon him

هذه بعض الفضائل كما أوردها المؤلف ولم يقوم بإسنادها تسهيلا لحفظها.

The author mentions some of the benefits of asking for blessings and peace upon the Prophet. To facilitate their memorization, he did not include their attributions.

- قال الله عز وجل ﴿إِنَّ اللَّهَ وَمَلَائِكَتَهُ يُصَلُّونَ عَلَى النَّبِيِّ يَا أَيُّهَا الَّذِينَ آمَنُوا صَلُّوا عَلَيْهِ وَسَلِّمُوا تَسْلِيمًا﴾ [33 الأحزاب :56]

God, Mighty and Sublime is He, says, "Truly, God and His angels bless the Prophet. O you who believe, ask God to bless him and grant him abundant peace." [Q 33:56]

- ويروى أن رسول الله صلى الله عليه وسلم جاء ذات اليوم والبشرى تُرى في وجهه فقال (إنه جاءني جبريل عليه السلام فقال أما ترضى يا محمد أن لا يصلي عليك أحد من أمتك إلا صليت عليه عشراً، ولا يسلم عليك أحد من أمتك إلا سلمت عليه عشراً).

It is reported that the Prophet, may God's blessings and peace be upon him, came one day with signs of good tidings on his face. He said: "Lo, Angel Gabriel, peace be upon him, said to me, 'Are you not contented, O Muhammad, whenever one of your nation asks God to bless you, God will bless him tenfold, and whenever one of your nation asks God to grant you peace, God will grant him peace tenfold.'"

- وقال صلى الله عليه وسلم: من قال حين يسمع الأذان والإقامة: اللهم رب هذه الدعوة التامة والصلاة والقائمة آت محمداً الوسيلة والفضيلة وأبعثه مقاماً محموداً الذي وعدته حلت له شفاعتي يوم القيامة.

The Prophet, may God's blessings and abundant peace be upon him, said: "Whoever hears the call to prayer and says, 'O God, Lord of this perfect call and this established prayer, grant Muhammad the Closest Access, Pre-Eminence and Lofty Rank, and the Most Praised Station You have promised him,' my intercession will be binding for him on the Day of the Rising Up."

- وقال صلى الله عليه وسلم: إن أولى الناس بي أكثرهم علي صلاةً.

The Prophet, may God's blessings and abundant peace be upon him, said: "The person nearest to me is the one who asks for the most blessings on me."

- وقال صلى الله عليه وسلم: من صلّى علي صلّت عليه الملائكة ما دام يصلّي علي فليُقلل عند ذلك أو ليكثر.

The Prophet, may God's blessings and abundant peace be upon him, also said: "Whoever asks for blessings upon me, angels bless him or her for as long as he asks, be it for a long time or for a short time."

- وقال صلى الله عليه وسلم: بحسب المرء من البخل أن أذكر عنده ولا يُصلّي علي.

The Prophet, may God's blessings and abundant peace be upon him, said: "A person is considered to be a miser if, when I am mentioned in his presence, he does not ask for blessings upon me."

- وقال صلى الله عليه وسلم: أكثروا الصلاة عليَ يوم الجمعة.

The Prophet, may God's blessings and abundant peace be upon him, said: "Ask for more blessings upon me on Fridays."

- وقال صلى الله عليه وسلم: من صلّى علي من أمتي كُتبت له عشر حسنات ومحيت عنه عشر سيئات.

The Prophet, may God's blessings and abundant peace be upon him, said: "Whoever of my nation asks for blessings on me once, ten good deeds are written down for him, and ten sins are erased."

- وقال صلى الله عليه وسلم من صلّى عليّ في كتاب لم تزل الملائكة تصلي عليه ما دام إسمي في ذلك الكتاب.

The Prophet, may God's blessings and abundant peace be upon him, said: "Whoever asks for blessings on me in a book, the angels bless him for as long as my name is in that book."

- وقال أبو سليمان الداراني من أراد أن يسأل الله حاجته فليكثر بالصلاة على النبي صلى الله عليه وسلم ثم يسأل الله

حاجته وليختم بالصلاة على النبي صلى الله عليه وسلم فإن الله يقبل الصلاتين وهو أكرم من أن يدع ما بينهما.

Abu Suleiman Ad-Darani (may God be pleased with him) said, "Whoever wishes to request something from God, let him increase his asking for blessings upon the Prophet, may God's blessings and peace be upon him. And then he may ask God about his affair and seal his request by once more asking for blessings upon the Prophet, may God's blessings and abundant peace be upon him. God will then accept the two requests for blessings upon the Prophet, and this is something nobler than whatever he asks for in between."

- وروي عنه صلى الله عليه وسلم أنه قال من صلى علي يوم الجمعة مائة مرة غفرت له خطيئة ثمانين سنة.

It is related that the Prophet, may God's blessings and peace be upon him, said: "Whoever asks God one hundred times to bless me on a Friday, they will be forgiven the sins of eighty years."

- وعن أبي هريرة رضي الله عنه أن رسول الله صلى الله عليه وسلم قال للمصلي عليّ نور على الصراط ومن كان على

الصراط من أهل النور لم يكن من أهل النار.

Abu Hurairah (may God be contented with him) narrated, "The Messenger of God, may God's blessings and abundant peace be upon him, said, 'For the one who asks for blessings upon me, there is a light on the path, and whoever of the People of Light is on the path, they will not be among the People of the Fire.'"

- وقال صلى الله عليه وسلم من نسي الصلاة على فقد أخطأ طريق الجنة. وإنما أراد بالنسيان الترك وإذا كان التارك يُخطئ

طريق الجنة كان المصلي عليه سالكاً إلى الجنة.

The Prophet, may God's blessings and abundant peace be upon him, said, "Whoever deliberately neglects to ask for blessings on me has missed the path to the Garden. The route to the Garden will be barred for such a negligent one, whereas it will be open for him who asks for blessings upon me."

- وفي رواية عبد الرحمن بن عوف رضي الله عنه قال قال رسول الله ﷺ جاءني جبريل عليه السلام فقال يا محمد لا يصلي

عليك أحد إلا صلّى الله سبعون ألف ملك ومن صلّت عليه الملائكة كان من أهل الجنة.

'Abd Ar-Rahman bin 'Awf (may God be pleased with him) reported that the Prophet, may God's blessings and abundant peace be upon him, said, "Angel Gabriel (peace be upon him) said: 'O Muhammad, whenever anyone from your nation asks for blessings on you, seventy thousand angels bless him. And whoever is blessed by angels will be one of the People of the Garden.'"

- وقال صلى الله عليه وسلم أكثركم علي صلاة أكثركم أزواجاً في الجنة.

The Prophet, may God's blessings and abundant peace be upon him, said, "The more you ask for blessings upon me, the more you will have in The Garden."

- وروي عنه صلى الله عليه وسلم أن قال من صلي علي صلاةً تعظيماً لحقي خلق الله عز وجل من ذلك القول ملكاً له

جناح بالمشرق والآخر بالمغرب ورجلاه مقرورتان في الأرض السابعة السفلى وعنقه ملتوية تحت العرش يقول الله عز

وجل له صل علي عبدي كما صلى علي نبي فهو يصلي عليه إلى يوم القيامة.

It is related that the Prophet, may God's blessings and abundant peace be upon him, said, "Whenever someone asks for blessings on me, extolling my right, God, Mighty and Sublime is He, creates from his words an angel. This angel has wings stretching from the East to the West, with his feet connected to the lowest part of the seventh earth and his neck bent beneath The Throne. God, Mighty and Sublime is He, says to him, 'Bless My servant as he asks for blessings on My Prophet,' and thereupon the angel will bless him until the Day of the Rising-Up."

- وروى عنه صلى الله عليه وسلم أنه قال ليردن على الحوض يوم القيامة أقوام ما أعرفهم إلا بكثرة الصلاة علي.

It is related that the Prophet, may God's blessings and abundant peace be upon him, said, "Nations will come to my Pool on the Day of the Rising-Up whom I will know only because of their frequent asking for blessings upon me."

- وروى عنه صلى الله عليه وسلم أنه قال من صلى علي مرة واحدة صلى الله عليه عشر مرات ومن صلى علي عشر مرات

صلى الله عليه مائة مرة ومن صلى علي مائة مرة صلى الله عليه ألف مرة ومن صلى علي ألف مرة حرّم الله جسده وثبته

بالقول الثابت في الحياة الدنيا وفي الآخرة عند المسألة وأدخله الجنة وجاءته صلواته علي نوراً له يوم القيمة على الصراط

مسيرة خمسمائة عام وأعطاه الله بكل صلاة صلاه قصراً في الجنة قل ذلك أو كثر.

It is related that the Prophet, may God's blessings and peace be upon him, said, "Whoever asks God to bless me, God will bless him ten times. And whoever asks God ten times to bless me, God will bless him one hundred times. And whoever asks God one hundred times to bless me, God will bless him one thousand times. And whoever asks God to bless me one thousand times, God will prohibit The Fire from touching his body. And his word on any matter will be made enduring in this world and the next. He will enter The Garden and, on the Day of the Rising-Up, his request for blessings on me will be a light for him on the path, a light visible at a distance of five hundred years. And God will grant him, for every blessing upon me asked for, a palace in The Garden, regardless of how many."

- وقال النبي صلى الله عليه وسلم ما من عبد صلى علي إلا خرجت الصلاة مسرعة من فيه فلا يبقى بر ولا بحر ولا شرق ولا غرب إلا وتمر به وتقول أن صلاة فلان بن فلان صلى على محمد المختار خير خلق الله فلا يبقى شيء إلا وصلى عليه ويُخلق من تلك الصلاة طائر له سبعون ألف جناح في كل جناح سبعون ألف ريشة في كل ريشة سبعون ألف وجه في كل وجه سبعون ألف فم في كل فم سبعون ألف لسان كل لسان يسبح الله تعالى بسبعين ألف لغة ويكتب الله له ثواب ذلك كله.

The Prophet, may God's blessings and abundant peace be upon him, said, "Whenever a servant of God asks for blessings on me, his request leaves him quickly, passing over land and sea and through East and West, saying 'I am the blessing on Muhammad, the Chosen One, the Best of God's Creation, asked for by so and so.' Everything asks for blessings on him. From these blessings a bird is created with seventy thousand wings, each with seventy thousand feathers. Each feather has seventy thousand heads, on each of which are seventy thousand faces. Each face has seventy thousand mouths, and there are seventy thousand tongues in every mouth. Each tongue glorifies God the Exalted in seventy thousand languages, and God will then write the reward for all of that for him."

- وعن علي بن أبي طالب رضي الله عنه قال قال رسول الله صلى الله عليه وسلم من صلى علي يوم الجمعة مائة مرة جاء يوم القيامة ومعه نور لو قُسم ذلك النور بين الخلق كلهم لوسعهم.

Imam Ali bin Abu Talib (may God bless him) narrated, "The Messenger of God, may God's blessings and abundant peace be upon him, said, 'Whoever asks God one hundred times on a Friday to bless me, on the Day of the Rising-Up a light will come for him, a light which, if it were divided among them, would be sufficient for all of creation.'"

- ذكر في بعض الأخبار مكتوب على ساق العرش من إشتاق إلى رحمته ومن سألني أعطيته ومن تقرّب إلي بالصلاة على محمد غفرت له ذنوبه ولو كانت مثل زبد البحر.

It is mentioned in the good tidings: "It is written on the leg of The Throne, 'Whoever yearns for Me, I am merciful to him. Whoever asks Me, I will grant him his wish. Whoever draws near to Me by asking for blessings upon My Beloved Muhammad, I will forgive him, even if his sins are as plentiful as the foam on the surface of the ocean.'"

- وروي عن بعض الصحابة رضوان الله عليهم أجمعين أنه قال ما من مجلس يصلى فيه على محمد صلى الله عليه وسلم إلا قامت منه رائحة طيبة حتى تبلغ عنان السماء فتقول الملائكة هذا مجلس صُلي فيه على محمد صلى الله عليه وسلم.

One of the Companions, may God be pleased with him, related, "There is no gathering in which blessings upon Muhammad, may God's blessings and peace be upon him, are asked for but that a beautiful fragrance rises from them and reaches the clouds in the sky. The angels then say, 'This is a gathering in which blessings upon Muhammad, may God's blessings and abundant peace be upon him, are being asked for.'"

- ذُكر في بعض الأخبار أن العبد المؤمن أو الأمة المؤمنة إذا بدأ بالصلاة على محمد صلى الله عليه وسلم فتحت له أبواب السماء والسرادقات حتى إلى العرش فلا يبقى ملك في السموات إلا صلى على محمد ويستغفرون لذلك العبد أو الأمة ما شاء الله.

Other reports mention, "The Gates of Heaven will be opened for a believing servant, male or female, who will start by asking for blessings upon Muhammad (ﷺ). The Pavilions are then opened as far as The Throne, and all the angels will bless Muhammad, may God's blessings and abundant peace be upon him, and they will ask for forgiveness for that believing servant for as long as God wishes."

- وقال صلى الله عليه وسلم: من عثرت عليه حاجة فليكثر بالصلاة علي فإنها تكشف الهموم والغموم والكروب وتكثر الأرزاق وتقضي الحوائج.

The Prophet, may God's blessings and abundant peace be upon him, said: "Whoever is troubled by some matter should increase his asking for blessings upon me. This will remove his anxieties, sorrows and cares, increase his provision and satisfy all his needs."

- وعن بعض الصالحين أنه قال كان لي جار نسّاخ فمات فرأيته في المنام فقلت له ما فعل الله بك فقال غفر لي فقلت فبم ذلك فقال كنت إذا كتبت إسم محمد صلى الله عليه وسلم في كتاب صليت عليه فأعطاني ربي ما لا عين رأيت ولا أذن سمعت ولا خطر على قلب بشر.

One of the Righteous reported, " A neighbour of mine was a scribe, and he died. After he died, I saw him in a dream and asked how God had treated him. He replied, 'He has forgiven me.' I asked, 'For what reason has He forgiven you?' He said, 'Whenever I wrote the name of Muhammad, may God's blessings and peace be upon him, in a book, I asked God to bless him. And, therefore, My Lord has given me what no eye has ever seen, no ear has ever heard and what no mortal has ever imagined.'"

- وعن أنس رضي الله عنه قال قال رسول الله صلى الله عليه وسلم لا يؤمن أحدكم حتى أكون أحب إليه من نفسه وماله وولده ووالده والناس أجمعين.

Anas, may God be pleased with him, related that the Prophet, may God's blessings and peace be upon him, said, "None of you truly believe until I am dearer to him than his self, his wealth, his children, his parents and all other people."

- وفي حديث عمر بن الخطاب رضي الله عنه أنت أحب إلي يا رسول الله من كل شيء إلا نفسي التي بين جنبي فقال له صلى الله عليه وسلم لا تكون مؤمنا حتى أكون أحب إليك من نفسك فقال عمر والذي أنزل عليك الكتاب لأنت أحب إليّ من نفسي التي بين جنبي فقال رسول الله صلى الله عليه وسلم الآن يا عمر تم إيمانك.

Umar, may God be pleased with him, reported that he said to the Prophet, "You are dearer to me, O Messenger of God, than everything I possess except myself, which is within me." The Prophet, may God's blessings and abundant peace be upon him, replied, "You will not be a true believer until I am dearer to you than yourself." Umar replied, "By Him Who revealed to you the Book, you are dearer to me than myself." The Prophet, may God's blessings and abundant peace be upon him, said, "Now, O Umar, your faith is complete."

- وقيل لرسول الله صلى الله عليه وسلم متى أكون مؤمناً وفي لفظ آخر مؤمناً صادقاً قال إذا أحببت الله ومتى أُحب الله قال إذا أحببت رسوله فقيل ومتى أُحب رسوله قال إذا اتبعت طريقته واستعملت سنته وأحببت بحبه وأبغضت ببغضه وواليت بولايته وعاديت بعداوته ويتفاوت الناس في الإيمان على قدر تفاوتهم في محبتي ويتفاوتون في الكفر على قدر تفاوتهم في بغضي. ألا لا إيمان لمن لا محبة له ألا لا إيمان لمن لا محبة له.

The Prophet, may God's blessings and abundant peace be upon him, was asked, "When will I attain faith?" (In another version: "When will I attain true faith?") He replied, "When you love God." It was asked, "When will I love God?" He said, "When you love His Messenger." It was then asked, "And when will I love His Messenger?" He answered: "When you follow his path, adhere to his way, love what he loves, befriend whom he befriends, hate what he hates, and oppose whom he opposes. According to their hatred of me, people will be distinguished from one another in their disbelief. Surely, there is no faith for those who have no love.".

- وقيل لرسول الله صلى الله عليه وسلم نرى مؤمناً يخشع ومؤمناً لا يخشع ما السبب في ذلك فقال من وجد لإيمانه حلاوة خشع ومن لم يجدها لم يخشع. فقيل بم توجد أو تنال وتكتسب قال بصدق الحب في الله فقيل وبم يوجد حب الله أو بم يكتسب فقال بحب رسوله فالتمسوا رضاء الله ورضاء رسوله في حبهما.

Can there be faith for one who does not love the Prophet, may God's blessings and peace be upon him?

It was said to the Messenger of God, may God's blessings and abundant peace be upon him, "We see humble believers and believers who are not humble. What is the reason for this?" He (ﷺ) replied: "The one finds his faith adorned with humility, while the other does not." It was asked: "How can we find such faith, obtain it or earn it? He (ﷺ) replied: "By sincerely loving God." It was asked, "How can we find or earn the love of God?" He (ﷺ) said, "By loving His Messenger. So, seek out the contentment of God and the contentment of His Messenger by loving them."

- وقيل لرسول الله صلى الله عليه وسلم من آلُ محمد الذين أُمرنا بحبهم وإكرامهم والبرور بهم فقال أهل الصفاء والوفاء من ءامن بي وأخلص فقيل وما علاماتهم فقال إيثار محبتي على كل محبوب وإشتغال الباطن بذكري بعد ذكر الله ✳ وفي أخرى علامتهم إدمان ذكري والإكثار من الصلاة عليّ.

It was asked of the Messenger of God, may God's blessings and abundant peace be on him, "Who are Muhammad's family whom we are ordered to love, honour and treat with reverence?" He replied, "They are the People of Purity and Fidelity who sincerely believe in me." It was asked, "What are their signs?" He said: "Traces of my love are on every lover, and their inner life is busy with remembering me and remembering God." (In another version, the words are, "Their signs are being devoted to remembering me and constantly asking for blessings upon me.")

- وقيل لرسول الله صلى الله عليه وسلم من القويّ في الإيمان بك فقال من آمن بي ولم يرني فإنه مؤمن بي على شوق منه وصدق في محبتي وعلامة ذلك منه أنّه يود رؤيتي بجميع ما يملك وفي أخرى بملء الأرض ذهباً ذلك المؤمن بي حقاً والمخلص في محبتي صدقاً.

A man asked the Messenger of God, may God's blessings and abundant peace be on him, "Who is he who is strongest in his love for you?" He replied, "He is the one who believes in me without having seen me, for he is sincere in his love for me and is a believer in me through yearning. A sign of this is that he hopes for a vision of me more than anything he owns. (In another version, the words are, "… more than all the gold in the world.") He is a true believer in me, whose love for me is true and sincere".

- وقيل لرسول الله صلى الله عليه وسلم أرأيت صلاة المصلين عليك ممن غاب عنك ومن يأتي بعدك ما حالهما عندك فقال أسمع صلاة أهل محبتي وأعرفهم وتُعرض على صلاة غيرهما عرضاً.

A person asked the Messenger of God, may God's blessings and abundant peace be on him, "Are you aware of the blessings on you asked for by those who are not with you or those who will come after you? What is their status regarding you?" He said, "I hear the blessings of those who love me, and I know them. And others' blessings are presented to me."

افتتاح دلائل الخيرات

بِسْمِ اللَّهِ الرَّحْمَٰنِ الرَّحِيمِ الْحَمْدُ لِلَّهِ رَبِّ الْعَالَمِينَ، حَسْبِيَ اللهُ وَنِعْمَ الْوَكِيلُ، وَلَا حَوْلَ وَلَا قُوَّةَ إِلَّا بِاللهِ الْعَلِيِّ الْعَظِيمِ. اللَّهُمَّ إِنِّي أَبْرَأُ مِنْ حَوْلِي وَقُوَّتِي إِلَى حَوْلِكَ وَقُوَّتِكَ. اللَّهُمَّ إِنِّي أَتَقَرَّبُ إِلَيْكَ بِالصَّلَاةِ عَلَى سَيِّدِنَا مُحَمَّدٍ عَبْدِكَ وَنَبِيِّكَ وَرَسُولِكَ سَيِّدِ الْمُرْسَلِينَ صَلَّى الله تَعَالَى وَسَلَّمَ عَلَيْهِ وَعَلَيْهِمْ أَجْمَعِينَ امْتِثَالاً لِأَمْرِكَ وَتَصْدِيقاً لَهُ وَمَحَبَّةً فِيهِ وَشَوْقاً إِلَيْهِ وَتَعْظِيماً لِقَدْرِهِ وَلِكَوْنِهِ صَلَّى اللهُ عَلَيْهِ وَسَلَّمَ أَهْلاً لِذَلِكَ فَتَقَبَّلْهَا مِنِّي بِفَضْلِكَ وَاجْعَلْنِي مِنْ عِبَادِكَ الصَّالِحِينَ وَوَفِّقْنِي لِقِرَاءَتِهَا عَلَى الدَّوَامِ بِجَاهِهِ عِنْدَكَ وَصَلَّى اللهُ عَلَى سَيِّدِنَا مُحَمَّدٍ وَآلِهِ وَصَحْبِهِ أَجْمَعِينَ.

bis°mi allahi al-raḥ°ma°ni al-raḥīmi al-ḥam°du lilahi rabi al-ʿālamīna, ḥas°bīa allahu wani°ma al-wakīlu, walā ḥaūla walā quwa°ta īlwā billhi al-ʿalīu al-ʿaẓīmi. allahuma īnī āb°ra'au min° ḥaū°lī waquwatī īlai ḥaū°lika waquwatika allahuma īnī ātaqarabu īlaī°ka bilṣalāti ʿalai saīidinā muḥammad° ʿab°dika wanabīika warasūlika saīidi al-mur°salīna ṣala allhu taʿālai wasalama ʿalaī°hi waʿalaī°him° āğ°maʿīna im°tiṯhālā°n li'ām°rika wataṣ°dīqā°n lahu wamaḥabaī°n fīhi washaū°qā°n ilaī°hi wata°zīmā°n liqad°rihi walikaū°nihi ṣalla allhu ʿalaī°hi wasalama āh°lā°n lizalika fataqabal°hā minī bifaḍ°lika wāğ°al°anī min° ʿibādika al-ṣāliḥīna wawafiq°nī liqirā'atihā ʿalai al-dawāmi biğāhihi ʿin°daka waṣallai allahu ʿala saīyidinā muḥammad° wa'ālihi waṣaḥ°bihi ājmaina.

The Opening of Dala'il Al-Khayrat

All praise belongs to God, the Lord of all the Worlds. God is enough for me and the best Protector. There is no power nor strength except from God, the Most High, the Immense. Dear God, I relinquish my power and strength in favour of Your Power and Your Strength. Dear God, I draw near to You by the prayer for our noble master Muhammad, Your Servant, Prophet and Messenger, the Master of the Messengers, may God Almighty bless him and grant him and all of them peace. I do so in obedience to Your Command, loving him, affirming him, yearning for him, respecting his worth and the fact that he, may God bless him and grant him abundant peace, is worthy of all that. Accept this from me by Your Grace and make me one of Your righteous servants. By his rank with You, give me success in reading it (Dala'il Al Khayrat) continuously. May God bless the noble master Muhammad and his family and all his Companions.

The Most Beautiful Names of God

In God's name, The Rahman, The Merciful

#	Arabic Name Transliterated	Arabic Name	English Translation
1	Ar-Raḥmān	الرَّحمنُ	The Rahman
2	Ar-Raḥīm	الرحيمُ	The Merciful
3	Al-Malik	الملكُ	The King
4	Al-Quddūs	القدُّوسُ	The Holy
5	As-Salām	السَّلامُ	The Peace
6	Al-Mu'min	المؤمنُ	The Faithful
7	Al-Muhaymin	المُهَيْمنُ	The Dominator
8	Al-'Azīz	العزيزُ	The Glorious
9	Al-Jabbār	الجبَّارُ	The Ever-Compelling
10	Al-Mutakabbir	المتَكبِّرُ	The Lofty
11	Al-Khāliq	الخالقُ	The Creator
12	Al-Bari'	البارئُ	The Maker
13	Al-Musawwir	المصوِّرُ	The Fashioner
14	Al-Ghaffār	الغفَّارُ	The Ever-Forgiving
15	Al-Qahhār	القهَّارُ	The Ever-Subduing
16	Al-Wahhāb	الوَهَّابُ	The Ever-Endowing
17	Ar-Razzāq	الرَّزَّاقُ	The Ever-Sustaining
18	Al-Fattāh	الفتَّاحُ	The Ever-Opening
19	Al-'Alīm	العليمُ	The Omniscient
20	As-Sami'	السَّميعُ	The All-Hearing
21	Al-Basir	البصيرُ	The All-Seeing
22	Al-Latīf	اللَّطيفُ	The Gracious
23	Al-Khabīr	الخبيرُ	The All-Knowing
24	Al-Halīm	الحَليمُ	The Ever-Forbearing
25	Al-'Azīm	العظيمُ	The Great
26	Al-Ghafūr	الغَفورُ	The All-Forgiving
27	Ash-Shakūr	الشَّكورُ	The All-Thankful

#	Arabic Name Transliterated	Arabic Name	English Translation
28	Al-'Alī	العليُّ	The Most High
29	Al-Kabīr	الكبيرُ	The Grand
30	Al-Hafīz	الحفيظُ	The All-Preserving
31	Al-Muqīt	المقيتُ	The All-Providing
32	Al-Hasīb	الحسيبُ	The All-Reckoning
33	Al-Karīm	الكريمُ	The Munificent
34	Ar-Raqīb	الرَّقيبُ	The Watchful
35	Al-Mujīb	المُجيبُ	The Answerer
36	Al-Wāsiᶜ	الواسعُ	The Broad
37	Al-Hakīm	الحَكيمُ	The Wise
38	Al-Wadud	الودودُ	The Ever-Loving
39	Al-Majeed	المجيدُ	The Glorious
40	Ash-Shahīd	الشَّهيدُ	The All-Witness
41	Al-Haqq	الحقُّ	The Truth
42	Al-Wakīl	الوَكيلُ	The Advocate
43	Al-Qawī	القويُّ	The Almighty
44	Al-Matīn	المتينُ	The Firm
45	Al-Walī	الوليُّ	The Patron
46	Al-Hamīd	الحميدُ	The Praiseworthy
47	Al-Ḥayy	الحيُّ	The Ever-Living
48	Al-Qayyūm	القيُّومُ	The Ever-Rising
49	Al-Wāḥid	الواحدُ	The One
50	Al-Aḥad	الأَحَدُ	The Unique
51	As-Ṣamad	الصَّمَدُ	The Steadfast
52	Al-Qādir	القادِرُ	The Powerful
53	Al-Muqtadir	المقتَدِرُ	The Omnipotent
54	Al-Awwal	الأَوَّلُ	The First
55	Al-Ākhir	الآخرُ	The Last
56	Az-Ẓāhir	الظَّاهرُ	The Manifest
57	Al-Bāṭin	الباطنُ	The Unmanifest

#	Arabic Name Transliterated	Arabic Name	English Translation
58	Al-Muta'ali	المتَعالِ	The Transcendent
59	Al-Barr	البَرُّ	The Beneficent
60	Al-Tawwāb	التَّوَّابُ	The Ever Accepting of Repentance
61	Al-ᶜAfū	العفَوُّ	The Pardoner
62	Ar-Ra'ūf	الرَّءوفُ	The Compassionate
63	Al-Ghanī	الغَنيُّ	The Rich
64	Al-Wārith	الوَارثُ	The Inheritor
65	Al-Qābid	القابضُ	The Constrictor
66	Al-Bāsit	الباسِطُ	The Expander
67	Al-Hakam	الحكَمُ	The Judge
68	Al-Muqaddim	المقدِّمُ	The Advancer
69	Al-Mu'akhkhir	المؤخِّرُ	The Delayer
70	Al-Khāfid	الخافضُ	The Demoter
71	Ar-Rāfi	الرَّافعُ	The Promoter
72	Al-Mu'izz	المعِزُّ	The Exalting
73	Al-Mudhill	المذلُّ	The Humiliator
74	Al-'Adl	العَدلُ	The Just
75	Al-Jalīl	الجَليلُ	The Majestic
76	Al-Bā'ith	الباعثُ	The Resurrector
77	Al-Muḥṣī	المُحصي	The Reckoner
78	Al-Mubdi'	المبدئُ	The Initiator
79	Al-Mu'īd	المعيدُ	The Restorer
80	Al-Muḥyi	المُحيي	The Life-Giver
81	Al-Mumīt	المميتُ	The Life-Taker
82	Al-Wājid	الواجِدُ	The Author
83	Al-Mājid	الماجِدُ	The Glory-Giver
84	Al-Wali	الوالي	The Ordainer
85	Al-Muntaqim	المنتقِمُ	The Avenger
86	Mālik al-Mulk	مالك المالِكُ	The Owner of Dominion
87	Dhu'l Jalāl wa'l-Ikrām	ذُو الجلالِ والإكْرام	The Majestic and Bounteous One

#	Arabic Name Transliterated	Arabic Name	English Translation
88	Al-Muqsiṭ	المقسِطُ	The Equitable
89	Al-Jāmi'	الجامِعُ	The Gatherer
90	Al-Mughnī	المُغني	The Enricher
91	Al-Māni'	المانعُ	The Preventer
92	Al-Nāfic	النَّافِعُ	The Propitious
93	Al-Ḍārr	الضَّارُّ	The Distresser
94	Al-Nūr	النُّورُ	The Light
95	Al-Hādī	الهادي	The Guide
96	Al-Badīc	البَديعُ	The Originator
97	Al-Bāqī	الباقي	The Everlasting
98	Ar-Rashīd	الرَّشيدُ	The All-Guiding
99	As-Ṣabūr	الصَّبورُ	The All-Patient

الَّذِي تَقَدَّسَتْ عَنِ الْأَشْبَاهِ ذَاتُهُ وَتَنَزَّهَتْ عَنْ مُشَابَهَةِ الْأَمْثَالِ صِفَاتُهُ وَاحِدٌ لَا مِنْ قِلَّةٍ وَمَوْجُودٌ لَا مِنْ عِلَّةٍ، بِالْبِرِّ مَعْرُوفٌ

وَبِالْإِحْسَانِ مَوْصُوفٌ مَعْرُوفٌ بِلَا غَايَةٍ وَمَوْصُوفٌ بِلَا نِهَايَةٍ أَوَّلٌ بِلَا ابْتِدَاءٍ وَآخِرٌ بِلَا إِنْتِهَاءٍ لَا يُنْسَبُ إِلَيْهِ الْبَنُونَ وَلَا يُفْنِيهِ تَدَاوُلُ

الْأَوْقَاتِ وَلَا تُوهِنُهُ السِّنُونَ كُلُّ الْمَخْلُوقَاتِ قَهْرُ عَظَمَتِهِ وَأَمْرُهُ بِالْكَافِ وَالنُّونِ بِذِكْرِهِ أَنِسَ الْمُخْلَصُونَ وَبِرُؤْيَتِهِ تَقَرُّ الْعُيُونُ

وَبِتَوْحِيدِهِ ابْتَهَجَ الْمُوَحِّدُونَ هَدَى أَهْلَ طَاعَتِهِ إِلَى صِرَاطٍ مُسْتَقِيمٍ وَأَبَاحَ أَهْلَ مَحَبَّتِهِ جَنَّاتِ النَّعِيمِ وَعَلِمَ عَدَدَ أَنْفَاسِ مَخْلُوقَاتِهِ بِعِلْمِهِ

الْقَدِيمِ وَيَرَى حَرَكَاتِ أَرْجُلِ النَّمْلِ فِي جُنْحِ اللَّيْلِ الْبَهِيمِ يُسَبِّحُهُ الطَّائِرُ فِي وَكْرِهِ وَيُمَجِّدُهُ الْوَحْشُ فِي قَفْرِهِ مُحِيطٌ بِعَمَلِ الْعَبْدِ سِرِّهِ

وَجَهْرِهِ وَكَفِيلٌ لِلْمُؤْمِنِينَ بِتَأْيِيدِهِ وَنَصْرِهِ وَتَطْمَئِنُّ الْقُلُوبُ الْوَجِلَةُ بِذِكْرِهِ وَكَشْفِ ضُرِّهِ وَمِنْ آيَاتِهِ أَنْ تَقُومَ السَّمَاءُ وَالْأَرْضُ بِأَمْرِهِ

أَحَاطَ بِكُلِّ شَيْءٍ عِلْماً وَغَفَرَ ذُنُوبَ الْمُذْنِبِينَ كَرَماً وَحِلْماً لَيْسَ كَمِثْلِهِ شَيْءٌ وَهُوَ السَّمِيعُ الْبَصِيرُ.

Allazī taqadasat' 'ani al-˚'āshbāhi ḏhātuhu wātanazahat 'an' mushābahatil al-˚ amthāli ṣifātuhu wāḥidun lā min' qillaṫen wamauġūdun lā min' 'illaṫ, bilbirri ma'rūfun wabil iḥsāni mauṣūf'ma'rūfun bilā ġāiaṫjn wa-mauṣūf'bilā nihāiaṫjn āwwal'bilā abtidā', wa ākhirun bilāntihā'in lā yunsabu ilayhil banūna walā yufnīhi tadāwulul awqāti walā tūhinuhus sinūna kullul makhlūqāti qahru 'aẓamatihi wa amruhu bilkāfi wan nūni bidhikrihi anisal mukhliṣūna wa biru'yatihi taqarrul 'uyūnu wa bitawḥīdihibtahajal muwaḥḥidūna hadā ahla ṭā'atihi ilā ṣirāṭim mustaqīmin wa abāḥa ahla maḥabbatihi jannātin na'īmi wa 'alima 'adada anfāsi makhlūqātihi bi'ilmihil qadīmi wa yarā ḥarakāti arjulin namli fī junḥil laylil bahīmu yusabbiḥuhuṭ ṭā'iru fī wakrihi wa yumajjiduhul waḥshu fī qafrihi muḥīṭun bi'amalil 'abdi sirrihi wajahrihi wa kafīlun lilmu'minīna bita'yīdihi wa naṣrihi wa taṭma'innul qulūbul wajilatu bidhikrihi wa kashfi ḍurrihi wa min āyātihi an taqūmas samā'u wal arḍu bi amrihi aḥāta bikulli shay'in 'ilman wa ghafara dhunubal mudhnibīna karaman waḥ ilman laysa kamithlihi shay'un wa huwas samī'ul baṣīr.

His Essence is pure beyond any likeness, and His Attributes are exalted beyond any resemblance to another. He is One, not among any one or thing, and He Exists but is not begotten. He is acclaimed for His Kindness and renowned for giving the best of Generosity, and this attribute is boundless.

He is the First, without beginning, and the Last, without end. Sons are not ascribed to Him. The passage of time does not alter Him, nor do the years affect Him. All of creation is subject to His Grandeur. His Command is the kaf and the nun ("kun" – Be). The sincere believers are familiar with the remembrance of Him, and their eyes delight in His proximity.

The people believe He is One. He guides the obedient to Him onto a straight path. And He bestows the Gardens of Bliss upon the people He loves. He knows the number of breaths of His creatures by His eternal and infinite Knowledge. And He sees the movements of the feet of ants in the dark night. The birds glorify Him in their nests, and wild animals celebrate His glory in the wilderness.

He has complete knowledge of His servants' actions, both in secret and in public. He guarantees the believers His support and help. Fearful hearts are put at rest by the remembrance of Him, and harm is removed. Among His signs is that His Command sustains the heavens and the earth. His Knowledge encompasses all things, and He forgives the wrong actions of those who commit them out of His Generosity and Forbearance. There is nothing that is like Him, and He is the All-Hearing, the All-Seeing.

اللَّهُمَّ اكْفِنَا السُّوءَ بِمَا شِئْتَ وَكَيْفَ شِئْتَ إِنَّكَ عَلَى مَا تَشَاءُ قَدِيرٌ (3) يَا نِعْمَ الْمَوْلَى وَيَا نِعْمَ النَّصِيرُ غُفْرَانَكَ رَبَّنَا وَإِلَيْكَ الْمَصِيرُ

وَلَا حَوْلَ وَلَا قُوَّةَ إِلَّا بِاللهِ الْعَلِيِّ الْعَظِيمِ. سُبْحَانَكَ لَا نُحْصِي ثَنَاءً عَلَيْكَ أَنْتَ كَمَا أَثْنَيْتَ عَلَى نَفْسِكَ جَلَّ وَجْهُكَ وَعَزَّ جَاهُكَ

يَفْعَلُ اللهُ مَا يَشَاءُ بِقُدْرَتِهِ وَيَحْكُمُ مَا يُرِيدُ بِعِزَّتِهِ. يَا حَيُّ يَا قَيُّومُ يَا بَدِيعَ السَّمَاوَاتِ وَالْأَرْضِ يَا ذَا الْجَلَالِ وَالْإِكْرَامِ لَا إِلَهَ إِلَّا أَنْتَ

بِرَحْمَتِكَ نَسْتَغِيثُ وَمِنْ عَذَابِكَ نَسْتَجِيرُ يَا غَيَاثَ الْمُسْتَغِيثِينَ لَا إِلَهَ إِلَّا أَنْتَ بِجَاهِ سَيِّدِنَا مُحَمَّدٍ صَلَّى اللهُ عَلَيْهِ وَسَلَّمَ أَغِثْنَا وَارْحَمْنَا.

رَحْمَةُ اللهِ وَبَرَكَاتُهُ عَلَيْكُمْ أَهْلَ الْبَيْتِ إِنَّهُ حَمِيدٌ مَجِيدٌ ﴿ إِنَّمَا يُرِيدُ اللهُ لِيُذْهِبَ عَنْكُمُ الرِّجْسَ أَهْلَ الْبَيْتِ وَيُطَهِّرَكُمْ تَطْهِيراً ﴾ ؛ ﴿ إِنَّ

اللهَ وَمَلَائِكَتَهُ يُصَلُّونَ عَلَى النَّبِيِّ يَا أَيُّهَا الَّذِينَ آمَنُوا صَلُّوا عَلَيْهِ وَسَلِّمُوا تَسْلِيماً ﴾ .

اللَّهُمَّ صَلِّ أَفْضَلَ صَلَاةٍ عَلَى أَسْعَدِ مَخْلُوقَاتِكَ سَيِّدِنَا مُحَمَّدٍ وَعَلَى آلِهِ وَصَحْبِهِ وَسَلِّمْ عَدَدَ مَعْلُومَاتِكَ وَمِدَادَ كَلِمَاتِكَ كُلَّمَا ذَكَرَكَ

الذَّاكِرُونَ وَغَفَلَ عَنْ ذِكْرِهِ الْغَافِلُونَ.

Allāhummaikfinās sū'a bimā shi'ta wa kayfa shi'ta innaka ʿalā mā tashā'u qadīrun (3) yā niʿmal mawlā wa yā niʿman naṣīr ghufrānaka rabbanā wa ilaykal maṣīr wā lā ḥawla wā lā quwwata illā biLlahil ʿaliyyil ʿaẓīm. Subḥānaka lā nuḥṣī thanā'an ʿalayka 'anta kamāthnayta ʿalā nafsika jalla wajhuka waʿazza jāhuka yafʿaluLlāhu mā yashā'u biqudratihi wa yaḥkumu mā yurīdu biʿizzatihi. Yā ḥayyu yā qayyūm yā badīʿas samāwāti wal arḍi yā dhāl jalāli wal ikrāmi lā ilāha illā anta biraḥmatika nastaghīthu wa min ʿadhabika nastajīru yā ghayyāthal mustaghīthīna lā ilāha illā anta bijāhi sayyidinā Muḥammadin ṣallAllāhu ʿalayhi wasallama aghithnā warḥamnā. RaḥmatuLlāhi wa barakātuhu ʿalaykum ahlal bayti innahu ḥamīdun majīdun: innamā yurīduLlāhu liyudh-hiba ʿankumur rijsa ahlal bayti wa yuṭahhirakum taṭhīran; innaLlāha wamalā'ikatahu yuṣallūna ʿalān nabiyyi yā ayyuhāl ladhīna āmanū ṣallū ʿalayhi wasallimū taslīman. Allāhumma ṣalli afḍala ṣalātin ʿalā asʿadi makhlūqātika Sayyidinā Muḥammadin wa ʿalā 'ālihi wa ṣaḥbihi wa sallim ʿadada maʿlūmātika wa midāda kalimātika kullamā dhakarakadh dhākirūna wa ghafala ʿan dhikrihil ghāfilūn.

Dear God! Save us from the evils ordained, for indeed You bring to fruition whatsoever You will (3 times). O the Best Protector, O the Best Helper, Forgive us, our Lord. The ultimate end is to You. There is no power nor strength except from God, the Most High, the Immense. Glory be to You. We cannot number Your praises as You praise Yourself. Your Face is Majestic, and Your Honour is exalted. God does whatsoever He wishes by His Power and judges what He wills by His Might. The Ever-Living, the Self-Sustaining. O Originator of the heavens and the earth. O Lord of Majesty and Honour!

There is no deity but You. We seek help by Your Mercy and Protection from Your punishment. O You Who helps those who ask for help. There is no god but You. By honouring our noble master Muhammad, may God's blessings and peace be upon him, give us support and show us mercy. "God's mercy and blessings be upon you, O People of the House." [Q 11:73] You are the Praiseworthy, the Glorious. "God desires to remove all impurity from you, O People of the House, and to purify you completely." [Q 33:33] "Truly, God and His angels invoke blessings on the Prophet. O you who believe! Invoke blessings on him and greetings of peace!" [Q 33:53]

Dear God, send Your best blessings to the happiest of Your creatures, our noble master Muhammad and his family and Companions, and grant him peace - in number as great as what You know, and the ink that writes Your words, and when those who remember You, remember; and those who neglect him, neglect.

201 Names of our noble master and Prophet, Muhammad - may God grant him peace and bestow His blessings upon him

اللَّهُمَّ صَلِّ وَسَلِّمْ وَبَارِكْ عَلَى مَنْ أَشْرَفُ الْأَسْمَاءِ سَيِّدُنَا مُحَمَّدٌ صَلَّى اللهُ عَلَيْهِ وَسَلَّمْ

Allāhumma ṣalli wa sallim wa bārik ʿalā man ashraful asmāʾi sayyidunā Muḥammadun ṣallAllāhu ʿalayhi wasallam.

Dear God! Bless and support, grant peace and sanctify the one with the noblest of names, our noble lord Muhammad, may God bless him and grant him peace.

#	Arabic Name	Arabic Name Transliterated	English Translation
1	محمد	Muhammad	The Praised One, God's blessing and peace be upon him
2	أَحْمَدُ	Ahmad	The Most Praised, God's blessing and peace be upon him
3	حَامِدُ	Haamid	The Praiser, God's blessing and peace be upon him
4	مَحْمُودُ	Mahmud	The Most Highly Praised, God's blessing and peace be upon him
5	أَحِيدُ	Aheed	The Repeller of Punishment on the Day of Judgment, God's blessing and peace be upon him
6	وَحِيدُ	Wahid	Unique, God's blessing and peace be upon him
7	مَاحٍ	Maahi	The Effacer, God's blessing and peace be upon him
8	حَاشِرُ	Hashir	The Gatherer, God's blessing and peace be upon him
9	عَاقِبُ	Aqib	The Last in Succession, God's blessing and peace be upon him
10	طَهَ	Ta Ha	(name of a Surah of the Holy Quran), God's blessing and peace be upon him
11	يَس	Ya Sin	(name of a Surah of the Holy Quran), God's blessing and peace be upon him
12	طَاهِرُ	Tahir	Pure, God's blessing and peace be upon him
13	مُطَهَّرُ	Mutahir	The Purifier, God's blessing and peace be upon him
14	طَيِّبُ	Tayyeb	The Good, God's blessing and peace be upon him
15	سَيِّدُ	Saiyed	The Master, God's blessing and peace be upon him
16	رَسُولُ	Rasool	The Messenger, God's blessing and peace be upon him

#	Arabic Name	Arabic Name Transliterated	English Translation
17	نَبِيٌّ	Nabi	The Prophet, God's blessing and peace be upon him
18	رَسُولُ الرَّحْمَةِ	Rasool ar-Rahmah	The Messenger of Mercy, God's blessing and peace be upon him
19	قَيِّمٌ	Qayim	Upright, God's blessing and peace be upon him
20	جَامِعٌ	Jami	Gatherer, God's blessing and peace be upon him
21	مُقْتَفِي	Muqtafin	Follower, God's blessing and peace be upon him
22	مُقَفَّى	Muqaffi	The Best Example, God's blessing and peace be upon him
23	رَسُولُ الْمَلَاحِم	Rasool al-Malahim	The Messenger of Fierce Battles, God's blessing and peace be upon him
24	رَسُولُ الرَّاحَةِ	Rasool ur-Rahah	The Messenger of Rest, God's blessing and peace be upon him
25	كَامِلٌ	Kamil	The Perfect, God's blessing and peace be upon him
26	إِكْلِيلٌ	Iklil	The Crown, God's blessing and peace be upon him
27	مُدَّثِّرٌ	Mudathir or Mudasir	The Covered, God's blessing and peace be upon him
28	مُزَّمِّلٌ	Muzzamil	The Wrapped, God's blessing and peace be upon him
29	عَبْدُ اللَّهِ	Abdullah	The Servant of God, God's blessing and peace be upon him
30	حَبِيبُ اللَّهِ	Habibullah	The Beloved of God, God's blessing and peace be upon him
31	صَفِيُّ اللَّهِ	Safiyullah	The Intimate of God, God's blessing and peace be upon him
32	نَجِيُّ اللَّهِ	Najiyullah	The Confidant of God, God's blessing and peace be upon him
33	كَلِيمُ اللَّهِ	Kalimullah	Spoken to by God, God's blessing and peace be upon him
34	خَاتِمُ الْأَنْبِيَاء	Khatim al-Ambiya	Seal of the Prophets, God's blessing and peace be upon him
35	خَاتِمُ الرُّسُلِ	Khatim ar-Rasool	Seal of the Messengers, God's blessing and peace be upon him
36	مُحْيِي	Muhyi	Reviver, God's blessing and peace be upon him
37	مُنْجِ	Munjin	Rescuer, God's blessing and peace be upon him

#	Arabic Name	Arabic Name Transliterated	English Translation
38	مُذَكِّرٌ	Mudhakkir or Muzakkir	Reminder, God's blessing and peace be upon him
39	نَاصِرٌ	Naasir	Helper, God's blessing and peace be upon him
40	مَنْصُورٌ	Mansoor	Victorious, God's blessing and peace be upon him
41	نَبِيُّ الرَّحْمَةِ	Nabiy ar-Rahmah	The Prophet of Mercy, God's blessing and peace be upon him
42	نَبِيُّ التَّوْبَةِ	Nabiy at-Tawba	The Prophet of Repentance, God's blessing and peace be upon him
43	حَرِيصٌ عَلَيْكُمْ	Haris Alaykum	Watchful over You, God's blessing and peace be upon him
44	مَعْلُومٌ	Ma'lum	The Known, God's blessing and peace be upon him
45	شَهِيرٌ	Shahir	The Famous, God's blessing and peace be upon him
46	شَاهِدٌ	Shaahid	The Witness, God's blessing and peace be upon him
47	شَهِيدٌ	Shaheed	Witnesser, God's blessing and peace be upon him
48	مَشْهُودٌ	Mashhood	The Attested, God's blessing and peace be upon him
49	بَشِيرٌ	Bashir	The Bringer of Good News, God's blessing and peace be upon him
50	مُبَشِّرٌ	Mubashir	The Spreader of Good News, God's blessing and peace be upon him
51	نَذِيرٌ	Nadhir	The Warner, God's blessing and peace be upon him
52	مُنْذِرٌ	Mundhir	The Admonisher, God's blessing and peace be upon him
53	نُورٌ	Nur	Light, God's blessing and peace be upon him
54	سِرَاجٌ	Siraj	The Lamp, God's blessing and peace be upon him
55	مِصْبَاحٌ	Misbah	The Lantern, God's blessing and peace be upon him
56	هُدَىً	Huda	The Guidance, God's blessing and peace be upon him
57	مَهْدِيٌّ	Mahdi	The Rightly Guided, God's blessing and peace be upon him
58	مُنِيرٌ	Munir	The Illumined, God's blessing and peace be upon him

#	Arabic Name	Arabic Name Transliterated	English Translation
59	دَاعٍ	Da'a	The Inviter, God's blessing and peace be upon him
60	مَدْعُوٌّ	Madu'u	The Called, God's blessing and peace be upon him
61	مُجِيبٌ	Mujib	The Answerer, God's blessing and peace be upon him
62	مُجَابٌ	Mujaab	The Answered, God's blessing and peace be upon him
63	حَفِيٌّ	Hafiy	The Welcoming, God's blessing and peace be upon him
64	عَفُوٌّ	'Afw	The Pardoning, God's blessing and peace be upon him
65	وَلِيٌّ	Wali	The Guardian, God's blessing and peace be upon him
66	حَقٌّ	Haqq	Truth, God's blessing and peace be upon him
67	قَوِيٌّ	Qawiy	Strong, God's blessing and peace be upon him
68	أَمِينٌ	Amin	The Trustworthy, God's blessing and peace be upon him
69	مَأْمُونٌ	Ma'mun	The Trusted, God's blessing and peace be upon him
70	كَرِيمٌ	Karim	Generous, God's blessing and peace be upon him
71	مُكَرَّمٌ	Mukarram	The Honoured, God's blessing and peace be upon him
72	مَكِينٌ	Makin	The Unshakable, God's blessing and peace be upon him
73	مَتِينٌ	Matin	The Stable, God's blessing and peace be upon him
74	مُبِينٌ	Mubin	The Evident, God's blessing and peace be upon him
75	مُؤَمَّلٌ	Mu'ammil	The Hoped for, God's blessing and peace be upon him
76	وَصُولٌ	Wasul	The Connection, God's blessing and peace be upon him
77	ذُو قُوَّةٍ	Dhu Quwatin	Possessor of Power, God's blessing and peace be upon him
78	ذُو حُرْمَةٍ	Dhu Hurmahtin	Possessor of Honour, God's blessing and peace be upon him
79	ذُو مَكَانَةٍ	Dhu Makanatin	The Possessor of High Status, God's blessing and peace be upon him

#	Arabic Name	Arabic Name Transliterated	English Translation
80	ذُو عِزٍّ	Dhu 'Azzin	Possessor of Might, God's blessing and peace be upon him
81	ذُو فَضْلٍ	Dhu Fadl	Possessor of Grace, God's blessing and peace be upon him
82	مُطَاعٌ	Muta'	The Obeyed, God's blessing and peace be upon him
83	مُطِيعٌ	Muti'	The Obedient, God's blessing and peace be upon him
84	قَدَمُ صِدْقٍ	Qadim Sidq	The Foot of Sincerity, God's blessing and peace be upon him
85	رَحْمَةٌ	Rahmah	Mercy, God's blessing and peace be upon him
86	بُشْرَى	Bushra	The Good News, God's blessing and peace be upon him
87	غَوثٌ	Ghawth or Gawsu	Redeemer, God's blessing and peace be upon him
88	غَيْثٌ	Ghayth	Helper, God's blessing and peace be upon him
89	غِيَاثٌ	Ghiyath	Help, God's blessing and peace be upon him
90	نِعْمَةُ اللَّهِ	Ni'matullah	The Blessing of God, God's blessing and peace be upon him
91	هَدِيَّةُ اللَّهِ	Hadiyatullah	The Gift of God, God's blessing and peace be upon him
92	عُرْوَةٌ وُثْقَى	'Urwatu Wuthqa	The Trusty Handhold, God's blessing and peace be upon him
93	صِرَاطُ اللَّهِ	Siratuallah	The Path of God, God's blessing and peace be upon him
94	صِرَاطُ مُسْتَقِيمٌ	Siratumustaqim	The Straight Path, God's blessing and peace be upon him
95	ذِكْرُ اللَّهِ	Dhikrullah or Zikrullah	Remembrance of God, God's blessing and peace be upon him
96	سَيْفُ اللَّهِ	Sayfullah	The Sword of God, God's blessing and peace be upon him
97	حِزْبُ اللَّهِ	Hizbullah	The Party of God, God's blessings and peace be upon him
98	النَّجْمُ الثَّاقِبُ	Al-Najm ath-thaqib	The Piercing Star, God's blessings and peace be upon him
99	مُصْطَفًى	Mustafa	The Chosen, God's blessings and peace be upon him
100	مُجْتَبًى	Mujtaba	The Elect, God's blessings and peace be upon him

#	Arabic Name	Arabic Name Transliterated	English Translation
101	مُنْتَقَى	Muntaqa	The Eloquent, God's blessing and peace be upon him
102	أُمِّيّ	Umiy	The Unlettered, God's blessing and peace be upon him
103	مُخْتَارٌ	Mukhtar	The Chosen, God's blessing and peace be upon him
104	أَجِيرٌ	Ajeer	The Rewarded, God's blessing and peace be upon him
105	جَبَّارٌ	Jabbar	Compelling, God's blessing and peace be upon him
106	أَبُو القَاسِم	Abu Qasim	Father of Qasim, God's blessing and peace be upon him
107	أَبُو الطَّاهِرِ	Abu at-Tahir	Father of Tahir, God's blessing and peace be upon him
108	أَبُو الطَّيِّبِ	Abu at-Tayyeb	Father of Tayyeb, God's blessing and peace be upon him
109	أَبُو إِبْرَاهِيمَ	Abu Ibrahim	Father of Ibrahim, God's blessing and peace be upon him
110	مُشَفَّعٌ	Mushaffa	Accepted Intercessor, God's blessing and peace be upon him
111	شَفِيعٌ	Shaafi'	The Interceder, God's blessing and peace be upon him
112	صَالِحٌ	Salih	The Righteous, God's blessing and peace be upon him
113	مُصْلِحٌ	Muslih	The Peace-maker, God's blessing and peace be upon him
114	مُهَيْمِنٌ	Muhaymin	Guardian, God's blessings and peace be upon him
115	صَادِقٌ	Sadiq	Truthful, God's blessing and peace be upon him
116	مُصَدَّقٌ	Musaddaq	The Confirmer, God's blessing and peace be upon him
117	صِدْقٌ	Sidq	The Sincere, God's blessings and peace be upon him
118	سَيِّدُ المُرْسَلِينَ	Sayyed al-Mursalin	Master of the Messengers, God's blessing and peace be upon him
119	إِمَامُ المُتَّقِينَ	Imam al-Muttaqeen	Leader of the Pious, God's blessing and peace be upon him
120	قَائِدُ الغُرِّ المُحَجَّلِينَ	Qayid al-Ghur al-Muhajjilin	Guide of the Brightly Shining Ones, God's blessing and peace be upon him
121	خَلِيلُ الرَّحمنِ	Khalil ar-Rahman	Friend of the Ever-Merciful, God's blessing and peace be upon him

#	Arabic Name	Arabic Name Transliterated	English Translation
122	بَرٌّ	Barr	The Pious, God's blessing and peace be upon him
123	مَبَرٌّ	Mubirr	The Venerated, God's blessing and peace be upon him
124	وَجِيهٌ	Wajih	The Eminent, God's blessing and peace be upon him
125	نَصِيحٌ	Nasseh	The Adviser, God's blessing and peace be upon him
126	نَاصِحٌ	Naasih	The Counsellor, God's blessing and peace be upon him
127	وَكِيلٌ	Wakeel	The Advocate, God's blessing and peace be upon him
128	مُتَوَكِّلٌ	Mutawakil	The Reliant on God, God's blessing and peace be upon him
129	كَفِيلٌ	Kafeel	The Guarantor, God's blessing and peace be upon him
130	شَفِيقٌ	Shafeeq	The Tender, God's blessing and peace be upon him
131	مُقِيْمُ السُّنَّةِ	Muqeem as-Sunna	Establisher of the Way, God's blessing and peace be upon him
132	مُقدَّسٌ	Muqaddis	The Sacred, God's blessing and peace be upon him
133	رُوحُ القُدُسِ	Ruh al-Qudus	The Holy Spirit, God's blessing and peace be upon him
134	رُوحُ الحَقِّ	Ruh al-Haqq	The Spirit of Truth, God's blessing and peace be upon him
135	رُوحُ القِسْطِ	Ruh al-Qist	The Spirit of Justice, God's blessing and peace be upon him
136	كَافٍ	Kaaf	The Sufficient, God's blessing and peace be upon him
137	مُكْتَفٍ	Muktaf	The Broad-Shouldered, God's blessing and peace be upon him
138	بَالِغٌ	Baaligh	The Proclaimer, God's blessing and peace be upon him
139	مُبَلِّغٌ	Mubaligh	The Informer, God's blessing and peace be upon him
140	شَافٍ	Shaaf	The Healer, God's blessing and peace be upon him
141	وَاصِلٌ	Waasil	The Inseparable Friend, God's blessing and peace be upon him
142	مَوْصُولٌ	Mawsool	The One Bound to God, God's blessing and peace be upon him

#	Arabic Name	Arabic Name Transliterated	English Translation
143	سَابِقٌ	Saabiq	The Foremost, God's blessing and peace be upon him
144	سَائِقٌ	Saa'iq	The Driver, God's blessing and peace be upon him
145	هَادٍ	Haadin	The Guide, God's blessing and peace be upon him
146	مُهْدٍ	Muhd	The Guided, God's blessing and peace be upon him
147	مُقَدَّمٌ	Muqaddam	Overseer, God's blessing and peace be upon him
148	عَزِيزٌ	Aziz'	Glorious, God's blessing and peace be upon him
149	فَاضِلٌ	Fadhil	The Outstanding, God's blessing and peace be upon him
150	مُفَضَّلٌ	Mufaddhil	The Favoured, God's blessing and peace be upon him
151	فَاتِحٌ	Fatih	Opener, God's blessing and peace be upon him
152	مِفْتَاحٌ	Miftah	The Key, God's blessing and peace be upon him
153	مِفْتَاحُ الرَّحْمَةِ	Miftah ar-Rahman	Key of Mercy, God's blessing and peace be upon him
154	مِفْتَاحُ الجَنَّةِ	Miftah al-Jannah	Key to the Garden, God's blessing and peace be upon him
155	عَلَمُ الإِيمَانِ	'Alam al-Iman	Banner of the Faith, God's blessing and peace be upon him
156	عَلَمُ اليَقِينِ	'Alm al-Yaqeen	Banner of Certainty, God's blessing and peace be upon him
157	دَلِيلُ الخَيْرَاتِ	Dalail al-Khayrat	Guide to Goodness, God's blessing and peace be upon him
158	مُصَحِّحُ الحَسَنَاتِ	Musahih al-Hasanat	Verifier of Good Deeds, God's blessing and peace be upon him
159	مُقِيلُ العَثَرَاتِ	Muqeel al-'Atharat	Forewarner of False Steps, God's blessing and peace be upon him
160	صَفُوحٌ عَنِ الزَّلَّاتِ	Safooh 'an az-Zallat	Pardoner of Missteps, God's blessing and peace be upon him
161	صَاحِبُ الشَّفَاعَةِ	Sahib ash-Shafa'h	Possessor of Intercession, God's blessing and peace be upon him
162	صَاحِبُ المَقَام	Sahib al-Maqam	Possessor of the Honoured Station, God's blessing and peace be upon him
163	صَاحِبُ القَدَم	Sahib al-Qadam	Owner of the Footprint, God's blessing and peace be upon him

#	Arabic Name	Arabic Name Transliterated	English Translation
164	مَخْصُوصٌ بِالْعِزِّ	Makhsoosun bil-'Azz	Distinguished with Might, God's blessing and peace be upon him.
165	مَخْصُوصٌ بِالْمَجْدِ	Makhsoosun bil-Majd	Distinguished with Glory, God's blessing and peace be upon him
166	مَخْصُوصٌ بِالشَّرَفِ	Makhsoosun bish-Sharaf	Distinguished with Honour, God's blessing and peace be upon him
167	صَاحِبُ الوَسِيلَةِ	Sahib al-Waseelah	Possessor of the Closest Access, God's blessing and peace be upon him
168	صَاحِبُ السَّيْفِ	Sahib as-Sayf	Owner of the Sword, God's blessing and peace be upon him
169	صَاحِبُ الفَضِيلَةِ	Sahib al-Fadeelah	Possessor of Pre-eminence, God's blessing and peace be upon him
170	صَاحِبُ الإِزَارِ	Sahib al-Izar	Owner of the Cloth, God's blessing and peace be upon him
171	صَاحِبُ الحُجَّةِ	Sahib al-Hujjah	Possessor of Proof, God's blessing and peace be upon him
172	صَاحِبُ السُّلْطَانِ	Sahib as-Sultan	Possessor of Authority, God's blessing and peace be upon him
173	صَاحِبُ الرِّدَاءِ	Sahib ar-Rida'	Owner of the Robe, God's blessing and peace be upon him
174	صَاحِبُ الدَّرَجَةِ الرَّفِيعَةِ	Sahib ad-Darajat ar-Rafi'	Possessor of the Lofty Rank, God's blessing and peace be upon him
175	صَاحِبُ التَّاجِ	Sahib at-Taj	Possessor of the Crown, God's blessing and peace be upon him
176	صَاحِبُ المِغْفَرِ	Sahib al-Migfir	Possessor of Forgiveness, God's blessing and peace be upon him
177	صَاحِبُ اللِّوَاءِ	Sahib al-Liwa'	Possessor of the Banner, God's blessing and peace be upon him
178	صَاحِبُ المِعْرَاجِ	Sahib al-Mi'raj	Master of the Night Journey, God's blessing and peace be upon him
179	صَاحِبُ القَضِيبِ	Sahib al-Qadheeb	Owner of the Staff, God's blessing and peace be upon him
180	صَاحِبُ البُرَاقِ	Sahib al-Buraq	Owner of Buraq, God's blessing and peace be upon him
181	صَاحِبُ الخَاتَمِ	Sahib al-Khaatim	Owner of the Ring, God's blessing and peace be upon him
182	صَاحِبُ العَلَامَةِ	Shahib al-'Alamah	Owner of the Sign, God's blessing and peace be upon him
183	صَاحِبُ البُرْهَانِ	Sahib al-Burhan	Possessor of the Evidence, God's blessing and peace be upon him
184	صَاحِبُ البَيَانِ	Sahib al-Bayan	Possessor of Evident Proofs, God's blessing and peace be upon him
185	فَصِيحُ اللِّسَانِ	Faseeh al-Lisan	Good Communicator, God's blessing and peace be upon him

#	Arabic Name	Arabic Name Transliterated	English Translation
186	مُطَهَّرُ الجَنَان	Mutahhir al-Jannan	Purified Heart, God's blessing and peace be upon him
187	رَؤُوفٌ	Ra'uf	Compassionate, God's blessing and peace be upon him
188	رَحِيمٌ	Raheem	Merciful, God's blessing and peace be upon him
189	أُذُنُ خَيْرٍ	Udhun Khayr	Good Listener, God's blessing and peace be upon him
190	صَحِيحُ الإِسْلَام	Saheeh al-Islam	Corrector of Islam, God's blessing and peace be upon him
191	سَيِّدُ الكَوْنَيْنِ	Sayyed al-Khawnain	Master of the Two Universes, God's blessing and peace be upon him
192	عَيْنُ النَّعِيم	'Ayn al-Na'eem	Spring of Bliss, God's blessing and peace be upon him
193	عَيْنُ الغُرِّ	'Ayn al-Ghur	Spring of Beauty, God's blessing and peace be upon him
194	سَعْدُ اللهِ	Sa'dullah	Joy of God, God's blessing and peace be upon him
195	سَعْدُ الخَلْقِ	Sa'd al-Khalq	Joy of Creation, God's blessing and peace be upon him
196	خَطِيبُ الأُمَم	Khateeb al-Umam	Preacher to the Nations, God's blessing and peace be upon him
197	عَلَمُ الهُدَى	'Alam al-Huda	Teacher of Guidance, God's blessing and peace be upon him
198	كَاشِفُ الكُرَبِ	Khashif al-Kurab	Remover of Hardships, God's blessing and peace be upon him
199	رَافِعُ الرُّتَبِ	Rafi'ar-Rutab	Elevator of Ranks, God's blessing and peace be upon him
200	عِزُّ العَرَبِ	'Izz al-'Arab	Might of the Arabs, God's blessing and peace be upon him
201	صَاحِبُ الفَرَج	Sahib al-Faraj	Possessor of Relief, God's blessing and peace be upon him

اللَّهُمَّ يَا رَبِّ بِجَاهِ نَبِيِّكَ المُصْطَفَى وَرَسُولِكَ المُرْتَضَى طَهِّرْ قُلُوبَنَا مِنْ كُلِّ وَصْفٍ يُبَاعِدُنَا عَنْ مُشَاهَدَتِكَ وَمَحَبَّتِكَ وَأَمِتْنَا عَلَى السُّنَّةِ وَالجَمَاعَةِ وَالشَّوْقِ إِلَى لِقَائِكَ يَا ذَا الجَلَالِ وَالإِكْرَامِ وَصَلَّ اللهُ عَلَى سَيِّدِنَا مُحَمَّدٍ وَعَلَى آلِهِ وَصَحْبِهِ وَسَلَّمَ تَسْلِيماً وَالحَمْدُ لِلهِ رَبِّ العَالَمِينَ.

Allāhumma yā rabbi bijāhi nabiyyikal muṣṭafā wa rasulikal murtaḍā ṭahhir qulūbanā min kulli waṣfin yubāʿidunā ʿan mushāhadatika wa maḥabbatika wa amitnā ʿalās sunnati wal jamāʿati wash shawqi ʾilā liqāʾika yā dhāl jalāli walʾikrāmi wa ṣallAllāhu ʿalā sayyidinā Muhammadin wa ʿalā ʾālihi wa ṣaḥbihi wa sallama taslīman wal ḥamdu liLlāhi rabbil ʿālamīna.

God! Our Lord! By honouring Your Chosen Prophet and Approved Messenger, purify our hearts from everything that keeps us away from Your contemplation and love. And have us pass away following his traditions and in his community, longing to meet You, O Lord of Majesty and Honour. May God bless our noble lord Muhammad and his family and Companions and grant them peace. All praise belongs to God, Lord of all the worlds.

A Description of al-Rawdah

Adjacent to the tomb of the Prophet, may God's blessings and peace be upon him

عن أبو هريرة ما بيْنَ بَيْتي ومِنْبَري رَوْضَةٌ مِن رِياضِ الجنَّةِ، ومِنْبَري علَى حَوْضِي. ⁽¹⁾

Abu Hurairah (may God be content with him) narrated that God's Messenger (ﷺ) said, "Between my house and my pulpit, there is a garden from one of the Gardens of Paradise. And my pulpit is over my Pool (Kawthar)."

This is a description of al-Rawda, where the Messenger of God is buried, God's blessings and abundant peace be upon him, and his Companions Abu Bakr and 'Umar, may God be pleased with them. Thus, Urwa ibn az-Zubayr (may God be pleased with him) narrated, "The Messenger of God, may God's blessings and abundant peace be upon him, is buried in an alcove. And Abu Bakr (may God be contented with him) is buried behind the Messenger of God, may God's blessings and abundant peace be upon him. 'Umar ibn al-Khattab (may God be contented with him) is buried at the feet of Abu Bakr. The nook's eastern side is left empty, and there is another tomb. They say, and God knows best, that 'Isa bin Maryam, peace be upon him, will be buried there, and this was part of the good news brought by the Messenger of God, may God's blessings and abundant peace be upon him".

'Aisha (may God be contented with her) narrated, "I saw three moons fall into my room. I related my vision to Abu Bakr (may God be pleased with him), and he said: 'O 'Aisha, three (persons) will be buried in your house, and they are better than all the people of the earth.' When the Messenger of God, may God's blessings and abundant peace be upon him, passed away, he was buried in my house. Abu Bakr said, 'This is one of your moons, and he is the best of them,' God's blessings and abundant peace be upon him and his family."

---

(1) The speaker: Al-Bukhari – Source: Sahih Al-Bukhari – page or number: 6588. Conclusion of the speaker: sound.

دعاء بدء دلائل الخيرات

اللَّهُمَّ إِنِّي نَوَيْتُ بِالصَّلاَةِ عَلَى النَّبِيِّ ﷺ ، امْتِثَالاً لأَمْرِكَ، وَتَصْدِيقاً لِنَبِيِّكَ سَيِّدِنَا مُحَمَّدٍ ﷺ، وَمَحَبَّةً فِيهِ، وَشَوْقاً إِلَيْهِ، وَتَعْظِيماً لِقَدْرِهِ، وَلِكَوْنِهِ أَهْلاً لِذَلِكَ. فَتَقَبَّلْهَا مِنِّي بِفَضْلِكَ وَإِحْسَانِكَ. وَأَزِلْ حِجَابَ الغَفْلَةِ عَنْ قَلْبِي وَاجْعَلْنِي مِنْ عِبَادِكَ الصَّالِحِينَ.

اللَّهُمَّ زِدْهُ شَرَفاً عَلَى شَرَفِهِ الَّذِي أَوْلَيْتَهُ، وَعِزّاً عَلَى عِزِّهِ الَّذِي أَعْطَيْتَهُ، وَنُوراً عَلَى نُورِهِ الَّذِي مِنْهُ خَلَقْتَهُ، وَأَعْلِ مَقَامَهُ فِي مَقَامَاتِ المُرْسَلِينَ وَدَرَجَتَهُ فِي دَرَجَاتِ النَّبِيِّينَ.

وَأَسْأَلُكَ رِضَاكَ وَرِضَاهُ يَا رَبَّ العَالَمِينَ مَعَ العَافِيَةِ الدَّائِمَةِ وَالمَوْتِ عَلَى الكِتَابِ وَالسُّنَّةِ وَالجَمَاعَةِ وَكَلِمَتَيِ الشَّهَادَةِ عَلَى تَحْقِيقِهَا مِنْ غَيْرِ تَبْدِيلٍ وَلَا تَغْيِيرٍ. وَاغْفِرْ لِي مَا ارْتَكَبْتُهُ بِفَضْلِكَ وَجُودِكَ وَكَرَمِكَ يَا أَرْحَمَ الرَّاحِمِينَ. وَصَلَّى اللهُ عَلَى سَيِّدِنَا مُحَمَّدٍ خَاتِمِ النَّبِيِّينَ وَإِمَامِ المُرْسَلِينَ وَعَلَى آلِهِ وَصَحْبِهِ أَجْمَعِينَ وَسَلامٌ عَلَى المُرْسَلِينَ وَالحَمْدُ للهِ رَبِّ العَالَمِينَ.

Allahumma any nwaytu balslat āla alnby eamtthalan lamrka wtsdyqaa lnbyka mhmd wa wmhbtn fyh wshwqaa āalah wtzymaa lqdrh wlkwnh ahlaa ldhlk ftqblha mny bfdlk wahsank wazl hjab alghflt n qlby wajlny mn badk alsalhyn. Allahumma zidhu shrfaa āla shrfh aldhy awālath w'idha āla izh aldhy atyth wnwraa āla nwrh aldhy mnh khlqth, wali mqamh fy mqamati almursālan, wdrjth fy drjati alnbyyn, wasalk rdak wrdah ya rab alalmyn, ma alafyt aldaymt walmwti āla alktab walsnt waljmat wklmty alshhadt āla thqyqha mn ghyr tbdyl wla tghyyr waghfr āla ma artkbth, bfdlk wjwdk wkrmk ya arhm alrahmyn, wsāla allh āla saydna mohamdin khatm alnbyyn weamam almrsaleen, wāla alh wshbh ajmyn, wslam āla almrsaleen, walhamd lilah rab alalamyn.

The Supplication of Intention

In God's Name, the Compassionate, the Merciful

Dear God! I intend to request blessings upon the Prophet (ﷺ), in obedience to Your Command and with faith in Your Prophet, our noble master Muhammad (ﷺ). (I do so) with love for him, yearning for him, and exalting his rank as he merits. Accept this from me by Your Grace and Benevolence, remove the veil of forgetfulness from my heart and join me with Your righteous servants.

Dear God! Increase him in honour above the honour You have given him, and with might beyond the might You have given him, and give him a light beyond his light from which You created him. Elevate his station among the Messengers' stations and his rank among the ranks of the Prophets.

I ask You for Your contentment, and his gratification, O Lord of all the Worlds, perpetual well-being, and a death in obedience to The Book and the Prophet's traditions, with the fulfillment of my shahadah without alteration. Forgive me, by Your favour, bounty and generosity, for what I have done, O Most Merciful of the merciful. May God bless our noble master Muhammad, Seal of the Prophets and Leader of the Messengers, and his family and Companions, and grant them abundant peace. Peace be upon the Messengers, and all praise belongs to God, the Lord of all the Worlds.

الحزبُ الأولُ وردُ يومِ الاثنين

بسمِ اللهِ الرحمنِ الرحيم

صلى اللهُ على سيدنا ومولانا محمدٍ وعلى آلهِ وصحبهِ وسلمَ، اللهمَّ صلِّ على سيدنا محمدٍ وأزواجهِ وذريتهِ كما صليتَ على سيدنا إبراهيمَ، وباركْ على سيدنا محمدٍ وأزواجهِ وذريتهِ كما باركتَ على آل سيدنا إبراهيمَ إنكَ حميدٌ مجيدٌ، اللهمَّ صلِّ على سيدنا محمدٍ وعلى آلهِ كما صليتَ على سيدنا إبراهيمَ، وباركْ على سيدنا محمدٍ وعلى آلِ سيدنا محمدٍ كما باركتَ على آلِ سيدنا إبراهيمَ في العالمينَ إنكَ حميدٌ مجيدٌ، اللهمَّ صلِّ على سيدنا محمدٍ وآلِ سيدنا محمدٍ كما صليتَ على سيدنا إبراهيمَ، وباركْ على سيدنا محمدٍ وآلِ سيدنا محمدٍ كما باركتَ على سيدنا إبراهيمَ إنكَ حميدٌ مجيدٌ،

Sallallahu āla sayyidina wa-maulana Muhammad-in wa āla āalihi wa sahbihi wa sallam Allahumma salli āla sayyidina Muhammad-in wa-azwajihii wa-zurriyyatihii kama sallaita āla sayyidina wa-maulanaa ibraahiimaa wa-barik āla sayyidina wa-maulana Muhammad-in-Wa-azwajihii wa-zurriyyatihii kama barakta āla Āli sayyidina wa-maulanaa Ibraahima innaka hamidum-majid

Allahumma salli āla sayyidina wa-maulana Muhammad-in wa āla ālihi kama sallaita āla sayyidina wa-maulanaa Ibrahima wa-barik āla sayyidina wa maulana Muhammad-in wa āla Āli sayyidina wa-maulana Muhammad-in kama barakta āla Āli sayyidina wa-maulana Ibrahiima fil 'alamina Innaka hamidum-majid

Allahumma salli āla sayyidina wa maulana Muhammad-in wa Āli sayyidina Wa maulana Muhammad-in kama sallaita āla sayyidina Ibraahima wa-barik āla sayyidina Muhammad-in-wa Āli sayyidina Muhammad-in kama barakta āla sayyidina Ibraahima Innaka hamidum-majid

The First Part to be read on Monday

BISMILLA HIRRAHMAAN NIRRAHIM

God's blessings and support be upon our noble master Muhammad and his family and Companions.

Dear God! Bless and support our noble master Muhammad and his wives and descendants, just as You blessed our noble master Abraham. And sanctify our noble master Muhammad and his wives and descendants, just as You sanctified our noble master Abraham. You are the Praiseworthy, the Glorious.

Dear God! Bless and support our noble master Muhammad and his family, just as You blessed our noble master Abraham. And sanctify our noble master Muhammad and his family, just as You sanctified our noble master Abraham and his family in all the worlds. You are the Praiseworthy, the Glorious.

Dear God! Bless and support our noble master Muhammad and his family, just as You blessed our noble master Abraham. And sanctify our noble master Muhammad and his family, just as You sanctified our noble master Abraham in all the worlds. You are the Praiseworthy, the Glorious.

اللهمَّ صلِّ على سيدنا محمدٍ النبيِّ الأميِّ وعلى آلِ سيدنا محمدٍ، اللهمَّ صلِّ على سيدنا محمدٍ عبدِكَ ورسولِكَ، اللهمَّ صلِّ على

سيدنا محمدٍ وعلى آلِ سيدنا محمدٍ كما صليتَ على سيدنا إبراهيمَ وعلى آلِ سيدنا إبراهيمَ إنكَ حميدٌ مجيدٌ، اللهمَّ باركْ على سيدنا

محمدٍ وعلى آلِ سيدنا محمدٍ كما باركتَ على سيدنا إبراهيمَ وعلى آلِ سيدنا إبراهيمَ إنكَ حميدٌ مجيدٌ، اللهمَّ وترحمْ على سيدنا محمدٍ

وعلى آلِ سيدنا محمدٍ كما ترحمتَ على سيدنا إبراهيمَ وعلى آلِ سيدنا إبراهيمَ إنكَ حميدٌ مجيدٌ، اللهمَّ وتحننْ على سيدنا محمدٍ وعلى

آلِ سيدنا محمدٍ كما تحننتَ على سيدنا إبراهيمَ وعلى آلِ سيدنا إبراهيمَ إنكَ حميدٌ مجيدٌ، اللهمَّ وسلمْ على سيدنا محمدٍ وعلى آلِ سيدنا

محمدٍ كما سلمتَ على سيدنا إبراهيمَ وعلى آلِ سيدنا إبراهيمَ إنكَ حميدٌ مجيدٌ،

Allahumma salli āla sayyidina Muhammadi-nin-nabiyyil-ummiyyi wa āla Āli sayyidina Muhammad Allahumma salli āla sayyidina Muhammad-in 'abdika wa rasulik

Allahumma salli āla sayyidina Muhammad-in- wa āla Āli sayyidina Muhammad-in kama sallaita āla sayyidina Ibraahima wa āla Āli sayyidina Ibraahima innaka Hamidum-majid

Allahumma barik āla sayyidina Muhammad-in wa āla Āli sayyidina Muhammad-in kama barakta āla sayyidina Ibraahima wa āla Āli sayyidina Ibraahima Innaka hamidum-majid

Allahumma watarah-ham āla sayyidina Muhammad-in wa āla Āli sayyidina Muhammad-in kama tarah-hamta āla sayyidina Ibraahima wa āla Āli sayyidina Ibraahima Innaka hamidum-majid

Allahumma wata-hannan āla sayyidina Muhammad-in wa āla Āli sayyidina Muhammad-in kama tahan-nanta āla sayidina Ibraahima wa āla Āli sayyidina Ibraahima Innaka hamidum-majid

Allahumma wa-sallim āla sayyidina Muhammad-in wa āla ali sayyidina Muhammad-in kama sallamta āla sayyidina Ibraahima wa āla Āli sayyidina Ibraahima Innaka hamidum-majid

God! Bless and support our noble master Muhammad, the Prophet sent to all nations, and his family. Dear God! Bless and support our noble master Muhammad, Your Servant and Messenger. Dear God! Bless and support our noble master Muhammad and his family, just as You blessed our noble master Abraham and his family. You are the Praiseworthy, the Glorious. Dear God! Sanctify our noble master Muhammad and his family, just as You sanctified our noble master Abraham and his family. You are the Praiseworthy, the Glorious. Dear God! Be merciful to our noble master Muhammad and his family, just as You were merciful to our noble master Abraham and his family. You are the Praiseworthy, the Glorious. Dear God! Be kind to our noble master Muhammad and his family, just as You were kind to our noble master Abraham and his family. You are the Praiseworthy, the Glorious. Dear God! Grant peace to our noble master Muhammad and his family, just as You granted peace to our noble master Abraham and his family. You are the Praiseworthy, the Glorious.

اللهمَّ صلِّ على سيدنا محمدٍ وعلى آلِ سيدنا محمدٍ، وارحمْ سيدنا محمداً وآلَ سيدنا محمدٍ، وباركْ على سيدنا محمدٍ وعلى آلِ سيدنا محمدٍ، كما صليتَ ورحمتَ وباركتَ على سيدنا إبراهيمَ وعلى آلِ سيدنا إبراهيمَ في العالمينَ إنكَ حميدٌ مجيدٌ، اللهمَّ صلِّ على سيدنا محمدٍ النبيِّ وأزواجهِ أمهاتِ المؤمنينَ، وذريتهِ وأهلِ بيتهِ، كما صليتَ على سيدنا إبراهيمَ إنكَ حميدٌ مجيدٌ، اللهمَّ باركْ على سيدنا محمدٍ وعلى آلِ سيدنا محمدٍ كما باركتَ على سيدنا إبراهيمَ إنكَ حميدٌ مجيدٌ، اللهمَّ داحِيَ المدْحُوَّاتِ، وبارئَ المسْموكاتِ، وجبارَ القلوبِ على فطرتِها، شقيِّها وسَعيدِها، اجعلْ شرائفَ صلواتِكَ، ونوامِيَ بركاتِكَ، ورأفةَ تحنُّنِكَ على سيدنا محمدٍ عبدكَ ورسولكَ،

Allahumma salli āla sayyidina Muhammad-in wa āla Āli sayyidina Muhammad-in warham sayyidina Muhammad-anw wa ʿaala sayyidina Muhammad-in wa barik āla sayyidina Muhammad-in-wa āla Āli sayyidina Muhammad-in kama sallaita wa rahimta wa barakta āla sayyidina Ibraahima wa-'ala Āli sayyidina Ibraahima fi -al ʿalamiina innaka hamidum-majid

Allahumma salli ʿalā sayyidinaa Muḥammadin innabiy wa azwajihi ummahatil mu'minina, wa zurriyyatihi wa ahli baitihi, kamā ṣallayta ʿalā sayyidinaa 'Ibrāhīma innaka ḥamīdun-majīd.

Allahumma barik āla sayyidina Muhammad-in -wa āla Āli sayyidina Muhammad-in kama barakta āla sayyidina Ibraahima innaka hamidu-mmajid

Allahumma dahiyal-mad-huwwati wa baariy- al-masmukate wa jabbaral-qulube āla fitratiha shaqiyyiha wasa'iidihaj ʿal sharaa'ifa salawatika wana-wamiya barakatika wa raʿ fata tahannunika āla sayyidina Muhammad-in 'abdika wa rasulik

Dear God! Bless and support our noble master Muhammad and his family, and be merciful to our noble master Muhammad and his family. And sanctify our noble master Muhammad and his family, just as You blessed, were gracious to, and sanctified our noble master Abraham and his family in all the worlds. You are the Praiseworthy, the Glorious.

Dear God! Bless and support our noble master Muhammad the Prophet, his wives - the Mothers of the Believers – his offspring, and the family of his household, just as You blessed our noble master Abraham. You are the Praiseworthy, the Glorious.

Dear God! Sanctify our noble master Muhammad and his family, just as You sanctified our noble master Abraham. You are the Praiseworthy, the Glorious.

Dear God! Maker of the Firmament, Leveller of the Plains, and Molder of Hearts into the good and the miserable. Give Your noblest blessings, most fruitful favours, and most loving-kindness to our noble master Muhammad, Your Servant and Messenger.

الفاتِح لِما أغلقَ، والخاتِم لِما سبقَ، والمعلنِ الحقَّ بالحقِّ والدامغ لِجيشاتِ الأباطيلِ كما حُمِّلَ، فاضطلعَ بأمرِكَ بطاعتِكَ،

مُستَوْفِزاً في مرضاتِكَ، واعياً لوحْيِكَ، حافِظاً لعهدِكَ، ماضِياً على نفاذِ أمرِكَ، حتى أوْرَى قبساً لقابسٍ آلاءُ اللهِ تصلُ بأهلهِ أسبابَهُ،

بهِ هُدِيَتِ القلوبُ بعدَ خوضاتِ الفتنِ والإثمِ، وأبهجَ موضِحاتِ الأعلامِ، ونائراتِ الأحكامِ ومنيراتِ الإسلامِ، فهو أمينُكَ

المأمونُ، وخازِنِ عِلْمِكَ المخزونُ، وشهيدُكَ يومَ الدينِ، وبعيثُكَ نعمةً، ورسولُكَ بالحقِّ رحمةً، اللهمَّ أفْسِحْ لهُ في عَدْنِكَ، واجزِهِ

مُضاعَفاتِ الخيرِ مِن فضلِكَ مُهنَّئاتٍ لهُ غيرَ مُكَدَّراتٍ، مِن فَوْزِ ثوابِكَ المحلولِ، وجزيلِ عطائِكَ المعلولِ، اللهمَّ أعلِ على بناءِ

الناسِ بناءَهُ، وأكرِمْ مثواهُ لديك ونُزُلَهُ، وأتِمّ لهُ نُورَهُ، واجزِهِ مِن ابتعائِكَ لهُ مقبولَ الشهادةِ ومَرْضِيَّ المقالةِ، ذا منطقٍ عدلٍ

وخُطَّةٍ فصلٍ، وبرهانٍ عظيمٍ، (إنَّ اللهَ ومَلائِكَتَهُ يُصَلُّونَ على النَّبِيِّ يَأَيُّها الذينَ آمَنُوا صَلُّوا عليهِ وسَلِّموا تسليماً)،

Al- fatihi lima ughliqa wal khatimi lima sabaqa wal mu'linil-haqqa bil haqqi waddamighi le-jaishatil-abatili kama hummila fadh-tala‘a bi amrika bito-‘atika mustaufizan fi mardhatika waa ‘iyanl-liwahyika hafizal-li‘ahdika madhiyan āla nafazi ‘āmrika

hatta āura qabasan liqabisin alaā ‘ullahi tasilu bi āhlihi asbabahu bihi hudiatil qulubu ba’da khaudatil-fitani wal ‘ithmi wa abhaja mudhihati al-‘alami wa naa‘iratil-ahkami wa muniratil-islami fahuwa aminukal-ma‘muunu wa khazinu ‘ilmika AL-makhzuni wa shahiduka yaumaddiini wa ba'ii-thuka ni’matan warasuluka bilhaqqi rahmah Allahumma Af-seh lahu fi 'adnika wajzihii mudha ‘afatil-khayri min fadlika muhannatin-lahu ghaira mukaddaratin-min fauzi thawabikal-mahluli wajazili ‘ataa ‘ikal-ma’-luul

Allahumma ‘Āli āla ala bina'i-nasi binaa'ahu wa akrim mathwahu ladaika wa nuzulahu wa atmim lahu nurahu Wajzihe minibti‘athika lahu maqbula-sh-shahadati wamardiyyal-maqalati tha mantiqin ādlin-wa khottatin faslin waburhanin āziim (Inna allaha wa mala'aikatahu yusalluuna ‘alan-nabi Ya ‘āyyuhalladhina ‘āamanu sallu ‘alaihi wa sallimu taslima)

The Opener of the locked, the Seal One of whatever came before, the Declarer of Right with Right, and the Rebuter of the forces of Untruth. He carried the responsibility of Your Order in obedience to You, speedily seeking Your contentment and earnestly heeding Your Revelation. He preserved Your Promise and executed Your Command so that, by kindling a burning brand for the seeker, his family gained access, through him, to Your blessings. He guided hearts after they had struggled with trials and sins and gladdened with evident signs, enlightening laws and illuminating Islam. He is Your trustworthy one and safe-keeper of Your Secret, Your Omniscience, Your Witness on the Day of Judgement, Your Envoy, Your Messenger, in truth, a blessing and a Mercy for us.

Dear God! Expand for him his place in Your Eden and reward him doubly with the goodness of Your Favour. Grant him untarnished felicitations from the victory of Your Reward, which is plentiful and fitting and from Your Lofty Gift.

Dear God! Raise higher that which he built over all that others have built. Exalt his place and his stay with You. Perfect his light and reward him with Your acceptance so that his statements are accepted, and his word is fair to You, making him the one whose utterances are just, whose course is defined, and whose argument is Glorious.

"Indeed, God and His Angels give their blessings and support to the Prophet. O you who believe, ask God to bless him and grant him abundant peace." [Q 33:56]

لبيكَ اللهمَّ ربِّ وسعديكَ، صلواتُ اللهِ البَرِّ الرحيمِ، والملائكةِ المقربينَ، والنبيِّينَ والصدِّيقينَ والشُّهداءِ والصالحينَ، وما

سبَّحَ لكَ من شيءٍ يا رَبَّ العالمينَ، على سيدنا محمدِ بن عبد اللهِ خاتمِ النبيينَ، وسيدِ المرسلينَ، وإمامِ المتقينَ، ورسولِ رَبِّ

العالمينَ، الشاهدِ البشيرِ، الداعي إليك بإذنِكَ السِّراجِ المنيرِ، عليهِ السلامُ، اللهمَّ اجعلْ صلواتِكَ وبركاتِكَ ورحمتِكَ على سيدِ

المرسلينَ، وإمامِ المتقينَ، وخاتمِ النبيينَ سيدنا محمدٍ عبدِكَ ورسولِكَ، إمامِ الخيرِ، وقائدِ الخيرِ، ورسولِ الرحمةِ، اللهمَّ ابعثهُ مقاماً

محموداً يغبطهُ فيهِ الأولونَ والآخرونَ، اللهمَّ صلِّ على سيدنا محمدٍ وعلى آلِ سيدنا محمدٍ كما صليتَ على سيدنا إبراهيمَ إنكَ حميدٌ

مجيدٌ، اللهمَّ باركْ على سيدنا محمدٍ وعلى آلِ سيدنا محمدٍ كما باركتَ على سيدنا إبراهيمَ إنكَ حميدٌ مجيدٌ،

Labbaika Allahumma rabbi wasaadayka salawaatullahi Al-barrirrahiimi wal-malaaikatil-mukarrabiina wannabiyyena was-siddiqiina wash-shuhadaa'i was-sāalihiina

wama sabbaha laka min shay-in-yaa rabbal 'alamiina āla sayyidina Muhammad-in ibn abd'illahi khaatamin-nabiyyiina wasayda almursalina Wa 'imamil-muttaqina warasuli rabbil-'alamiina āsh-shahidil-bashiri-ddaa'i 'ilaika bi-iznikas-sirajil-muniri wa 'ālaihis-salam

Allahumma-aj'al salawatika wabarakatika warahmateka āla saiyidil-mursalina wa imamil-muttaqiina wa khatamin-nabiyyina sayyidina Muhammad-in 'abdika warasulika imamil-khairi waqaa'idil-khairi warasulir-rahmah

Allahummab 'ath-hu maqaman-mahmuday- yaghbituhu fiihil-awwaluna wal-akhirun

Allahumma salli āla sayyidina Muhammadin-inw wa āla Āli sayyidina Muhammad-in kama sallaita āla sayyidina Ibraahima innaka hamiidum- majid

Allahumma barik āla sayyidina Muhammad-in wa āla Āli sayyidina Muhammad-in kama barakta āla sayyidina Ibraahima innaka hamiidum majid

Dear God! I am here at Your service and Your Command, my Lord. I ask for the blessings of God, the Infinitely Good, the Most Merciful, and His closest angels, the Prophets, the sincere ones, the martyrs, the righteous, and whatever else glorifies You.

O the Lord of all the worlds, grant Your blessings, support and peace upon our noble master Muhammad, son of Abdullah, Seal of the Prophets and noble master of the Messengers, Leader of the Pious, Messenger of the Lord of all the worlds, the Witness, the Bearer of Good News, the Caller to You by Your leave, the Lamp, the Illuminated One.

Dear God! Grant Your blessings, favours and mercy upon the noble master of the Messengers. He is the Leader of the Pious, Seal of the Prophets, our noble master Muhammad, Your Servant and Messenger, the Pioneer and Guide to Goodness, the Messenger of Mercy.

Dear God! Grant him the Honoured Station, the longing of those who came first and those who will come last. Dear God! Bless and support our noble master Muhammad and his family, just as You blessed and supported our noble master Abraham, for You are the Praiseworthy, the Glorious.

Dear God! Sanctify our noble master Muhammad and his family, just as You sanctified our noble master Abraham, for You are the Praiseworthy, the Glorious.

اللهمَّ صلِّ على سيدنا محمدٍ وعلى آلهِ وأصحابهِ وأولادهِ وأزواجهِ وذريتهِ وأزواجهِ وذريتهِ وأهلِ بيتهِ وأصهارهِ وأنصارهِ وأشياعهِ ومحبيهِ وأمتهِ وعلينا معهم أجمعينَ، يا أرحمَ الراحمينَ، اللهمَّ صلِّ على سيدنا محمدٍ عددَ مَنْ صلى عليهِ، وصلِّ على سيدنا محمدٍ عددَ مَنْ لم يصلِّ عليهِ، وصلِّ على سيدنا محمدٍ كما أمرتَنا بالصلاةِ عليهِ، وصلِّ عليه كما يُحِبُّ أن يُصلى عليهِ، اللهمَّ صلِّ على سيدنا محمدٍ وعلى آلِ سيدنا محمدٍ كما أمرتنا أن نُصلي عليهِ، اللهمَّ صلِّ على سيدنا محمدٍ وعلى آلِ سيدنا محمدٍ كما هو أهلُهُ، اللهمَّ صلِّ على سيدنا محمدٍ وعلى آلِ سيدنا محمدٍ كما تُحِبُّ وترضاهُ لهُ، اللهمَّ يا رَبَّ سيدنا محمدٍ وآلِ سيدنا محمدٍ، صلِّ على سيدنا محمدٍ وآلِ سيدنا محمدٍ، وأعطِ سيدَنا محمداً الدرجةَ والوسيلةَ في الجنةِ، اللهمَّ يا رَبَّ سيدنا محمدٍ وآلِ سيدنا محمدٍ، اجزِ سيدَنا محمداً ﷺ ما هو أهلُهُ،

Allahumma salli āla sayyidina Muhammad-in wa āla ālihi wa āshabihi wa āuladihi wa āzwaajihi wa zurriyyatihi wa āhli baitihi wa as-harehi wa ansarehi wa ashya-'ihi wa muhibbihi wa ummatihi wa 'alaina ma'ahum ajma'ina ya arhamar-rahimina. Allahumma salli āla sayyidina Muhammad-in 'adada man salla 'alaihi wa salli āla sayyidina Muhammad-in 'adada manl-lam yusalli 'alaihi wa salli āla sayyidina Muhammad-in kama amartana bissalati 'alaihi wasalli 'alaihi kama tuhibbu an-yusalla 'alaih

Allahumma salli āla sayyidina Muhammad-in wa āla Āli sayyidina Muhammad-in kama amartanaa annusalliya 'alaihi Allahumma salli āla sayyidina Muhammad-in wa āla Āli sayyidina Muhammad-in kama huwa ahluh Allahumma salli āla sayyidina Muhammad-in wa āla Āli sayyidina Muhammad-in kama tuhibbu watardhahu Lah Allahumma yaa rabba sayyidina Muhammad-in wa Āli sayyidina Muhammad-in salli āla sayyidina Muhammad-in wa Āli sayyidina Muhammad-in wa 'ati sayidana Muhammada-niddarajata walwasilata filjannah Allahumma yaa rabba sayyidina Muhammad-in wa Āli sayyidina Muhammadin ijzi sayyidina Muhammad-an sallallahu 'alaihi wa sallama ma huwa ahluh

Dear God! Bless and support our noble master Muhammad, his family and Companions, his wives and children, his descendants, the People of his Household, and his relations by marriage. And bless and support his Helpers, adherents, his nation and everyone who loves him, and all of us along with them, O the Most Merciful of the Merciful.

Dear God! Bless and support our noble master Muhammad as many times as those who have asked for blessings upon him, and bless and support our noble master Muhammad as many times as those who have neglected to ask for blessings upon him. And bless and support him as You have ordered us to ask for blessings upon him, and bless him as You like him to be blessed.

Dear God! Bless and support our noble master Muhammad and his family, as You have ordered us to ask for blessings upon him. Dear God! Bless and support our noble master Muhammad and his family, as he deserves.

Dear God! Bless and support our noble master Muhammad and his family, just as You like and just as You are contented with him. Dear God! O Lord of our noble master Muhammad and his family, bless our noble master Muhammad and his family. Grant our noble master Muhammad the highest rank in the Garden. Dear God! Grant our noble master Muhammad the station of Pre-Eminence and the noblest and greatest rank. Dear God! O Lord of our noble master Muhammad and his family. Reward our noble master Muhammad, bless him and give him peace, just as he deserves.

اللهم صل على سيدنا محمد وعلى آل سيدنا محمد وعلى أهل بيته، اللهمَّ صلِّ على سيدنا محمدٍ وعلى آلِ سيدنا محمدٍ حتى لا يبقى من الصلاةِ شيءٌ، وارحمْ سيدَنا محمداً وآلَ سيدنا محمدٍ حتى لا يبقى من الرحمةِ شيءٌ، وباركْ على سيدنا محمدٍ وعلى آلِ سيدنا محمدٍ حتى لا يبقى من البركةِ شيءٌ، وسَلِّمْ على سيدنا محمدٍ وعلى آلِ سيدنا محمدٍ حتى لا يبقى من السلامِ شيءٌ، اللهمَّ صلِّ على سيدنا محمدٍ في الأوَّلينَ، وصلِّ على سيدنا محمدٍ في الآخِرينَ، وصلِّ على سيدنا محمدٍ في النبيينَ، وصلِّ على سيدنا محمدٍ في المُرْسَلينَ، وصلِّ على سيدنا محمدٍ في الملإِ الأعلى إلى يومِ الدينِ، اللهمَّ أعطِ سيدَنا محمداً الوسيلةَ والفضيلةَ والشرفَ والدرجةَ الكبيرةَ،

Allahumma salli āla sayyidina Muhammad-in-wa āla Āli sayyidina Muhammad-in-wa āla ahli baiti

Allahumma salli āla sayyidina Muhammad-in wa āla Āli sayyidina Muhammad-in hatta la yabqaa mina As-salaati sha'i

War ham sayidana Muhammad-anw wa aala sayyidina Muhammad-in hatta la yabqa minarrahmati shai 'un

Wa barik āla sayyidina Muhammad-in wa āla Āli sayyidina Muhammad-in hatta la yabqaa minal-barakati shai-'un

Wa sallim āla sayyidina Muhammad-in wa āla Āli sayyidina Muhammad-in hatta la yabqa minassalami shai'un

Allahumma salli āla sayyidina Muhammad-in fil-awwalin Wasalli'ala sayyidina Muhammadin fil-akhirin

Wa salli āla sayyidina Muhammad-in fin-nabiyyiin Wa salli āla sayyidina Muhammad-in Fil mursalin Wa salli āla sayyidina Muhammad-in filmala-il-'ala ila yaumiddiin

Allahumma 'aati sayidana Muhammada-nil -wasilata wal fadhilata washrafa waddarajatal-kabirat

Dear God! Bless and support our noble master Muhammad, his family, and the People of his House. Dear God! Bless and support our noble master Muhammad and his family for all of eternity. Dear God! Favour our noble master Muhammad and his family for all of eternity. Dear God! Have mercy upon our noble master Muhammad and his family for all eternity. Dear God! Grant peace to our noble master Muhammad and his family for all eternity. Dear God! Bless and support our noble master Muhammad among the First and the Last. Dear God! Bless and support our noble master Muhammad among the Prophets and Messengers. Dear God! Bless and support our noble master Muhammad among the Highest Host until the Day of Reckoning. Dear God! Bless and support our noble master Muhammad and grant him the Pre-eminent Station, the Closest Access and the Most Honoured Rank.

اللهمَّ إني آمنتُ بسيدنا محمدٍ ولمْ أرهْ، فلا تحرمني في الجنانِ رُؤْيَتَهُ، وارزقني صُحْبَتَهُ، وتوفني على مِلّتِهِ، واسقني من حوضِهِ مشرباً رَوِيّاً، سائغاً هنيئاً، لا نَظْمأُ بعدَهُ أبداً إنكَ على كلِّ شيءٍ قديرٌ، اللهمَّ أبلِغْ روحَ سيدنا محمدٍ مني تحيةً وسلاماً، اللهمَّ وكما آمنتُ بسيدنا محمد ولمْ أرهْ، فلا تحرمني في الجنانِ رُؤْيَتَهُ، اللهمَّ تقبلْ شفاعةَ سيدنا محمدٍ الكبرى وارفعْ درجتَهُ العُلْيا، وآتِهِ سُؤْلَهُ في الآخرةِ والأولى، كما آتيتَ سيدَنا إبراهيمَ وسيدَنا موسى، اللهمَّ صلِّ على سيدنا محمدٍ وعلى آلِ سيدنا محمدٍ كما صليتَ على سيدنا إبراهيمَ وعلى آلِ سيدنا إبراهيمَ، وبارِكْ على سيدنا محمدٍ وعلى آلِ سيدنا محمدٍ كما باركتَ على سيدنا إبراهيمَ وعلى آلِ سيدنا إبراهيمَ إنكَ حميدٌ مجيدٌ،

Allahumma inni aamantu bisayyidina Muhammad-in-walam arahu fala tahrimni filjinani ru'-yatahu warzuqni suhbatahu wata waffani āla mellatihi wa-asqini min hauddehi mashraban-rawiyyan saa'ighan hanii'ann la-nazma'u ba'dahu ābadan innaka āla kulli shai-in qadiir

O Allahumma abligh ruha sayyidina Muhammad-im-minni tahiyyatanw-wasalama Allahumma Wakama amantu bisayyidina Muhammad-in-wa lam arahu fala tahrimni filjinani ru'uyatah

Allahumma taqabbal shafa'ata sayyidina Muhammadin il-kubra warfa' darajatahul-'ulya wa 'atihii su'lahu fil akhirati wal ula kama 'ataita sayidana Ibraahima wa sayidana musa

Allahumma salli āla sayyidina Muhammmad-inw-wa āla Āli sayyidina Muhammad-in kama sallaita āla sayyidina Ibraahima wa āla Āli sayyidina Ibraahima wa barik āla sayyidina Muhammad-in-wa āla Āli Muhammad-in kama barokta āla sayyidina Ibraahima wa āla Āli sayyidina Ibraahima innaka hamidum-majid

Dear God! Just as I have believed in our noble master Muhammad without seeing him, do not deprive me of a vision of him in Paradise. Make me one of his companions and let me die on his path. Lead me to drink plentifully, blissfully and heartily from his Pool, a drink after which I will never feel thirst. You are the Most Powerful over all things.

Dear God! Send my greetings and salutations to the soul of our noble master Muhammad. I have believed in our noble master Muhammad without seeing him, so do not deprive me of a vision of him in Paradise.

Dear God! Accept the most extraordinary intercession of our noble master Muhammad, raise his rank high and grant him what he asks for in the Hereafter and this present life just as You gave to our noble masters Abraham and Moses.

Dear God! Bless and support our noble master Muhammad and his family, just as You blessed our noble master Abraham and his family. And sanctify our noble master Muhammad and his family, just as You sanctified our noble master Abraham and his family, for You are the Praiseworthy, the Glorious.

اللهمَّ صلِّ وسَلِّمْ وبارِكْ على سيدِنا محمدٍ نبيِّكَ ورسولِكَ، وسيدنا إبراهيمَ خليلِكَ وصفيِّكَ، وسيدنا موسى كليمِكَ ونجيِّكَ، وسيدنا عيسى روحِكَ وكلمتِكَ، وعلى جميعِ مَلائِكَتِكَ ورُسِلِكَ وأنبيائِكَ، وخيرتِكَ من خلقِكَ وأصفيائِكَ وخاصتِكَ وأوليائِكَ، من أهلِ أرضِكَ وسمائِكَ، وصلى اللهُ على سيدِنا محمدٍ عددَ خلقِهِ ورضاءَ نفسِهِ، وزِنَةَ عرشِهِ ومدادَ كلماتِهِ، وكما هو أهلُهُ، وكلما ذكرَهُ الذَّاكرونَ، وغفلَ عن ذكرِهِ الغافلونَ وعلى أهلِ بيتِهِ وعترتِهِ الطاهرينَ، وسَلِّمْ تسليماً، اللهمَّ صلِّ على سيدِنا محمدٍ وعلى أزواجِهِ وذريتِهِ، وعلى جميعِ النبيينَ والمرسلينَ والمَلائِكَةِ والمقرَّبينَ، وجميعِ عبادِ اللهِ الصالحينَ، عددَ ما أمطرتِ السماءُ منذُ بنيتَها، وصلِّ على سيدِنا محمدٍ عددَ ما أنبتتِ الأرضُ منذُ دحوتَها، وصلِّ علىٰ سيدِنا محمدٍ عددَ النجومِ في السماءِ فإنكَ أحصيتَها، وصلِّ على سيدِنا محمدٍ عددَ ما تنفستِ الأرواحُ منذُ خلقتَها، وصلِّ على سيدِنا محمدٍ عددَ ما خلقتَ وما تخلُقُ وما أحاط به علمُكَ، وأضعافَ ذلكَ،

Allahummasalliwa sallim wa barik āla sayyidina Muhammad-in-nabiyyika warasulik Wa sayyidina Ibraahima khalilika wa safiyyika wa sayyidina Musa kaliimika wanajiyyik Wa sayyidina 'isaa ruhika wa kalimatika wa āla jamii'i malaaikatika warusulika wa ambiyaa'ika wa khiyaratika min khalqika wa asfiyaa'ika wa khassatika wa awliyaa 'ika min ahli ardika wa samaa'ik

Wa sallallahu āla sayyidina Muhammad-in 'adada khalqihii waridha'a nafsihi wazinata arshihi wa Midada kalimatehi wa kama huwa āhluhu wa-kullama dhakarahu-aldhakeruna waghafala 'an dhikrihil-ghafiluna wa āla ahli baitihi wa itratihit-tahirina wa sallama taslima

Allahumma salli āla sayyidina Muhammad-in wa āla azwaajihii wa zurriyatihii wa āla jamii'in-nabiyyina wal-mursalina walmala'ikatil-muqarrabina wajami'i 'ibad'illahis-sālihina. 'adada ma amtarati-ssamaa'u munzu banaitaha wa salli āla sayyidina Muhammad-in 'adada maa anbatatil-arudhu munzu dahautah Wa salli āla sayyidina Muhammad-in 'adadan- nujumi Fissamaa'i fa innaka ahsaitah Wa salli āla sayyidina Muhammad-in 'adada ma tanaffasatil-arwahu munzu khalaqtah Wa salli āla sayyidina Muhammad-in 'adada ma khalaqta wa ma takhluqu wa ma 'ahata bihi 'ilmuka wa adh 'afa zalik

Dear God! Bless, sanctify and grant peace to our noble master Muhammad, Your Prophet and Messenger. And also our noble master Abraham, Your Friend and Pure One, and our noble master Moses, whom You called out to and selected. And also our noble master Jesus, Your Spirit and a Word from You. And all Your Angels, Prophets and Messengers, Righteous Ones from Your creation, the Pure Ones, the Elected Ones and Your Saints from the people of Your earth and Your heavens.

May God's blessings and support be upon our noble master Muhammad as many times as the number of His creation and to the extent of His contentment. And as much as the weight of His Throne, to the extent of the ink for His words, and to the measure he deserves. And whenever those who remember him do so, and those who are heedless to remember him. And may these blessings also be for the People of his Household and the Pure descendants, on whom be peace, over and over again.

Dear God! Bless and support our noble master Muhammad and his wives and progeny, all the Prophets and Messengers, the closest angels, and all the righteous servants of God in all the rain the sky has rained since it was formed. Bless and support our noble master Muhammad in everything the Earth has produced since it was spread out.

And bless and support our noble master Muhammad as the number of stars in the sky, for You alone are their counter. And bless and support our noble master Muhammad in every breath of every soul from the moment You created them. And bless and support our noble master Muhammad in everything You have created and in what You will create. And in whatever is encompassed by Your Omniscience, and then double all of that.

اللهمَّ صلِّ عليهم عددَ خلقِكَ ورضاءَ نفسِكَ، وزِنَةَ عرشِكَ ومِدادَ كلماتِكَ، ومبلغَ علمِكَ وآياتِكَ، اللهمَّ صلِّ عليهم صلاةً تفوقُ وتفضُلُ صلاةَ المُصلينَ عليهم من الخلقِ أجمعينَ، كفضلِكَ على جميعِ خلقِكَ، اللهمَّ صلِّ عليهم صلاةً دائمةً مستمرةَ الدوامِ على مَرِّ الليالي والأيامِ متصِلةَ الدوامِ لا انقِضاءَ لها ولا انْصِرامَ، على مَرِّ الليالي والأيامِ، عددَ كُلِّ وابِلٍ وطَلٍّ، اللهمَّ صلِّ على سيدنا محمدٍ نبيكَ، وسيدنا إبراهيمَ خليلِكَ، وعلى جميعِ أنبيائِكَ وأصفيائِكَ، من أهلِ أرضِكَ وسمائِكَ، عددَ خلقِكَ ورضاءَ نفسِكَ، وزِنَةَ عرشِكَ ومِدادَ كلماتِكَ ومنتهى علمِكَ وزِنَةَ جميعِ مخلوقاتِكَ، صلاةً مكررةً أبداً، عددَ ما أحصى علمُكَ، ومِلْءَ ما أحصى علمُكَ، وأضعافَ ما أحصى علمُكَ، صلاةً تزيدُ وتفوقُ وتفضُلُ صلاةَ المصلينَ عليهم من الخلقِ أجمعينَ، كفضلِكَ على جميعِ خلقِكَ.

Allahummasalli'alaihim 'adada khalqika waridha'a nafsika wazinata arshika wamidada kalimatika wa mablagha' 'ilmika wa ayatik Allahummasalli'alaihim salatan tafuqu wa tafdhulu salatal-musallina 'alaihim minal-khalqi ajma'ina kafadlika -'ala jami'i khalqik

Allahummasalli'alaihim solawatan daa 'imatan- mustamirratad-dawami āla marr'illayali wal ayyami muttasilatad-dawami lan-qidhaa'a laha walan-sirama āla marrilliyali wal ayyami 'adada kulli waabil-inw watolli

Allahumma salli āla sayyidina Muhammad-in nabiyyika wa saiyidina ibraahima khalilika wa āla jamii'i anbiya'ika wa asfiyaa 'ika min ahli ardika wasamaa'ika 'adada khalqika wa rida'a nafsika wazinata 'arshika wa-midada kalimatika wa-muntaha 'ilmika wazinata jami'i makhluqatika Salatan-mukarraratan ābadan 'adada ma ahsa 'ilmuka wa mil'a ma ahsa 'ilmuka wa ad'afa ma ahsa 'ilmuka salatan tazidu wa-tafuqu wa-tafdulu salatal-musallina 'alaihim minal-khalqi 'ajma'iina kafadlika āla jamii'i khalqik

Dear God! Bless and support him in all of Your Creation and as much as it pleases You. And as much as the weight of Your Throne, and the ink for Your Words is, and to the extent of Your Omniscience and Signs. Dear God! Bless and support him with excellent and more gracious blessings equal to all the requests for blessings declared by the whole of creation just as, in like measure, the whole of creation enjoys Your favour.

Dear God! Bless and support him with endless and eternal blessings for as long as the duration of all future days and nights, never-ending and perpetual. And with blessings equal to the duration of all the days and nights which have already passed. And with blessings as copious as the rain contained in every downpour and shower that has ever fallen.

Dear God! Bless and support our noble master Muhammad, Your Prophet, and our noble master Abraham - Your Friend, and all the Prophets and Pure Ones from the people of Your Earth and Your Heavens. And in all of Your creation and as it contents You, in the weight of Your Throne, as much as the ink for Your words is, to the extent of Your Omniscience and Beauty of Your created beings, with blessings repeated eternally as much as Your Omniscience. And to the depth of Your Omniscience and then double this with blessings abundant, gracious and excellent. And blessings equal to all the requests for blessings ever declared by the whole of Your creation just as, in like measure, all of creation enjoys Your favour.

ثم تدعو بهذا الدعاء فإنه مرجو الإجابة إن شاء الله تعالى بعد الصلاة على النبي ﷺ:

اللهمَّ اجعلني ممن لَزِمَ مِلَّةَ نبيِّكَ سيدنا محمدٍ ﷺ، وعَظَّمَ حُرْمَتَهُ، وأعَزَّ كلمتَهُ، وحَفِظَ عهدَهُ وذِمَّتَهُ، ونصرَ حِزْبَهُ ودعوَتَهُ،

وكَثَّرَ تابعِيهِ وفِرْقَتَهُ، ووافى زُمرتَهُ، ولم يُخالِفْ سبيلَهُ وسُنَّتَهُ، اللهمَّ إني أسألُكَ الاستمساكَ بسُنَّتِهِ، وأعوذُ بِكَ من الانحرافِ عما

جاءَ بِهِ اللهمَّ إني أسألُكَ من خيرِ ما سألَكَ منهُ سيدُنا محمدٌ نبيُّكَ ورسولُكَ ﷺ، وأعوذُ بِكَ من شَرِّ ما استعاذَكَ منهُ سيدُنا محمدٌ

نبيُّكَ ورسولُكَ ﷺ، اللهمَّ اعصِمْني من شَرِّ الفتنِ وعافِني من جميعِ المِحنِ، وأصْلِحْ مني ما ظَهَرَ وما بَطَنَ، ونَقِّ قلبي من الحقدِ

والحسدِ، ولا تجعلْ عَلَيَّ تباعةً لأحدٍ،

Thumma tad'u bihzad-dua'i fa innahu marjuwwul-lijabati inshaa 'allaahu ta'laa ba'das-salaati 'alan-nabiyyi sallallahu 'alaihi wa sallam

Allahummaj 'alni mimman-lazima m'illata nabiyyik sayyidina Muhammad-in sallallahu 'alaihi wasallama wa 'azzoma hurmatahu wa-'azza kalimatahu wa-hafidha 'ahdahu wa-dhimmatahu wa-nasara hizbahu wada'watahu wa qathara taabi'iihi wafirqatahu wa wafa zumratahu wa lam yukhalif sabilahu wasunnatahu

Allahumma inni as'alukal-istimsaka bisunnatihi wa a'uzubika minal-inhirafi 'amma jaa 'a bih

Allahumma inni as'aluka min khairi ma sa'alaka minhu saiyiduna Muhammadun-nabiyyuka wa-rasuluka sallallahu 'alaihi wa-sallama wa-a'uzubika min sharri mastu'adhaka minhu saiyiduna Muhammadun-nabiyyuka wa-rasuluka sallallahu 'alaihi wasallama

Allahumma' aesimny min sharri - alfitani Wa 'afini min jamii'il-mihani wa aslih minni ma zahara wama batana wanaqqi qalbi minal-hiqdi wal hasadi wala taj'al 'alayya taba'atan-li Ahad

Then, dear reader, make the following supplications, for it is to be hoped they will be answered, God willing, after asking for blessings upon the Prophet, may God grant him peace.

Dear God! Grant me to be among those who stay close to the Way of Your Prophet, our noble master Muhammad, and Your blessings be always on him. Strengthen his holiness, enable his words, protect his promise and security, and give triumph to his party. Increase those who pledge their allegiance to him and his company. Grant that we die in his company and do not allow us to stray from his Path and Way.

Dear God! I ask You to keep me on his Way and to seek refuge in You from all deviations from it.

Dear God! I ask You for the good our noble master Muhammad, Your Prophet and Messenger, asked of You. And I ask for refuge in You from the evil our noble master Muhammad, Your Prophet and Messenger, sought refuge. May You grant him peace and bless him.

Dear God! Protect me from the evil of discord, absolve me from all tests, purify me from within and without, cleanse my heart from hatred and envy, and do not allow anyone to oppress me.

اللهمَّ إني أسألُكَ الأخذَ بأحسنِ ما تعلمُ، والتركَ لسيءٍ ما تعلمُ وأسألُكَ التكفُّلَ بالرزقِ والزهدِ في الكفافِ، والمَخْرجِ

بالبيانِ من كُلِّ شبهةٍ، والفلجَ بالصوابِ في كُلِّ حُجَّةٍ، والعدلَ في الغضبِ والرِّضاءِ، والتسليمَ لِما يَجري به القضاءُ، والاقتصادَ

في الفقرِ والغِنى، والتواضعَ في القولِ والفعلِ، والصِّدْقَ في الجِدِّ والهزلِ، اللهمَّ إن لي ذنوباً فيما بيني وبينَكَ، وذنوباً فيما بيني وبين

خَلقِكَ، اللهمَّ ما كان لكَ منها فاغفرهُ، وما كان منها لخلقِكَ فَتَحَمَّلهُ عني، وأغْنِني بفضلِكَ، إنكَ واسِعُ المغفرةِ، اللهمَّ نَوِّرْ

بالعلمِ قلبي، واستعملْ بطاعتِكَ بدني، وخَلِّصْ من الفتنِ سِرِّي، وأشْغِلْ بالاعتبارِ فِكري، وقِني شَرَّ وَساوِسِ الشيطانِ، وأجِرني

مِنْهُ يا رحمنُ، حتى لا يكونَ لهُ عَلَيَّ سلطانٌ.

Allahumma inni as'alukal-ākhza bi āhsani ma ta'lamu wattarkelisai'i ma ta'lamu wa-as'aluka-
ttakaffula birrizqi wazzuhdi filkafafi wal makhraji bilbayani min kulli shubhatin-walfalaja bi-ssawabi fi
kulli hujjatin-wal'adla fil-ghadabi warrida'i wattaslima lima yajri bihil qadaa'u wal-iqtisada fil-faqri wal-
ghina wat-tawadu'a fil-qauli Wal fi'li wassidqa fil-jiddi wal-hazl

Allahumma inna li zunuuban fima baini wabainaka wazunuban fima baini wabaina khalqi

Allahumma ma kana laka minha fa-ghfirhu wama kana minha likhalqika fa-tahammalhu 'anni wa a-
ghnini bifadlika inaka wasi-'ul-maghfirah Allahumma nawwir bil 'ilmi qalbi wasta'mil bita-'atika badani
Wa-khallis minal-fitani sirri Washghil bil-'itibari fikri Wa-qini sharra wasawisi esh-shaitan Wa ajirni
minhu yaa rahmaanu hatta la yakuna lahu 'Alayya sultan

Dear God! I ask You for the good that You know, and let me pass by the evil You know. I ask You
for provision, indifference to being physically satisfied, and a clear way out from every uncertainty. I
also ask You for a proper stance in every argument, justice in anger and contentment, peace with
whatever fate ordains, providence in poverty, freedom from want, humility in my words and actions, and
sincerity in my seriousness and my jesting.

Dear God! Indeed, there are sins I have committed, so please forgive them for me. And for the sins I
have committed against others of your creation, and whatever arises from them, bear them on my behalf.
And enrich me with Your favour as Your forgiveness spreads far and wide.

Dear God! Enlighten the knowledge of my heart, render my body obedient to You, and purify me
from inner discord. Occupy me with contemplation, protect me from Satan's whisperings, and save me
from him, O Merciful One, until he has no power over me.

بِسمِ اللهِ الرحمنِ الرحيمِ

اللهمَّ إني أسألكَ من خيرِ ما تعلمُ، وأعوذُ بِكَ من شرِّ ما تعلمُ، وأستغفرُكَ من كُلِّ ما تعلمُ، إنكَ تعلمُ ولا نعلمُ، وأنتَ علامُ الغيوبِ، اللهمَّ ارْحَمْني من زَمَاني هذا وإحْداقِ الفتنِ، وتطاوُلِ أهلِ الجُرْأةِ عَلَيَّ واستضعافهمْ إيَّايَ، اللهمَّ اجعلني منكَ في عياذٍ منيعٍ، وحِرْزٍ حصينٍ من جميعِ خلقِكَ حتى تُبَلِّغَني أجلي مُعافىً، اللهمَّ صلِّ على سيدنا محمدٍ وعلى آلِ سيدنا محمدٍ عددَ من صلى عليهِ، وصلِّ على سيدنا محمدٍ وعلى آلِ سيدنا محمدٍ عددَ من لم يصلِّ عليهِ، وصلِّ على سيدنا محمدٍ وعلى آلِ سيدنا محمدٍ كما تنبغي الصلاةُ عليهِ، وصلِّ على سيدنا محمدٍ وعلى آلِ سيدنا محمدٍ كما تَجِبُ الصلاةُ عليهِ،

Allahumma inni as'aluka min khairi ma ta'lamu wa a'uzu bika min sharri ma ta'lamu wa 'āstaghferuka min kulli ma ta'alamu 'innaka ta'alamu wala na'alamu wa 'anta 'allamul-ghuyub

Allahumma-arhamni min zamani hatha wa-ihdaqil-fitani wata-uli- ahlil-jur-ati 'Alaiya wastidh'a fihim iyya

Allahumma aj-'alni minka fi 'iyazim-mani'inw-wa hirzin hasinim-min jami'i khalqika hatta tuballighani ajali mu'afa Allahumma salli āla sayyidina Muhammad-in-wa-'ala Āli sayyidina Muhammad-in 'adada man salla 'alaih Wa salli āla sayyidina Muhammad-in-wa-'ala Āli sayyidina Muhammad-in 'adada mal-lam yusalli 'alaihi wa-salli āla sayyidina Muhammad-in-wa-'ala āalihii sayyidina Muhammad-in kama tambaghis-solatu 'alaihi wa salli āla sayyidina Muhammad-in- wa-'ala Āli sayyidina Muhammad-in kama tajibuss-solatu 'alaih

The Second Part to be read on Tuesday

BISMILLA HIRRAHMAAN NIRRAHIM

Dear God! I ask You for the good that You know. And I seek refuge in You from the evil of what You know. I ask Your forgiveness for everything You know. For indeed You know and we do not know. And indeed, You are the Omniscient of the Unwitnessed.

Dear God! I ask You to have mercy on me from the encirclement of discord, the oppression of the arrogant and disrespectful, their deficiencies, and all such ills.

Dear God! Give me safe refuge in You and impassable preservation with You from all of Your creation until I come to a virtuous end.

Dear God! Bless and support our noble master Muhammad and his family as often as those who have requested blessings upon him.

Dear God! Bless and support our noble master Muhammad and his family as often as those who have not asked for blessings upon him. And bless and support our noble master Muhammad and his family with as many blessings as are fitting for him and with as many blessings as are his due.

وصلِّ على سيدنا محمدٍ وعلى آلِ سيدنا محمدٍ كما أمرتَ أن يُصلى عليهِ، وصلِّ على سيدنا محمدٍ وعلى آلِ سيدنا محمدٍ الذي نُورُهُ من نورِ الأنوارِ، وأشرقَ بشُعاعِ سِرِّهِ الأسرارُ، اللهمَّ صلِّ على سيدنا محمدٍ وعلى آلِ سيدنا محمدٍ وعلى أهلِ بيتهِ الأبرارِ أجمعينَ، اللهمَّ صلِّ على سيدنا محمدٍ وعلى آلِهِ بحرِ أنوارِكَ، ومَعْدِنِ أسرارِكَ، ولِسانِ حُجَّتِكَ، وعَروسِ مملكتِكَ وإمام حَضْرَتِكَ، وخاتَم أنبيائِكَ، صلاةً تَدومُ بدوامِكَ، وتبقى ببقائِكَ، صلاةً تُرْضيكَ وتُرْضِيهِ، وتَرْضى بها عنا يا أرحمَ الراحمينَ، اللهمَّ رَبَّ الحِلِّ والحرامِ، ورَبَّ المشْعَرِ الحرامِ، ورَبَّ البيتِ الحرامِ، ورَبَّ الرُّكْنِ والمقامِ، أبلغ لسيدنا ومولانا محمدٍ منا السلامَ، اللهمَّ صلِّ على سيدنا ومولانا محمدٍ سيدِ الأَوَّلينَ والآخِرينَ اللهمَّ صلِّ على سيدنا ومولانا محمدٍ في كُلِّ وقتٍ وحينَ اللهمَّ صلِّ على سيدنا ومولانا محمدٍ في الملإِ الأَعلى إلى يومِ الدينِ،

Wa-salli āla sayyidina Muhammad-in-wa-'ala Āli sayyidina Muhammad-in kama amarta anyusallah 'alaihi Wa-salli āla sayyidina Muhammadi-n'illazi nuruhu minnuri -al-anwaari wa-ashraqa bi-shu'a 'i sirri-hil-asrar

Allahumma salli āla sayyidina Muhammad-in wa-'ala Āli sayyidina Muhammad-in wa-'ala aahli baitihil-abraari ajma'in

Allahumma salli āla sayyidina Muhammad-in wa-'alaa aalihi bahri 'anwarika wa ma'dani asrarika wa lisani hujatika -'arusi mamlakatika wa-imami hadratika wakhatemi ambiya'ika salatan tadumu bedawamika watabqa-bibaqa'ika salatan turdika waturdihi watarda biha 'anna Ya-'arhamar-rahimin

Allahumma rabbal-hille wal-harami warabbal-mash 'aril-harami wa rabbal-baitil harami warabbar-rukni walmaqami abligh li-sayyidina wa-maulana Muhammad-im- minnas-salam

Allahumma salli āla sayyidina wa maulana Muhammad-in sayyiddil awwalina wal-akhirin Allahumma salli āla sayyidina wa maulana Muhammad-in fi kulli waqtinw-wa-hiin Allahumma salli āla sayyidina wa maulana Muhammad-in filmala 'il āla ila yaumiddin

And bless and support our noble master Muhammad and his family as You have ordered him to be blessed.

And bless and support our noble master Muhammad and his family, whose light is from the Light of Lights and illuminates all secrets with a ray from his Secrets. Dear God! Bless and support our noble master Muhammad, his family, and all the Chosen People of his House.

Dear God! Bless and support our noble master Muhammad and his family. He is the Sea of Your Lights, the Mine of Your Secrets, the Tongue of Your Proofs. And he is the Bridegroom of Your Kingdom, Leader of Your Presence and the Seal of Your Prophets. Bless him with blessings that last for eternity. Bless him with blessings that please You, which please him, and which make You pleased with us, O the Most Merciful.

Dear God! Lord of the two hills and the Haram, Lord of the Sacred House, and Lord of the Corner and Station of Abraham. Send peace from us to our noble master Muhammad. Dear God! Bless and support our noble master Muhammad, master of the First and the Last. Dear God! Bless and support our noble master Muhammad at every moment and every instant. Dear God! Bless and support our noble master Muhammad in the Highest Host until the Day of Judgement.

اللهمَّ صلِّ على سيدنا ومولانا محمدٍ حتى تَرِثَ الأرضَ ومن عليها وأنتَ خيرُ الوارثينَ، اللهمَّ صلِّ على سيدنا محمدٍ النبيِّ الأميِّ وعلى آلِ سيدنا محمدٍ كما صَلَّيْتَ على سيدنا إبراهيمَ إنكَ حميدٌ مجيدٌ، وبارِكْ على سيدنا محمدٍ النبيِّ الأميِّ كما باركتَ على سيدنا إبراهيمَ إنكَ حميدٌ مجيدٌ، اللهمَّ صلِّ على سيدنا محمدٍ وعلى آلِ سيدنا محمدٍ عددَ ما أحاطَ بهِ عِلْمُكَ، وجَرَى بهِ قَلَمُكَ، وسَبَقَتْ بهِ مَشيئتُكَ، وصَلَّتْ عليهِ مَلائِكَتُكَ، صلاةً دائمةً بدَوامِكَ، باقيةً بفضلِكَ وإحسانِكَ، إلى أبدِ الأبَدِ، أبَداً لا نهايةَ لأبَدِيَّتِهِ، ولا فناءَ لِدَيْمُومِيَّتِهِ، اللهمَّ صلِّ على سيدنا محمدٍ وعلى آلِ سيدنا محمدٍ عددَ ما أحاطَ بهِ عِلْمُكَ، وأحصاهُ كِتابُكَ، وشَهِدَتْ بهِ مَلائِكَتُكَ، وارْضَ عن أصحابِهِ، وارحَمْ أُمَّتَهُ إنكَ حميدٌ مجيدٌ، اللهمَّ صلِّ على سيدنا محمدٍ وعلى آلِ سيدنا محمدٍ وعلى جميعِ أصحابِ سيدنا محمدٍ،

Allahumma salli āla sayyidina wa maulana Muhammadin hatta tarithal-'ardha wa man 'alaiha wa-anta khairul-warithin Allahumma salli āla saiyidinaa Muhammadi-nin-nabiyyil-ummiyyi wa-'ala Āli sayyidina Muhammad-in kama sallaita āla sayyidina Ibraahima innaka hamiidum majiid

Wa barik āla sayyidina Muhammadi-nin-nabiyyil-ummiyyi kama barakta āla sayyidina Ibraahima innaka hamiidum majiid

Allahumma salli āla sayyidina Muhammad-in-wa-'ala Āli sayyidina Muhammad-in 'adada ma 'ahata bihi 'ilmuka wajara bihi qalamuka wasabaqat bihi mashi-'atuka wa-sallat 'alaihi mala'ikatuka salatan daa'imatam-bidawamika baqiyatan bifadlika Wa ihsanika ilā abadel-abadi abadal-la nihayata liabadiyyatihi wala fana'a lidaimumiyyatih

Allahumma salli āla sayyidina Muhammad-in-wa āla Āli sayyidina Muhammad-in 'adada ma 'ahata bihi 'ilmuka wa ahsahu kitabuka washahidat bihi mala'ikatuka warda 'an as-habihi warham ummatahu innaka hamidum-majid

Allahumma salli āla sayyidina Muhammad-in-wa āla Āli sayyidina Muhammad-in-wa āla jamii'i ashabi sayyidina Muhammad-in

Dear God! Bless and support our noble master Muhammad until You inherit the earth and what is on it. You are the Best Inheritor. Dear God! Bless and support our noble master Muhammad, the prophet sent to all nations, just as You blessed our noble master Abraham. You are the Praiseworthy, the Glorious.

Dear God! Bless and support our noble master Muhammad and his family in all that Your Omniscience encompasses, in everything Your pen writes and Your Will pre-ordains, and as often as Your angels have blessed him. Bless him with eternal blessings, by Your Grace and Generosity, for all eternity, never-ending, with no beginning and no end, forever and ever.

Dear God! Bless and support our noble master Muhammad and his family as much as You know him, as much as Your Book has collected, and as much as Your angels witness. And be content with his Companions and be merciful to his nation. You are the Praiseworthy, the Glorious.

Dear God! Bless and support our noble master Muhammad and his family and all his Companions.

اللهمَّ صلِّ على سيدنا محمدٍ وعلى آلِ سيدنا محمدٍ كما صَلَّيْتَ على سيدنا إبراهيمَ، وباركْ على سيدنا محمدٍ وعلى آلِ سيدنا محمدٍ كما باركتَ على سيدنا إبراهيمَ وعلى آلِ سيدنا إبراهيمَ في العالمينَ إنكَ حميدٌ مجيدٌ، اللهمَّ صلِّ على سيدنا ومولانا محمدٍ عددَ ما أحاطَ بِهِ علمُكَ اللهمَّ صلِّ على سيدنا ومولانا محمدٍ عددَ ما أحصاهُ كتابُكَ، اللهمَّ صلِّ على سيدنا ومولانا محمدٍ عددَ ما نَفَذَتْ بِهِ قُدْرَتُكَ، اللهمَّ صلِّ على سيدنا ومولانا محمدٍ عددَ ما خصَّصَتْهُ إرادتُكَ، اللهمَّ صلِّ على سيدنا ومولانا محمدٍ عددَ ما تَوجَّهَ إليهِ أمْرُكَ ونَهْيُكَ، اللهمَّ صلِّ على سيدنا ومولانا محمدٍ عددَ ما وَسِعَهُ سَمْعُكَ، اللهمَّ صلِّ على سيدنا ومولانا محمدٍ عددَ ما أحاطَ بِهِ بصرُكَ، اللهمَّ صلِّ على سيدنا ومولانا محمدٍ عددَ ما ذكَرَهُ الذاكرونَ، اللهمَّ صلِّ على سيدنا ومولانا محمدٍ عددَ ما غَفَلَ عن ذكرِهِ الغافِلونَ،

Allahumma salli āla sayyidina Muhammad-in wa āla sayyidina Muhammadin Kama sallaita āla sayyidina Ibraahiima

wa barik k'illahumma āla sayyidina Muhamamd-inw-wa āla Āli sayyidina Muhamamd-in kama barakta āla sayyidina Ibrahiima wa āla Āli sayyidina Ibraahiima fil-'alamina innaka hamidum-majiid

Allahumma salli āla sayyidina wa maulana Muhamamdin 'adada maa ahata bihi 'ilmuka Allahumma salli āla sayyidina wa maulaana Muhamamd-in 'adada maa ahsahu kitabuk

Allahumma salli āla sayyidina wa maulana Muhammadin 'adada ma nafazat bihi qudratuk Allahumma salli āla Sayyidina wa maulana Muhammad-in 'adada ma khassa-sat-hu iradatuk

Allahumma salli āla sayyidina wa maulana Muhammadin 'adada ma tawajaha 'ilaihi 'amruka wa nahyuk Allahumma salli āla sayyidina wa maulana Muhamamd-in 'adada ma wasi'ahu sam'uk

Allahumma salli āla sayyidina wa maulana Muhammadin 'adada ma ahata bihi basaruk Allahumma salli āla sayyidina wa maulana Muhammad-in 'adada ma zakarahuz-zaakirun Allahumma salli āla sayyidina Muhammad-in 'adada ma ghafala 'an dhikrihil-ghafilun

Dear God! Bless and support our noble master Muhammad and his family, just as You blessed our noble master Abraham. And bless and support our noble master Muhammad and his family just as You blessed our noble master Abraham in all the worlds. You are the Praiseworthy, the Glorious.

Dear God! Bless and support our noble master Muhammad as much as Your Omniscience encompasses and as much as Your Book has enumerated. Dear God! Bless and support our noble master Muhammad as much as he is distinguished by Your will and as much as he is crowned by Your Command and Your prohibition.

Dear God! Bless and support our noble master Muhammad as much as all that is within range of Your Hearing and as much as all that Your Vision encompasses.

Dear God! Bless and support our noble master Muhammad as many times as those who remember him do so and as many times as those who are heedless to remember him.

اللهمَّ صلِّ على سيدنا ومولانا محمدٍ عددَ قَطْرِ الأمطارِ، اللهمَّ صلِّ على سيدنا ومولانا محمدٍ عددَ أوراقِ الأشجارِ، اللهمَّ صلِّ على سيدنا ومولانا محمدٍ عددَ دوابِّ القِفارِ، اللهمَّ صلِّ على سيدنا ومولانا محمدٍ عددَ دوابِّ البحارِ، اللهمَّ صلِّ على سيدنا ومولانا محمدٍ عددَ مياهِ البحارِ، اللهمَّ صلِّ على سيدنا ومولانا محمدٍ عددَ ما أظلمَ عليهِ الليلُ وأضاءَ عليهِ النهارُ، اللهمَّ صلِّ على سيدنا ومولانا محمدٍ بالغُدُوِّ والآصالِ، اللهمَّ صلِّ على سيدنا ومولانا محمدٍ عددَ الرَّمالِ، اللهمَّ صلِّ على سيدنا ومولانا محمدٍ عددَ النِّساءِ والرِّجالِ، اللهمَّ صلِّ على سيدنا ومولانا محمدٍ رِضاءَ نَفْسِكَ اللهمَّ صلِّ على سيدنا ومولانا محمدٍ مِدادَ كلِماتِكَ، اللهمَّ صلِّ على سيدنا ومولانا محمدٍ مِلْءَ سَمَاوَاتِكَ وأرْضِكَ،

Allahumma Salli āla sayyidina wa maulana Muhammad-in ‘adada qatril-amtar Allahumma salli āla sayyidina wa maulana Muhammad-in ‘adada auraqil-ashjar

Allahumma salli āla sayyidina wa maulana Muhammmad-in ‘adada dawaabbil-qifar Allahumma salli āla sayyidina wa maulana Muhammad-in ‘adada dawaab-bil-bihar

Allahumma salli āla sayyidina wa maulana Muhammad-in ‘adada miyahil-bihar Allahumma salli āla sayyidina wa maulana Muhammad-in ‘adada ma azlama ‘alaihil-lailu wa adha‘a ‘alaihin-nahar

Allahumma salli āla sayyidina wa maulana Muhammad-in bil-ghuduwwi wal-aasal Allahumma salli āla sayyidina wa maulana Muhammad-in ‘adadar-rimal Allahumma salli āla sayyidina wa maulana Muhammad-in ‘adadan-nisaa‘i warrijal

Allahumma salli āla sayyidina wa maulana Muhammad-ir-rida ‘a nafsik Allahumma salli āla sayyidina wa maulana Muhammad-im midada kalimatik Allahumma salli āla saiyidinaa wa maulaana Muhammad-im mil‘a samawatika wa ‘ardik

Dear God! Bless and support our noble master Muhammad as many times as there are raindrops. Dear God! Bless and support our noble master Muhammad as often as there are leaves on the trees. Dear God! Bless and support our noble master Muhammad as often as there are beasts in the desert. Dear God! Bless and support our noble master Muhammad as often as there are creatures in the sea. Dear God! Bless and support our noble master Muhammad as much as there is water in the sea. Dear God! Bless and support our noble master Muhammad as much as all the night has covered and the day has illuminated. Dear God! Bless and support our noble master Muhammad every morning and every evening. Dear God! Bless and support our noble master Muhammad as often as there are grains of sand. Dear God! Bless and support our noble master Muhammad as often as there are men and women.

Dear God! Bless and support our noble master Muhammad as much as pleases You. Dear God! Bless and support our noble master Muhammad as much as Your will has designated, and as much as the ink for Your words is. Dear God! Bless and support our noble master Muhammad to the fullness of Your Heavens and Your Earth.

اللهمَّ صلِّ على سيدنا ومولانا محمدٍ زِنَةَ عرشِكَ، اللهمَّ صلِّ على سيدنا ومولانا محمدٍ عددَ مخلوقاتِكَ اللهمَّ صلِّ على سيدنا ومولانا محمدٍ أفْضَلَ صلواتِكَ، اللهمَّ صلِّ على نبيِّ الرحمةِ، اللهمَّ صلِّ على شفيعِ الأمةِ، اللهمَّ صلِّ على كاشِفِ الغُمَّةِ، اللهمَّ صلِّ على مُجْلي الظُّلْمَةِ، اللهمَّ صلِّ على مُولي النِّعمةِ، اللهمَّ صلِّ على مُؤْتي الرَّحمةِ اللهمَّ صلِّ على صاحِبِ الحوضِ الموروِد، اللهمَّ صلِّ على صاحِبِ المقام المحمودِ، اللهمَّ صلِّ على صاحِبِ اللواءِ المعقودِ، اللهمَّ صلِّ على صاحِبِ المكانِ المشهودِ، اللهمَّ صلِّ على الموصوفِ بالكرمِ والجودِ، اللهمَّ صلِّ على مَنْ هو في السماءِ محمودٌ وفي الأرضِ سيدُنا محمدٌ، اللهمَّ صلِّ على صاحِبِ الشامةِ، اللهمَّ صلِّ على صاحِبِ العلامةِ، اللهمَّ صلِّ على الموصوفِ بالكرامةِ، اللهمَّ صلِّ على المخصوصِ بالزعامةِ،

Allhumma salli āla sayyidina wa maulaana Muhammad-in zinata 'arshi Allahumma salli āla sayyidina wa maulana Muhammad-in 'adada makhluqaatik Allahumma salli āla sayyidina Wa maulana Muhammad-in afdala salawaatik

Allahumma salli āla nabiyyir-rahmah Allahumma salli āla shafii'il-ummat Allahumma salli āla kashifil-ghummah Allahumma salli āla mujlil-zulmah Allahumma salli āla mulin-ni'mah

Allahumma salli āla mu'tir-rahmah Allahumma salli āla sahibil-hauzil-maurud Allahumma salli āla sahibil-maqamil-mahmud Allahumma salli āla saahibil-lilwaa'il ma'qud

Allahumma salli āla sahibi Makanil-mash hud Allahummasalli'alal-mausufi bilkarami waljud Allahummasalli'ala man huwa fissamaa 'i sayyiduna Mahmuduw-wafil 'ardi sayyidunaa Muhammad

Allahumma salli āla saahibish-shamah Allahumma salli āla sahibil-'alamah Allahummasalli'alal-mausufi bilkaramah Allahummasalli'alal-makhsusi bizza'amah

Dear God! Bless and support our noble master Muhammad as much as the weight of Your Throne.

Dear God! Bless and support our noble master Muhammad as many times as there are created beings. Dear God! Bless and support our noble master Muhammad with the best of Your blessings. Dear God! Bless and support the Prophet of Mercy and Intercessor of his nation. Dear God! Bless and support the Remover of grief and Clarifier of darkness. Dear God! Bless and support the noble master of Grace and Granter of Mercy. Dear God! Bless and support the Owner of the Visited Pool and Most Praised Station. Dear God! Bless and support the Owner of the Banner and site of Witnessing. Dear God! Bless and support the One adorned with Nobility and Generosity. Dear God! Bless and support the One called Mahmud in the Heavens and Muhammad on the Earth. Dear God! Bless and support the Possessor of the mole and distinguishing mark. Dear God! Bless and support the One dressed in miracles. Dear God! Bless and support the One with extraordinary leadership.

اللهمَّ صلِّ على من كان تُظِلُّهُ الغَمامةُ، اللهمَّ صلِّ على مَنْ كان يرى مَنْ خَلْفَهُ كما يرى مَنْ أمامهُ، اللهمَّ صلِّ على الشفيع المُشَفَّعِ يومَ القيامةِ، اللهمَّ صلِّ على صاحِبِ الضراعةِ، اللهمَّ صلِّ على صاحِبِ الشفاعةِ، اللهمَّ صلِّ على صاحِبِ الوسيلةِ، اللهمَّ صلِّ على صاحِبِ الفضيلةِ، اللهمَّ صلِّ على صاحِبِ الدرجةِ الرفيعةِ، اللهمَّ صلِّ على صاحِبِ الهِراوَةِ، اللهمَّ صلِّ على صاحِبِ النَّعْلَيْنِ، اللهمَّ صلِّ على صاحِبِ الحُجَّةِ، اللهمَّ صلِّ على صاحِبِ البُرْهانِ، اللهمَّ صلِّ على صاحِبِ السُّلْطانِ، اللهمَّ صلِّ على صاحِبِ التّاجِ، اللهمَّ صلِّ على صاحِبِ المِعْراجِ، اللهمَّ صلِّ على صاحِبِ القَضيبِ، اللهمَّ صلِّ على راكِبِ النَّجيبِ، اللهمَّ صلِّ على راكِبِ البُراقِ، اللهمَّ صلِّ على مُحْتَرِقِ السبع الطِّباقِ، اللهمَّ صلِّ على الشَّفيع في جَميع الأنامِ، اللهمَّ صلِّ على مَنْ سَبَّحَ في كَفِّهِ الطَّعامُ، اللهمَّ صلِّ على من بكى إليهِ الجِذْعُ وحَنَّ لفراقِهِ، اللهمَّ صلِّ على مَنْ تَوسَّلَ بِهِ طَيْرُ الفَلاةِ، اللهمَّ صلِّ على مَنْ سَبَّحَتْ في كَفِّهِ الحَصاةُ،

Allahumma salli āla man kana tuzziluhul- ghamamah Allahumma salli āla man kana yaraa khalfahu kama yara mann amamah Allahummasalli'Alash-shafii'il-mushaffa'i yaumal-qiyamah

Allahumma salli āla sahibid-dhora'ah Allahumma salli āla sahibish-shafa'ah Allahumma salli āla sahibil-wasilah Allahumma salli āla sahibil-fadhilah Allahumma salli āla sahibid-darajatir-rafi'ah

Allahumma salli āla sahibil-harawah Allahumma salli āla sahibin-na' lain Allahumma salli āla sahibil-hujjajah Allahumma salli āla sahibil-burhan Allahumma salli āla sahibis-sultaan Allahumma salli āla sahibit-taaj Allahumma salli āla sahibil-mi'raj Allahumma salli āla sahibil-qadiib

Allahumma salli āla rakibin-najiib Allahumma salli āla rakibil-buraaq Allahumma salli āla mukhtariqis-sab'ittibaq Allahummasalli'alash-shafii' fi jamii'il-anam Allahumma salli āla mann sabbaha fi kaffihit-ta'am Allahumma salli āla mann baka ilayhil-jiz'u wahanna lifiraqih Allahumma salli āla man tawassala bihi tairul-falat Allahummasalli'ala mann sabbahat fi kaffihil-hasah

Dear God! Bless and support the One shaded by the clouds. Dear God! Bless and support the One who sees equally from behind and in front of him. Dear God! Bless and support the One whose intercession will be accepted on the Day of the Rising-Up. Dear God! Bless and support the Possessor of humility.

Dear God! Bless and support the Possessor of Intercession for all creatures. Dear God! Bless and support the Possessor of the Closest Access. Dear God! Bless and support the Possessor of Pre-eminence and Lofty Rank. Dear God! Bless and support the Owner of the firm staff and the sandals.

Dear God! Bless and support the Possessor of sound argument and convincing reason. Dear God! Bless and support the Possessor of authority. Dear God! Bless and support the Owner of the turban. Dear God! Bless and support the noble master of the night journey. Dear God! Bless and support the noble Rider and the Rider of Buraq. Dear God! Bless and support the One who travelled across the Seven Heavens.

Dear God! Bless and support the One whose food glorified God while in his hand. Dear God! Bless and support the One for whom a palm trunk wept and sighed at its separation from him. Dear God! Bless and support the One whose mediation was sought by the birds of the desert. Dear God! Bless and support the One who held stones in his hand, which glorified God.

اللهمَّ صلِّ على مَنْ تشفعَ إليهِ الظبيُ بأفْصَحِ كلام، اللهمَّ صلِّ على مَنْ كَلَّمَهُ الضَّبُّ في مَجْلِسِهِ مَعَ أصحابِهِ الأعلام، اللهمَّ صلِّ على البَشيرِ النَّذيرِ، اللهمَّ صلِّ على السِّراجِ المُنيرِ، اللهمَّ صلِّ على مَنْ شكا إليهِ البَعيرُ، اللهمَّ صلِّ على مَنْ تَفَجَّرَ مِنْ بَيْنِ أَصابِعِهِ الماءُ النَّميرُ، اللهمَّ صلِّ على الطَّاهِرِ المُطَهَّرِ، اللهمَّ صلِّ على نُورِ الأنوارِ، اللهمَّ صلِّ على مَنِ انشقَّ لهُ القمرُ، اللهمَّ صلِّ على الطَّيِّبِ المُطَيَّبِ، اللهمَّ صلِّ على الرَّسولِ المُقَرَّبِ، اللهمَّ صلِّ على الفَجْرِ السَّاطِعِ، اللهمَّ صلِّ على النَّجْمِ الثَّاقِبِ، اللهمَّ صلِّ على العُرْوَةِ الوُثْقَى، اللهمَّ صلِّ على نذيرِ أهلِ الأرضِ، اللهمَّ صلِّ على الشفيعِ يومَ العرضِ، اللهمَّ صلِّ على الساقي للناسِ مِنَ الحَوْضِ، اللهمَّ صلِّ على صاحبِ لواءِ الحَمْدِ، اللهمَّ صلِّ على المُشَمِّرِ عَنْ ساعِدِ الجِدِّ، اللهمَّ صلِّ على المُسْتَعْمِلِ في مِرْضاتِكَ غَايَةَ الجُهْدِ، اللهمَّ صلِّ على النبيِّ الخاتَمِ،

Allahumma salli āla mann tashaffa'a ilaihiz-zabyu bi-afsahil-kalam Allahumma salli āla mann kallamahudh-dhabbu fi majlisihii ma'a ashaabihil-'alam Allahummasalli'alal-bashirin-nazir

Allahummasalli'alas-sirajil-munir Allahumma salli āla man shakaa ilaihil-ba'ir Allahuma salli āla man tafajjara mim baini asabi 'ihil-maa'un-namir Allahummasalli'alat-tahiril-mutahar

Allahumma salli āla nuril-anwaar Alahahumma salli āla manin-saqqa lahul-qamar Allahumma salli'alat-tayyibil-mutayyab Allahummasalli'alar-rasulil-muqarrab Allahummasalli'alal-fajris-saati'

Allahummasalli'alan-najmith-thaaqib Allahummasalli'alal-'ur-watil-wusqa Allahumma salli āla naziri ahlil-ardh Allahummasalli'alash-shafii 'i yaumal-ardh Allahummasalli'alas-saqi linnasi minal-haud

Allahumma salli āla saahibi liwaa'il-hamd Allahummasalli'alal-mushammiri 'ann sahidil-jidd Allahummasalli'alal-musta' aamili fi mardhotika ghayatal-juhd Allahummasalli'alan-nabiyyil-khatim

Dear God! Bless and support the One whose intercession was sought by the gazelles and whose request was made in human speech. Dear God! Bless and support the One to whom a lizard spoke at an open gathering of the most learned Companions. Dear God! Bless and support the Bearer of glad tidings and the Warner. Dear God! Bless the Brilliant Lamp.

Dear God! Bless and support the One to whom a camel made its complaint. Dear God! Bless and support the One for whom sparkling water burst forth from his fingertips for his Companions. Dear God! Bless and support the Pure One, the Purifier. Dear God! Bless and support the Light of Lights.

Dear God! Bless and support the One for whom the moon was split open. Dear God! Bless and support the One who was good and did good. Dear God! Bless and support the Messenger closest to You. Dear God! Bless the Breaking Dawn. Dear God! Bless the Piercing Star.

Dear God! Bless and support the Trusty Handhold. Dear God! Bless and support the Warner of those inhabiting the Earth. Dear God! Bless and support the Intercessor on the Day of Petition. Dear God! Bless and support the One who will allow people to drink from his Pool. Dear God! Bless and support the Owner of the Banner of happiness. Dear God! Bless and support the One who was ever ready for Your service. Dear God! Bless and support the One who strived his utmost for Your Contentment. Dear God! Bless and support the Prophet, the Seal One.

اللهمَّ صلِّ على الرسولِ الخاتَمِ، اللهمَّ صلِّ على المُصطفى القائِمِ، اللهمَّ صلِّ على رسولِكَ أبي القاسِمِ، اللهمَّ صلِّ على صاحِبِ الآياتِ، اللهمَّ صلِّ على صاحِبِ الدَّلالاتِ، اللهمَّ صلِّ على صاحِبِ الإشاراتِ، اللهمَّ صلِّ على صاحِبِ الكراماتِ، اللهمَّ صلِّ على صاحِبِ العلاماتِ، اللهمَّ صلِّ على صاحِبِ البيِّناتِ، اللهمَّ صلِّ على صاحِبِ المُعْجِزاتِ اللهمَّ صلِّ على صاحِبِ خوارِقِ العاداتِ، اللهم صل على من سلمت عليه الأحجار، اللهمَّ صلِّ على مَنْ سَجَدَتْ بَيْنَ يَدَيْهِ الأشجارُ، اللهمَّ صلِّ على مَنْ تَفَتَّقَتْ مِنْ نُورِهِ الأزهارُ، اللهمَّ صلِّ على مَنْ طَابَتْ بِبَرَكَتِهِ الثِّمارُ، اللهمَّ صلِّ على مَنِ اخضرَّتْ مِنْ بَقِيَّةِ وَضُوئِهِ الأشجارُ، اللهمَّ صلِّ على مَنْ فاضتْ مِنْ نُورِهِ جَميعُ الأنوارِ، اللهمَّ صلِّ على مَنْ بالصلاةِ عليهِ تُحَطُّ الأوزارُ، اللهمَّ صلِّ على مَنْ بالصلاةِ عليهِ تُنالُ منازلُ الأبرارِ،

Allahummasalli'alar-rasulil-khatim   Allahummasalli'alal-mustafal-qaaim   Allahumma   salli   āla rasulika abil-qasim Allahumma salli āla sahibil-ayat Allahumma salli āla sohibid-dalalat

Allahumma salli āla sahibil-isharat Allahumma salli āla sahibil-karamat Allahumma salli āla sahibil alamat Allahumma salli āla sahibil-bayyinaat

Allahumma salli āla Sahibil-mu'j'idhat Allahumma salli āla sahibi-khawariqil-'adat Allahumma salli āla mun sallamat 'alaihil-ahjaar Allahumma salli āla man sajadat baina yadaihil-ashjaar

Allahumma salli āla mann tafattaqat min nurihil-azhaar Allahumma salli āla mann tobat bibarkatihith-thimar Allahumma salli āla manikh-darrat mimm baqiyyati wadhuu 'i-hil-ashjaar

Allahummasalli'ala mann fadhat min-nurihi jami'ul-anwar Allahumma salli āla Mam bissolati 'alaihi tuhattul-auzar Allahumma salli āla mam bissalaati 'alaihi tunalu manazilul-abrar

Dear God! Bless and support Your Messenger, the Seal One, the Chosen One, the Upright One. Dear God! Bless and support the Messenger, father of Qasim. Dear God! Bless and support the Owner of Signs. Dear God! Bless and support the Owner of warnings and indicators. Dear God! Bless and support the Owner of miracles and marks. Dear God! Bless and support the Owner of evidence and marvels. Dear God! Bless and support the Owner of extraordinary events. Dear God! Bless and support the One who was greeted by rocks. Dear God! Bless and support the One before whom trees prostrated. Dear God! Bless and support the One from whose light blossoms unfolded. Dear God! Bless and support the One from whose blessings fruit ripened. Dear God! Bless and support the One from whose leftover ablution water trees became green. Dear God! Bless and support the One whose light engulfs all other lights. Dear God! Bless and support the One, the request for blessings upon whom lightens our every load. Dear God! Bless and support the one by whose prayer burdens are shed. Dear God! Bless and support the one by whose prayer degrees of the righteous are obtained.

اللهمَّ صلِّ على مَنْ بالصلاةِ عليهِ يُرْحَمُ الكِبَارُ والصِّغَارُ، اللهمَّ صلِّ على مَنْ بالصلاةِ عليهِ نَتَنَعَّمُ في هذهِ الدارِ وفي تلكَ الدارِ، اللهمَّ صلِّ على مَنْ بالصلاةِ عليهِ تُنالُ رحمةُ العَزيزِ الغَفَّارِ، اللهمَّ صلِّ على المنصورِ المُؤَيَّدِ، اللهمَّ صلِّ على المختارِ المُمَجَّدِ، اللهمَّ صلِّ على سيدنا ومولانا محمدٍ، اللهمَّ صلِّ على مَنْ كان إذا مشى في البَرِّ الأقْفَرِ تَعَلَّقَتِ الوُحوشُ بأذيالِهِ، اللهمَّ صلِّ عليهِ وعلى آلِهِ وصَحْبِهِ وسَلِّمْ تسليماً والحمدُ للهِ رَبِّ العالمينَ.

Allahumma salli āla mam bissalati 'alaihi yurhamul-kibaru wasighar Allahumma salli āla mam bissalati 'alaihi natana' 'amu fi hazihid-dari wa fi tilkad-dar Allahumma salli āla mam bissalati 'alaihi tunalu rahmatul-aziizil-ghaffar

Allahummasalli'alal-mansuril-mu'aiyad Allahummasalli'alal-mukhtaril-mumajjad Allahumma salli āla sayyidina wa maulana Muhammad Allahummasalli.'ala man kana 'idha mashaa fil barril-aqfari ta-'allaqatil-uhushu bi-azyalih Allahummasalli'alaihi wa āla ālihii wa sahbihi wa sallim taslii-maw-walhamdu l'illahi rabil-'alamiin

Dear God! Bless and support the one, the request for blessings upon whom grants mercy to young and old. Dear God! Bless and support the one, the request for blessings upon whom brings favour to this house and that house. Dear God! Bless and support the one, the request for blessings upon whom brings Mercy from the Glorious, the Ever-Forgiving. Dear God! Bless and support the victorious One, the confirmer. Dear God! Bless and support the chosen one, the extolled. Dear God! Bless and support the one who, when he walked in the desert, wild creatures would cling to the hem of his robe. Dear God! Bless, support, and grant abundant peace to him and his family and Companions, and the totality of Grace belongs to God, the Lord of all the worlds.

<h1 style="text-align:center">ابتداء الربع الثاني</h1>

الحمدُ للهِ على حِلمِهِ بَعْدَ عِلْمِهِ، وعلى عَفوِهِ بَعْدَ قُدْرَتِهِ، اللهمَّ إنِّي أعوذُ بِكَ مِنَ الفقرِ إلا إليكَ، ومِنَ الذُّلِّ إلا لَكَ، ومِنَ الخوفِ إلا مِنْكَ، وأعوذُ بِكَ أن أقولَ زُوراً، أو أغشى فُجوراً، أو أكونَ بِكَ مغروراً، وأعوذُ بِكَ مِنْ شماتةِ الأعداءِ، وعُضَالِ الدَّاءِ وخيبةِ الرَّجاءِ، وزوالِ النِّعْمَةِ، وفُجاءةِ النِّقْمَةِ، اللهمَّ صلِّ على سيدنا محمدٍ وسَلِّمْ عليه واجزِهِ عنا ما هو أهلُهُ حَبيبكَ (ثلاثاً) اللهمَّ صلِّ على سيدنا إبراهيمَ وسَلِّمْ عليه واجزِهِ عنا ما هو أهلُهُ خَليلُكَ (ثلاثاً)، اللهمَّ صلِّ على سيدنا محمدٍ وعلى آلِ سيدنا محمدٍ كما صَلَّيْتَ ورَحِمْتَ وباركتَ على سيدنا إبراهيمَ في العالمينَ إنَّكَ حميدٌ مجيدٌ، عددَ خلقِكَ ورضاءَ نفسِكَ وزِنةَ عَرْشِكَ ومِدادَ كلماتِكَ، اللهمَّ صلِّ على سيدنا محمدٍ عددَ مَنْ صلى عليه، اللهمَّ صلِّ على سيدنا محمدٍ عددَ مَنْ لم يصلِّ عليه، اللهمَّ صلِّ على سيدنا محمدٍ عددَ ما صُلِّيَ عليه، اللهمَّ صلِّ على سيدنا محمدٍ أضعافَ ما صُلِّيَ عليه، اللهمَّ صلِّ على سيدنا محمدٍ كما هو أهلُهُ، اللهمَّ صلِّ على سيدنا محمدٍ كما تُحِبُّ وترضى لهُ.

Alhamdu l'illahi āla hilmihi ba'da 'ilmihi wa āla 'afwihi ba'da qudratihi Allahumma 'inni 'auzu bika minal-faqri 'illa ''illaik Wamina-zzulli 'illa laka wa minal-kaufi 'illa minka Wa 'auzu-bika 'an aqula zura 'au 'aghsha fujura Au Akuna bika maghrura Wa 'auzu bika min shamatatil-'adaa'i Wa-'u-dalid-daa'i wa khaibatir-raja'i wa zawalin-ni'mati wafaja'atil-niqmati Allahumma salli āla sayyidina Muhammad-in-wa sallim 'alaihi wajzihi 'anna ma huwa āhluhu habiibuka (thalaatha) Allahumma salli āla sayyidina Ibraahima wa sallim 'alaihi wajzihi anna ma huwa āhluhu khaliluka (thalaatha) Allahumma salli āla sayyidina Muhammad-in-wa āla Āli sayyidina Muhammad-in kama sallaita wa rahmita wa barakta āla sayyidina Ibrahiima fil-'alamina innaka hamidum-majid 'Adada khalqika wa rida nafsika wazinata 'arshika wa midada kalimatika Allahumma salli āla sayyidina Muhammad-in 'adada mann salla 'alaih Allahumma salli āla sayyidina Muhammad-in 'adada man-lam yusalli 'alaih Allahumma salli āla sayyidina Muhammad-in 'adada ma sulliya 'alaih Allahumma salli āla sayyidina Muhammad-in adh-'aafa ma sulliya 'alaihi Allahumma salli āla sayyidina Muhammad-in kama huwa ahluh Allahumma salli āla sayyidina Muhammad-in kama tuhibbu watarda lahu

Beginning of the Second Quarter

All praise is due to God for His Forbearance despite His Complete Knowledge, Clemency and Absolute Power. Dear God! I seek refuge with You from all thoughts not directed to You, from all humility not for You, and from all fear not of You. And I seek refuge in You from perjuring myself, being dishonest, immoral or proud. And I seek refuge in You from rejoicing over the affliction of my enemies, any disease or sickness that becomes incurable, disappointment, the waning of Your Favour, and Your Grace being suddenly taken away from me. Dear God! Bless and support our noble master Muhammad, grant him peace, and reward him as much as he deserves, for he is Your Beloved. (three times) Dear God! Bless and support our noble master Abraham, grant him peace, and reward him as much as he deserves, for he is Your Friend. (three times)

Dear God! Bless and support our noble master Muhammad and his family, just as You blessed and were merciful to our noble master Abraham in all the worlds. You are the Praiseworthy, the Glorious. Dear God! Bless and support our noble master Muhammad and his family, as much as all of Your creation, to the extent of Your Contentment and the weight of Your throne. Dear God! Bless and support our noble master Muhammad as much as You have designated and as much as the ink for Your words is. Dear God! Bless and support our noble master Muhammad as often as those who have asked for blessings upon him. Dear God! Bless and support our noble master Muhammad as often as those who have not asked for blessings upon him. Dear God! Bless and support our noble master Muhammad as often as he has been blessed. Dear God! Bless and support our noble master Muhammad twice as many times as he has already been blessed. Dear God! Bless and support our noble master Muhammad just as he deserves. Dear God! Bless and support our noble master Muhammad as much as You love him and are contented with him.

<h1 align="center">الحزبُ الثالثُ وردِ يومِ الأربعاءِ</h1>

بسمِ اللهِ الرحمنِ الرحيمِ

اللهمَّ صلِّ على روحِ سيدنا محمدٍ في الأرواحِ، وعلى جسدِهِ في الأجسادِ، وعلى قبرِهِ في القبورِ، وعلى آلِهِ وصحبِهِ وسَلِّمْ، اللهمَّ صلِّ على سيدنا محمدٍ كلما ذكرَهُ الذاكرونَ، اللهمَّ صلِّ على سيدنا محمدٍ كلما غَفَلَ عَنْ ذكرِهِ الغَافلونَ، اللهمَّ صلِّ وسَلِّمْ وبارك على سيدنا محمدٍ النبيِّ الأميِّ وأزواجِهِ أمهاتِ المؤمنينَ، وذُرِّيَّتِهِ وأهلِ بيتِهِ صلاةً وسلاماً لا يُحصى عَدَدُهُما، ولا ينقطعُ مَدَدُهُما، اللهمَّ صلِّ على سيدنا محمدٍ عددَ ما أحاطَ بِهِ علمُكَ، وأحصاهُ كتابُكَ، صلاةً تكونُ لَكَ رضاءً، ولِحقِّهِ أداءً وأعطِهِ الوسيلَةَ والفضيلَةَ والدرجَةَ الرفيعَةَ، وابعثهُ اللهمَّ المقامَ المحمودَ الذي وعدتَهُ، واجزِهِ عنا ما هو أهلُهُ، وعلى جميعِ إخوانِهِ مِنَ النبيينَ والصِّدِّقينَ والشُّهداءِ والصَّالحينَ،

Allahumma salli āla ruhi sayyidina Muhammad-in fil-arwahi wa āla jasadihi fil-ajsadi wa āla qabrihi fil quburi wa'ala 'ālihi wasahbihi wa-sallim Allahumma salli āla sayyidina Muhammad-in kullama zakara-huz-zaakirun Allahumma salli āla sayyidina Muhammad-in kullama ghafala 'ann zikri-hil-ghaafilun Allahumma salli wa sallim wabarik āla sayyidina Muhammadi-nin- nabiyyil-ummiyyi wa-azwajihi ummaahatil-Mu'minina wazurriiyatihi wa-ahli baitihii salatan-wa-salamal-la Yuhsa 'adadu humaa walaa yuqta'u mada-duhuma

Allahumma salli āla sayyidina Muhammad-in 'adada ma 'ahata bihi 'ilmuka wa-'ahsau kitabuka salatan takunu laka ridan-wali-haqqihi ada'an- wa'atihil wasilata walfadilata wad-darajatal rafi'ata wab'ath-huallahummal maqama-lmahmudal-lazi wa'adtahu wajzihi 'anna ma huwa āhluhu wa āla jamii-'i- ikhwanihi minan-nabiyiina was-siddiqiina wash-shuhadaaa-'i was-sālihin

The Third Part on Wednesday

BISMILLA HIRRAHMAAN NIRRAHIM

Dear God! Bless the body and soul of our noble master Muhammad, and his grave. Bless him and grant abundant peace to him, his family and his Companions. Dear God! Bless and support our noble master Muhammad whenever those who remember him do so, and whenever those who are heedless do not remember him.

Dear God! Bless, support, sanctify and grant peace to our noble master Muhammad, the prophet sent to all nations, and his wives - the Mothers of the Believers, his descendants and the People of his House. Make such blessings and peace measureless and never-ending.

Dear God! Bless and support our noble master Muhammad in everything encompassed by Your Omniscience, and in everything Your Book has enumerated. Bless him with blessings that are a contentment for You and which he deserves. And grant him the Closest Access, Pre-eminence and Lofty Rank.

Dear God! Grant him the Most Praised Station You have promised him, and reward him on our behalf as he deserves. And, likewise, reward his Brother Prophets, the Truthful, the Martyrs and the Righteous Ones.

اللهمَّ صلِّ على سيدنا محمدٍ وأنزلهُ المُنْزَلَ المُقَرَّبَ يومَ القيامَةِ، اللهمَّ صلِّ على سيدنا محمدٍ، اللهمَّ تَوِّجْهُ بتاجِ العزِّ والرضا

والكرامَةِ، اللهمَّ أعطِ لسيدنا محمدٍ أفضلَ ما سَأَلَكَ لنفسِهِ، وأعطِ لسيدنا محمدٍ أفضلَ ما سَأَلَكَ لَهُ أحدٌ مِنْ خلقِكَ، وأعطِ

لسيدنا محمدٍ أفضلَ ما أنتَ مسؤولٌ لَهُ إلى يوم القيامَةِ، اللهمَّ صلِّ على سيدنا محمدٍ وسيدنا آدمَ وسيدنا نوحٍ، وسيدنا إبراهيمَ

وسيدنا موسى وسيدنا عيسى، وما بينهم مِنَ النبيينَ والمُرْسَلينَ، صلواتُ اللهِ وسلامُهُ عليهمْ أجمعينَ (ثلاثاً)، اللهمَّ صلِّ على

أبينا سيدنا آدمَ وأمنا سيدتنا حواءَ، صلاةَ مَلائِكَتِكَ، وأعطِهِما مِنَ الرِّضْوانِ حتى تُرْضِيَهُما، واجزِهِما اللهمَّ أفضلَ ما جزيتَ بِهِ

أباً وأماً عَنْ ولديهِما (ثلاثاً)، اللهمَّ صلِّ على سيدنا جبريلَ وسيدنا ميكائيلَ، وسيدنا إسرافيلَ وسيدنا عزرائيلَ، وحملةِ العرشِ،

وعلى المَلائِكَةِ والمُقَرَّبينَ، وعلى جميعِ الأنبياءِ والمرسلينَ، صلواتُ اللهِ وسلامُهُ عليهم أجمعينَ (ثلاثاً)،

Allahumma salli āla sayyidina Muhammad-in wa-anzilhul-manzilal mukarraba yaumal-qiyaamah Allahumma salli āla sayyidina Muhammad-in Allahumma tawwijhu bitajil-'izzi warrida walkaramah

Allahumma 'ati le-sayyidina Muhammad-in afdala masa-alaka le-nafsihi wa-'ati le-sayyidina Muhammad-in afdala masa-laka lahuuu ahadum-min-khalqika wa'ati li-sayyidina afdala maa anta mas'u-lun-lahuu ila yaumal-qiyaamah

Allahumma salli āla sayyidina Muhammad-in-wa sayyidina adaama wa sayyidina nuhinw-wasayyidina Ibrahiimaa wa sayyidina musaa wa sayyidina 'eisaa wama bainahum minan-nabiyina wal-mursalina salawatullahi wasalamuhu 'alaihim 'ajma'ina (thalatha)

Allahumma salli āla abiina sayyidina adama wa-umminaa sayyidatinaa hawwaaa-'a salata malaaa'ikatika wa'-'atihimaa minar-ridhwaani hattaa turdhiyahuma wajzihimalla-humma afdala ma jazaita bihi abanw-wa-umman 'an-waladai-hima (thalatha)

Allahuma salli āla sayyidina jibrila wasayyidina mikaa 'ilaaa wasayyidina israqiila wasayyidina 'izraa-'iilaaa wahamalatil-arshi wa'alal- malaaa'ikatil-muqarrabinaa wa'ala jamii-'il-ambiyaaa'i walmursalina salawatullahi wasalamuhu alaihim ajma'in (thalatha)

Dear God! Bless and support our noble master Muhammad and bestow upon him the nearest position to You on the Day of the Rising-Up. Dear God! Bless and support our noble master Muhammad. Dear God! Crown him with the crown of might, contentment and honour. Dear God! Grant our noble master Muhammad more than he has ever asked for himself. Grant our noble master Muhammad better than any of Your Creation has ever asked for him, and grant our noble master Muhammad more than You can be asked to give him until the Day of the Rising-Up.

Dear God! Bless and support our noble masters Muhammad, Adam, Abraham, Moses, Jesus, and all the Prophets and Messengers between them, and God's blessings and abundant peace be upon all of them. (three times).

Dear God! Bless our parents, father Adam and Mother Eve, with the blessings of Your angels, and grant them Your Contentment. And reward them, dear God, better than You have awarded any father and mother on behalf of their children. (three times).

Dear God! Bless and support our noble masters Gabriel, Michael, Israfeel and Azrael, the Bearers of the Throne, the Angels of Closeness and all the Prophets and Messengers, and the blessings and peace of God be upon all of them. (three times)

اللهمَّ صلِّ على سيدنا محمدٍ عددَ ما علمتَ ومِلْءَ ما علمتَ، وزِنَةَ ما علمتَ، ومِدادَ كلماتِكَ، اللهمَّ صلِّ على سيدنا محمدٍ صلاةً موصولةً بالمزيدِ، اللهمَّ صلِّ على سيدنا محمدٍ صلاةً لا تنقطعُ أبدَ الآبادِ ولا تبيدُ، اللهمَّ صلِّ على سيدنا محمدٍ صلاتَكَ التي صليتَ عليهِ، وسَلِّمْ على سيدنا محمدٍ سلامَكَ الذي سلمتَ عليهِ، واجزِهِ عنا ما هو أَهْلُهُ، اللهمَّ صلِّ على سيدنا محمدٍ صلاةً تُرْضِيكَ وتُرْضِيهِ وتَرْضى بها عنا، واجزِهِ عنا ما هو أَهْلُهُ، اللهمَّ صلِّ على سيدنا محمدٍ بحر أنوارِكَ، ومَعْدِنِ أَسرارِكَ، ولِسانِ حُجَّتِكَ، وعروسِ مملكتِكَ، وإمامِ حَضرتِكَ، وطِرازِ مُلْكِكَ، وخزائنِ رحمتِكَ وطريقِ شريعتِكَ، المُتَلَذِّذِ بتوحيدِكَ، إنسانِ عينِ الوجودِ، والسببِ في كل موجودٍ، عينِ أعيانِ خلقِكَ، المُتَقَدِّم مِنْ نُورِ ضِيائِكَ، صلاةً تدومُ بدوامِكَ، وتبقى ببقائِكَ، لا مُنتهى لها دونَ عِلْمِكَ، صلاةً تُرْضيكَ وتُرْضيهِ، وتَرْضى بها عنا يا رَبَّ العالمينَ، اللهمَّ صلِّ على سيدنا محمدٍ عددَ ما في عِلْمِ اللهِ، صلاةً دائِمَةً بدوامِ ملكِ اللهِ،

Allahumma salli āla sayyidina Muhammad-in. 'Adada ma 'alimta wamil'a ma 'alimta wazinata ma 'alimta wamidada kalimatik Allahumma salli āla sayyidina Muhammad-in salatan- mausulatan bilmazid Allahumma salli āla sayyidina Muhammad-in salaatalla tanqati 'u abadala-abaadi walaa tabiid

Allahumma salli āla sayyidina Muhammad-in salata-kallati sallaita 'alaiihi wa sallim āla sayyidina Muhammad-in salama-kalladhi sallamta 'alaihi wajzihii 'annaa maa huwa ahluh Allahumma salli āla sayyidina Muhammad-in salaatan turdika waturdihi watardho bihaq 'annaa Wajzihii anna maa huwa ahluh

Allahumma salli āla sayyidina Muhammadi-m bahri anwarika wa-ma'dini asrarika wa lisanika hujjatika wa 'urusi mamlakatika wa 'imami hadratika wa-tirazi mulkika wa-khazza'ini rahmatika wa-tariqi shari'atika-lmutalazizi bitauhidika insani 'ainil-wujudi w-assababi fi kulli maujudin 'aini 'ayani khalqika almutaqadimi min-nuri diyaa'ika salatan tadumu-bidawamika wa tabqa bibaqa'ika la mu'taha laha duna 'ilmika salatan turdika waturdihi watarda biha 'anna ya rabba -Al 'alamin Allahumma salli āla sayyidina Muhammad-in 'adada maa fi ilm'illahi salaatan daaa'imatan bidawami mulk'illah

Dear God! Bless and support our noble master Muhammad as much as Your Omniscience, the depths of Your Omniscience, the weight of Your Omniscience, and as much as Your Will has designated, and as much as the ink for Your words is. Dear God! Bless and support our noble master Muhammad with continuously abundant blessings.

Dear God! Bless and support our noble master Muhammad with blessings that are never-ending and unceasing. Dear God! Bless and support our noble master Muhammad with as many blessings as You have so far bestowed upon him. And grant as much peace to our noble master Muhammad with as much peace as You have so far given him and reward him on our behalf as he deserves. Dear God! Bless and support our noble master Muhammad with blessings that cause You to be contented, that make him content, and by which You are contented with us. And reward him as he deserves.

Dear God! Bless and support our noble master Muhammad, the Ocean of Your Lights, the Mine of Your Secrets, and the Tongue of Your Proof. He is the Bridegroom of Your Kingdom, the Head of Your Attendance, and the Weight of Your Sovereignty. The Safe of Your Mercy, the Way of Your Rules, the Contentment of Your Unity, and the Pupil of the Eye of Existence. He is the Cause of all Existence, the Most Eminent of Your Creation, and the Representative of the Light of Your Resplendence, with blessings that last forever. And blessings that are limitless apart from Your Omniscience, blessings which cause You to be contented, which make him contented and by which You are contented with us, O Lord of all the worlds. Dear God! Bless and support our noble master Muhammad as much as all that is within Your Omniscience, blessings that are eternal.

اللهمَّ صلِّ على سيدنا محمدٍ كما صليتَ على سيدنا إبراهيمَ، وبارِكْ على سيدنا محمدٍ وعلى آلِ سيدنا محمدٍ كما باركتَ على آلِ

سيدنا إبراهيمَ في العالمينَ إنَّكَ حميدٌ مجيدٌ، عددَ خلقِكَ ورِضا نفسِكَ وزِنَةَ عرشِكَ ومِدادَ كلماتِكَ، وعددَ ما ذكرَكَ بِهِ خلقُكَ فيما

مضى، وعددَ ما هم ذاكرونَكَ بِهِ فيما بقيَ في كل سنةٍ وشهرٍ وجمعةٍ ويومٍ وليلةٍ وساعةٍ مِنَ الساعاتِ، وشَمٍّ ونفسٍ وطرفةٍ ولَحْظةٍ،

مِنَ الأبدِ إلى الأبدِ، وآبادِ الدنيا وآبادِ الآخرةِ، وأكثرَ مِنْ ذلكَ، لا ينقطعُ أولُهُ، ولا ينفَدُ آخرُهُ، اللهمَّ صلِّ على سيدنا محمدٍ على

قدرِ حُبِّكَ فيهِ، اللهمَّ صلِّ على سيدنا محمدٍ على قدرِ عِنايَتِكَ بِهِ، اللهمَّ صلِّ على سيدنا محمدٍ حَقَّ قدرِهِ ومِقْدارِهِ، اللهمَّ صلِّ على

سيدنا محمدٍ صلاةً تُنَجِّينا بِها مِنْ جميعِ الأهوالِ والآفاتِ، وتقضي لنا بها جميعَ الحاجاتِ، وتُطَهِّرُنا بها مِنْ جميعِ السَّيِّئاتِ، وتَرْفَعُنا

بها أعلى الدرجاتِ، وتُبَلِّغُنا بها أقصى الغاياتِ مِنْ جميعِ الخيراتِ، في الحياةِ وبعدَ المماتِ،

Allahumma salli āla sayyidina Muhammad-in kama sallaita āla sayyidina Ibraahiimaa wabarik āla sayyidina Muhammad-in-wa āla Āli sayyidina Muhammad-in kama barakta āla aĀli sayyidina Ibraahima fil-'alamina innaka hamidum-majid

'Adada khalqika warida'a nafsika wazinata 'arshika wamidada kalimatika wa 'adada ma dhakaraka bihi khalquka fima mada wa 'adada ma hum dhakirunaka bihi fima baqiya fi kulli Sanatin-washarinw-wa jumu'atinw-wa yauminw-wa lailatinw-wa sa'atin-minassa'ati wa shammin wa nafsin wa tarfatin wa lamhatim-minal-abadi ila al-abadi wa abaadid-dunyaa wa abadil-aakhirati wa akthara min thalika la yanqati'u awwaluhu wala yanfadu aakhiruh

Allahumma salli āla sayyidina Muhammad-in āla qadri hubbika fiih Allahumma salli āla sayyidina Muhammad-in āla qadrii 'inayatika bih Allahumma salli āla sayyidina Muhammad-in haqqa qadrihii wamiqdarih Allahumma salli āla sayyidina Muhammad-in salaatan tunajjina biha minn jami'il ahwali Wal 'afati wataqdi lana biha jami'al-hajati watutahiruna biha minn jami'is-sayyi'aati watarfa'una biha 'aalal-darajati watuballighuna biha aqsal-ghayati min jami'il khairati fil- hayati wa ba'dal-mamat

Dear God! Bless and support our noble master Muhammad just as You blessed our noble master Abraham. And sanctify our noble master Muhammad and his family just as You sanctified the family of our noble master Abraham, in all the worlds, for You are the Praiseworthy, the Glorious.

Dear God! Bless and support him as much as all of Your creation, to the extent of Your Contentment, in the weight of Your Throne, and Your Will has designated. And as much as is the ink for Your Words, and as much as all of Creation has remembered You in the past, and as much as they will remember You throughout the rest of time. And bless him every year, every month, every week, every day, every night, and every hour. And in every sniff, breath, twinkling and glance, forever and ever, for the duration of this world, the duration of the Hereafter, and for all eternity.

Dear God! Bless and support our noble master Muhammad as much as Your love for him is, and as befits his legitimate rank.

Dear God! Bless and support our noble master Muhammad with blessings that serve as a sanctuary for us from all terror and oppression, that settle all our affairs, purify us from all sins, raise our ranks in Your Presence, and allow us to attain ultimate goodness in this life and the next.

اللهمَّ صلِّ على سيدنا محمدٍ صلاةَ الرِّضا، وارضَ عَنْ أصحابِهِ رِضاءَ الرِّضا، اللهمَّ صلِّ على سيدنا محمدٍ السابقِ للخلقِ نُورُهُ ورحمةٌ للعالمينَ ظُهُورُهُ، عددَ مَنْ مضى مِنْ خلقِكَ ومَنْ بقيَ، ومَنْ سَعِدَ منهم ومَنْ شقيَ، صلاةً تستغرقُ العَدَّ وتُحيطُ بالحَدِّ، صلاةً لا غايَةَ لها ولا مُنْتَهى ولا انقِضاءَ، صلاةً دائمةً بدوامِكَ، وعلى آلِهِ وصحبِهِ وسَلِّمْ تسليماً مثلَ ذلكَ، اللهمَّ صلِّ على سيدنا محمدٍ الذي مَلأَتَ قلبَهُ مِنْ جلالِكَ، وعينَهُ مِنْ جمالِكَ، فأصبَحَ فَرِحاً مُؤَيَّداً منصوراً، وعلى آلِهِ وصحبِهِ وسَلِّمْ تسليماً، والحمدُ لله على ذلكَ، اللهمَّ صلِّ على سيدنا ومولانا محمدٍ عددَ أوراقِ الزيتونِ وجميعِ الثِّمارِ، اللهمَّ صلِّ على سيدنا ومولانا محمدٍ عددَ ماَ كان وما يكونُ، وعددَ ما أظلمَ عليهِ الليلُ وأضاءَ عليهِ النهارُ اللهمَّ صلِّ على سيدنا ومولانا محمدٍ وعلى آلِهِ وأزواجِهِ وذُرِّيَّتِهِ، عددَ أنفاسِ أمتِهِ، اللهمَّ بِبركةِ الصلاةِ عليهِ، اجعلنا بالصلاةِ عليهِ مِنَ الفائزينَ، وعلى حوضِهِ مِنَ الوارِدِينَ الشَّارِبينَ، وبِسُنَّتِهِ وطاعتِهِ مِنَ العامِلينَ، ولا تَحُلْ بيننا وبينَهُ يومَ القيامةِ يا رَبَّ العالمينَ، واغفر لنا ولوالِدِينا ولِجميعِ المسلمينَ، الحمدُ لله رَبِّ العالمينَ.

Allahumma salli āla sayyidina Muhammad-in salaatar-ridaa war-dha 'anashabihi rida 'ar-ridaa Allahuma salli āla sayyidina Muhammadi-nis-saabiqi lil khalqi nuruhu warahmatun-lil-'alamiina zuhuruhu 'adada mam-mada min khalqika wa mam-baqiya wa man sa'ida minhum wa man shaqiya salatan tastaghriqu Al-adda watuhiitu bil-haddi salaatan la ghaayata laha wala muntahaa walan-qidhaaa 'a salaatan dhaaa 'imatam bidawamika wa āla āalihi wa sahbihi wasallim tasliiman-mithla zaalik

Allahumma salli āla sayyidina Muhammadi- Muhammadin-illadhi mala'ta qalbahu min jalalika wa 'ainahu min jamalika fa-'asbaha farihan-mu'ayyadam-mansura wa āla aalihi -wa sahbihi wasallim tasliman-walhamdu l'illahi āla zalik Allahumma salli āla sayyidina wa maulaana Muhammad-in 'adada auraaqiz-zaituuni wa jami'ith-thimaar Allahumma salli āla sayyidina wa maulaana Muhammad-in 'Adada ma kana wa ma yakunu wa 'adada ma adhlama 'alaihil-lailu wa adha 'a 'alaihin-nahar Allahumma salli āla sayyidina wa maulaana Muhammad-in wa āla āalihii wa azwaajihii wa zurriyatihi 'adada anfaasi ummati Allahumma bibarakatis-salaati 'alaihij-alna bissalaati 'alaihi minal-faaa'iziina wa āla haudihii minal-waaridii nash-shaaribiin Wabisunnatihii wata'atihii minal-'amiliin Wala tahul bainana wa bainahu yaumal-qiyamate ya rabbal-'alamiin Waghfirlana waliwaalidaina Wali jamii 'il-muslimina walhamdu l'illahi rabbil-'alamiin

Dear God! Bless and support our noble master Muhammad, a blessing of contentment, and be pleased with his Companions, a pleasure of contentment. Dear God! Bless and support our noble master Muhammad, whose light preceded all creation. And his appearance is a Mercy to all the worlds, as much as all Your Creation which has passed and as much as what is to come. And as much as Your Creation who are happy and those who shall be miserable. Blessings which exceed all enumeration and encompass all limits. Blessings with no utmost limit that are boundless, ceaseless and eternal. And likewise, bless his family and Companions, and grant him and them abundant peace in like measure.

Dear God! Bless and support our noble master Muhammad, whose heart is full of Your Glory, and whose eyes are full of Your Beauty that he came to be overjoyed, supported and victorious. And bless his family and Companions likewise, and grant him and them abundant peace. And the totality of Glory belongs to God for all of that. Dear God! Bless and support our noble master Muhammad as many times as there are leaves on the olive trees and all of their fruit. Dear God! Bless and support our noble master Muhammad as much as all that has been, and will be, and as much as all the night has shrouded in darkness, and the day has enlightened with its radiance.

Dear God! Bless and support our noble master Muhammad and his family, his wives and his descendants as many times as every breath of his nation. Dear God! Through the grace of asking for blessings upon him, make us among the victorious ones and the drinkers at his Pool. And make us observe his way and obey him. And keep us connected on the Day of the Rising-Up, O Lord of all the Worlds. And grant us forgiveness, and our parents and all those who have submitted themselves to You. All praise belongs to God, the Lord of all the Worlds.

ابتداء الثلث الثاني

اللهمَّ صلِّ وسَلِّمْ وبارِكْ على سيـدنا محمدٍ وعلى آلِ سيدنا محمدٍ أكرم خلقِكَ، وسِراج أفقِكَ، وأفضَل قائمٍ بحقِّكَ، المبعوثِ بتيسيرِكَ ورفقِكَ، صلاةً يتوالى تكرارُها، وتلوحُ على الأكوانِ أنوارُها، اللهمَّ صلِّ وسَلِّمْ وبارِكْ على سيدنا محمدٍ وعلى آلِ سيدنا محمدٍ أفضل ممدوح بقولِكَ وأشرفِ داعٍ للاعتصامِ بحبلِكَ، وخاتَمِ أنبيائِكَ ورُسُلِكَ، صلاةً تبلغنا بها في الدارين عميمَ فضـلِكَ، وكرامةَ رِضْـوانِكَ ووصلِكَ، اللهمَّ صلِّ وسَلِّمْ وبارِكْ على سيدنا محمدٍ وعلى آلِ سيدنا محمدٍ أكرم الكرماءِ مِنْ عبادِكَ، وأشرفِ المنادينَ لطرقِ رشادِكَ، وسِراج أقطارِكَ وبلادِكَ، صلاةً لا تفنى ولا تبيدُ، تبلغنا بها كرامةَ المـزيدِ، اللهمَّ صلِّ وسَلِّمْ وبارِكْ على سيـدنا محمدٍ وعلى آلِ سيدنا محمدٍ الرفيعِ مقامُهُ، الواجِبِ تعظيمُهُ واحترامُهُ، صلاةً لا تنقـطعُ أبداً ولا تفنى سرمداً، ولا تنحصرُ عدداً،

Allahumma salli wa sallim wa barik āla sayyidina Muhammad-in-wa āla Āli sayyidina Muhammad-in 'akrami khalqika wasiraji 'ufuqika wa 'afdali qa'imim bi haqqikal-mab'uuthi btaisirika warifqika salatan-yata wala tekraruha wataluhu alal-'akwaani anwaruha

Allahumma salli wasallim wabarik āla sayyidina Muhammad-in wa āla Āli sayyidina Muhammad-in afdala mamduuhim bi qaulika wa ashrafi da-'in-lil-'ihtisami bi hablika wa khatimi ambiya'ika wa rusulika salatan-tuballighuna fid-daraini 'amima fadlika wakaramata ridwanika wawaslika

Allahumma salli wa sallim wa barik āla sayyidina Muhammad-in-wa āla Āli sayyidina Muhammad-in 'akramil-kuramaa'i min 'ibadika wa 'ashrafil- munadina lituruqi rashadika wa siraji aqtarika wa biladika salatan la tafna wala tabidu tuballighuna biha karamatal-mazid

Allahummasalliwasallim Wa barik āla sayyidina Muhammad-in wa āla Āli sayyidina Muhammadi-nirrafii'i maqaamuhul-wajibi ta'ziimuhu wa-ihtiraamuhu salatan-la tanqati'u abadan-wala tafna sarmadan-wala tanhasiru 'adada

Beginning of the second Third

Dear God! Bless, support, sanctify and grant peace to our noble master Muhammad and his family, the Noblest of Your Creation, the Shining Lamp of the Horizons and best Upholder of Your Truth, the Envoy of Your Relief and Kindness. Bless him with blessings which continue, repeat, and permeate their light all over the universe.

Dear God! Bless, support, sanctify and grant peace to our noble master Muhammad and his family. And he is the one praised most by Your Words, the noble one calling for adherence to Your Bond, the Seal of Your prophets and messengers. Bless him with blessings that permit us to attain, both here and in the Hereafter, Your general Favour and the honour of Your Contentment and Union.

Dear God! Bless, support, sanctify and grant peace to our noble master Muhammad and his family. And he is the Noblest of Your Noble Servants, the Most Prominent of the Inviters to Your Guidance, and Shining Lamp of all regions and countries, with endless blessings which, through them, bring us great favours.

Dear God! Bless, support, sanctify and grant peace to our noble master Muhammad and the family of our noble master Muhammad, whose rank is high. It is our duty to exalt them and hold them in the highest esteem, with endless and immeasurable blessings that are never curtailed or finished.

اللهمَّ صلِّ على سيدنا محمدٍ وعلى آلِ سيدنا محمدٍ كما صليتَ على سيدنا إبراهيمَ وعلى آلِ سيدنا إبراهيمَ في العالمينَ إنَّكَ حميدٌ مجيدٌ، وصلِّ اللهمَّ على سيدنا محمدٍ وعلى آلِ سيدنا محمدٍ كلما ذكرَهُ الذاكرونَ، وغَفَلَ عَنْ ذكرِهِ الغافِلونَ، اللهمَّ صلِّ على سيدنا محمدٍ وعلى آلِ سيدنا محمدٍ، وارحمْ سيدَنا محمداً وآلِ سيدنا محمدٍ، وباركْ على سيدنا محمدٍ وآلِ سيدنا محمدٍ، كما صليتَ ورحمتَ وباركتَ على سيدنا إبراهيمَ وعلى آلِ سيدنا إبراهيمَ إنَّكَ حميدٌ مجيدٌ، اللهمَّ صلِّ على سيدنا محمدٍ النبيِّ الأميِّ الطَّاهِرِ المُطَهَّرِ، وعلى آلِهِ وسَلِّم، اللهمَّ صلِّ على من ختمتَ بِهِ الرسالةَ، وأيدتَّهُ بالنصرِ والكوثرِ والشفاعةِ، اللهمَّ صلِّ على سيدنا ومولانا محمدٍ نبيِّ الحُكْمِ والحِكْمَةِ، السراجِ الوهاجِ، المخصوصِ بالخلقِ العظيمِ، وخَتْمِ الرُّسُلِ ذي المعراجِ، وعلى آلِهِ وأصحابِهِ وأتباعِهِ السالِكينَ على منهجِهِ القويمِ،

Allahumma salli āla sayyidina Muhammad-in wa āla Āli sayyidina Muhammad-in kama sallaita āla sayyidina Ibraahima wa āla Āli sayyidina Ibraahima fil-'alamiina innaka hamiidun-majid

Wa salli āla sayidina Muhammad-in-wa āla Āli sayyidina Muhammad-in kullama zakarahuz-zaakiruuna wa ghafala 'an dhikrihil-ghafiluun

Allahumma salli āla sayyidina Muhammad-in wa āla Āli sayyidina Muhammad-in-warham sayyidina Muhammad-in wa-Āli sayyidina Muhammad-in-wa barik āla sayyidina Muhammadi-in wa āla Āli sayyidina Muhammad-in kama sallaita warahimta wabaarakta āla sayyidina Ibraahima wa āla Āli sayyidina Ibraahima innaka hamiidun-majid

Allahumma salli āla sayyidina Muhammadi-nin-nabiyyil-ummiyit-taahirih-mutahhir wa āla āalihi wasallim Allahumma salli āla mann khatamta bihir-risaalata wa-ayyadtahu binnasri wal-kauthari Wash-shafa'ah Allahumma salli āla sayyidina wa maulana Muhammad-in nabiyyil-hukmi wal-hikmatis-serajil-wahhajil-makhsusi bil khuluqil-'adhimi wa khatmu-rrusuli zil-mi'raji wa āla āalihi wa ashabihi wa-at ba'ihiis-hissalikina āla manhajihil-qawim

Dear God! Bless, support, sanctify and grant peace to our noble master Muhammad and his family, just as You blessed Abraham and his family in all the worlds, for You are the Praiseworthy, the Glorious.

Dear God! Bless and support our noble master Muhammad and his family whenever those who remember him do so and those who are heedless do not remember him.

Dear God! Bless and support our noble master Muhammad and his family. And have mercy upon our noble master Muhammad and his family. And sanctify our noble master Muhammad and his family, just as You blessed, sanctified, and had mercy upon our noble master Abraham and his family, for You are the Praiseworthy, the Glorious. Dear God! Bless, support and grant peace to our noble master Muhammad and his family. And he is the Prophet sent to all nations, the Pure One, the Immaculate.

Dear God! Bless and support the one with whom You stamped the Message, the one to whom You granted victory, the Pool known as Kawthar, and the Intercession. Dear God! Bless and support our noble master Muhammad, the Prophet of Judiciousness and Wisdom. And he is the Brilliant Lamp, the one with the Greatest Character, the Seal of the Messengers, the noble master of the Night Journey. And, likewise, bless his family, Companions, followers, and sincere travellers on the True Path.

فأعظِم اللهمَّ بِهِ مِنْهَاجَ نُجُومِ الإسلامِ، ومصابيحِ الظلام، المهتدى بِهِم في ظلمةِ ليلِ الشكِّ الداج، صلاةً دائمة مستمرةً ما تلاطمتْ في الأبحُرِ الأمواجُ، وطافَ بالبيتِ العتيقِ مِنْ كل فجٍ عميقٍ الحجاجُ، وأفضلُ الصلاةِ والتسليمِ، على سيدنا محمدٍ رسولِهِ الكريمِ، وصفوتِهِ مِنَ العبادِ، وشفيعِ الخلائِقِ في الميعادِ، صاحِبِ المقام المحمودِ، والحوضِ المورودِ، الناهِضِ بأعباءِ الرسالةِ والتبليغِ الأعمِّ، والمخصوصِ بشرفِ السعايةِ في الصلاح الأعظم، صلى اللهُ عليهِ وعلى آلهِ، صلاةً دائمة مستمرةَ الدوامِ، على مَرِّ الليالي والأيام، فهو سيدُ الأولينَ والآخرينَ، وأفضلُ الأولينَ والآخرينَ، عليهِ أفضلُ صلاةِ المصلينَ، وأزكى سلام المسلمينَ، وأطيبُ ذكرِ الذاكرينَ، وأفضلُ صلواتِ اللهِ، وأحسنُ صلواتِ اللهِ، وأجلُّ صلواتِ اللهِ، وأجملُ صلواتِ اللهِ، وأكملُ صلواتِ اللهِ، وأسبغُ صلواتِ اللهِ، وأتمُّ صلواتِ اللهِ، وأظهرُ صلواتِ اللهِ، وأعظمُ صلواتِ اللهِ، وأذكى صلواتِ اللهِ، وأطيبُ صلواتِ اللهِ، وأبركُ صلواتِ اللهِ،

Fa'azim'illahumma bihi minhaja nujumil-islami wa masabihiz-zalamil-muhtada bihim fi zulmatish-shakkid-daaajji salaatan daaa'imatam-mustamirratam-ma talatamat fil-abhuril-amwaaju wa tafa bil-baiti al-'attiiqi minn kulli fajjin 'amiqil-nilhujjaju

wa afdalus-salati wattasliimi āla sayyidina Muhammadir-rasulihil-karimi wasafwatihi minal-ibadi wa shafii 'il-khalaaa 'iqi fil mi'adi sahibil-maqamil-mahmudi wal haudil-maurudin-nahidhi bi 'aaba'irrisalati wattablighil-'ammi wal-makhsosi bi-sharafis-si'ayati fissalahil-'azam

salla allh alyh waealaa alhi, salatan daa'imatan mustamirrata aldwami, ealaa marr allayali walayami, Fahuwa sayidul-auwalina walakhiryna, wa Afdl alawlyn walakhiryna, Alyh afdl salat almuslyna, wa'azka salam almuslmyna, watyab zekr alzakiryna, wafdl salawat allhi, wahsan slwat allhi, waajll salawat allhi, waajml salawat allhi, waakml salawat allhi, waasbgh salawat allhi, waatmm salawat allhi, waazhr salawat allhi, waaezm salawat allhi, wa'adhkaa salawat allhi, waatyab salawat allhi, waabrk slwat allhi,

Dear God! Magnify, through him, the path of the Stars of Islam and the Lamps, the path signposted by them that dispels the darkness in the murky gloom of the night of doubt. And send eternal and continuous blessings, lasting for as long as the waves crash in the oceans and for as long as the Ancient House (the Holy Kaaba) is encircled by pilgrims who have come from a long distance. Your peace and the best of all blessings be upon our noble master Muhammad, the Munificent Messenger, Your Selected One among all Your servants, the one who will intercede for all Your creatures on the Day of the Rising-Up. Owner of the Most Praiseworthy Station and the Oft-Visited Pool, the one who took on the mission of Your Message and the responsibility of spreading it far and wide, the one destined for honour and the one who strove for the greatest righteousness.

The blessings and support of God be upon him and his family, continuous and eternal blessings, lasting as long as the passing of all days and nights. And he is the noble master and the best of the First and the Last. Upon him are the best blessings of those who blessed him. They give peace to those who ask for peace upon him. And the best thoughts are of those who remember him.

And the finest blessings of God. And the choicest blessings of God. And the greatest blessings of God. And the fairest blessings of God. And the fullest blessings of God. And the most abundant blessings of God. And the utmost blessings of God. And the clearest blessings of God. And the mightiest blessings of God. And the sweetest blessings of God. And the freshest blessings of God. And the holiest blessings of God.

وأزكى صلواتِ اللهِ، وأنمى صلواتِ اللهِ، وأوفى صلواتِ اللهِ، وأسنى صلواتِ اللهِ، وأعلى صلواتِ اللهِ، وأكثرُ صلواتِ اللهِ، وأجمعُ صلواتِ اللهِ، وأعمُّ صلواتِ اللهِ، وأدومُ صلواتِ اللهِ، وأبقى صلواتِ اللهِ، وأعزُّ صلواتِ اللهِ، وأرفعُ صلواتِ اللهِ، وأعظمُ صلواتِ اللهِ على أفضلِ خلقِ اللهِ، وأحسنِ خلقِ اللهِ، وأجلِّ خلقِ اللهِ، وأكرمِ خلقِ اللهِ، وأجملِ خلقِ اللهِ، وأكملِ خلقِ اللهِ، وأتمِّ خلقِ اللهِ، وأعظم خلقِ اللهِ عندَ اللهِ، رسولِ اللهِ ونبيِّ اللهِ، وحبيبِ اللهِ وصفيِّ اللهِ ونجيِّ اللهِ، وخليلِ اللهِ وليِّ اللهِ وأمينِ اللهِ، وخيرةِ اللهِ مِنْ خلقِ اللهِ، ونُخْبَةِ اللهِ مِنْ بريةِ اللهِ، وصفوةِ اللهِ مِنْ أنبياءِ اللهِ، وعروةِ اللهِ، وعصمةِ اللهِ، ونعمةِ اللهِ، ومفتاحِ رحمةِ اللهِ، المختارِ مِنْ رسلِ اللهِ، المنتخبِ مِنْ خلقِ اللهِ، الفائزِ بالمطلبِ فِي المرهبِ والمرغبِ، المُخْلِصِ فيما وُهِبَ، أكْرَمِ مبعوثٍ، أَصْدَقِ قائلٍ، أَنْجَحِ شافعٍ، أفْضَلِ مُشَفَّعٍ، الأمينِ فيما استودِعَ الصادقِ فيما بَلَّغَ، الصادعِ بأمرِ ربهِ، المضطلعِ بما حُمِّلَ، أقْرَبِ رسلِ اللهِ إلى اللهِ وسيلةً، وأعْظَمِهِمْ غداً عندَ اللهِ منزلةً وفضيلةً، وأكْرَمِ أنبياءِ اللهِ الكرامِ الصفوةِ على اللهِ، وأحَبِّهِمْ إلى اللهِ، وأقْرَبِهِمْ زلفى لدى اللهِ، وأكْرَمِ الخلقِ على اللهِ، وأحْظَاهُمْ وأرْضَاهُمْ لدى اللهِ،

Wa azka salawaat'illah Wa anmaa salawaat'illah Wa aufa salawaat'illah Wa asnaa salawaat'illah Wa āla salawat'illah Wa-aktharu salawat'illah Wa-ajma 'u salawat'illah Wa-'ammu salawat'illah wa-adwamu salawat'illah Wa-abqa salawat'illah wa 'a azzu salawat'illah Wa arfa'u salawat'illah Wa 'aazamu salawat'illah āla 'afdali khalq'illah Wa-ahsani khalq'illah Wa-a-ajalli khalq'illah Wa-akrami khalq'illah Wa-ajmali khalq'illah Wa-akmali khalq'illah Wa-atammi khalq'illah Wa-'azomi khalq'illahi indallah rasul-'illah nabiyy-'illah Wa Habibi-llah Wa-safiy'illah Wa-najiy'illah Wa-khalil'illah Wa- waliy'illah Wa-'amin'illah Wa-khiyarat'illahi min khalq'illah Wa-nukhabat'illahi min bari 'at'illah Wa-safwat'illahi min ambiyaa ''illah Wa-'urwat'illah Wa-'ismat'illah Wa-ni'mat'illah Wa-miftahi rahmat'illah Al-mukhtari Min-rusul'illah Al-muntakhabi min khalk'illahil-faaa'izi bil matlabi fil marhabe wal marghabe Al-mukhlase fi ma wuhib Akrame mab'uth Assdaqe qaaa'il Anjahe shaaf'i Afdali mushaffa'i n al-amini fi mastudi 'as-sadiqi fi ma ballaghas-sadi 'i bi amri rabbihi al-mudtoli'i bima hummil Aqrabi rusul'illahi ila allahi wasilatan wa-'aazamihim ghadan 'inda-allahi manzilatan wafadilah Wa 'akrami ambiya'a 'illahil-kiramis-safwati 'ala-allah w'ahabbihim 'ila allhi, w'aqrabihim zulfaa ladaa allhi, w'akram alkhlq ealaa allhi, w'ahzahum w'ardahum ladaa allhi,

And the purest blessings of God. And the richest blessings of God. And the sincerest blessings of God. And the matchless blessings of God. And the highest blessings of God. And the most lavish blessings of God. And the myriad blessings of God. And the universal blessings of God. And the longest-lasting blessings of God. And the longest remaining blessings of God. And the strongest blessings of God. And the loftiest blessings of God. And the mightiest blessings of God upon the best of God's creation.

The finest of God's creation. The greatest of God's creation. The noblest of God's creation. The fairest of God's creation. The most perfect of God's creation. The most flawless of God's creation. The mightiest of God's creation in the sight of God. The Messenger of God. The Prophet of God. The Beloved of God. The Intimate of God. The Confidant of God.

The Friend of God. The Loved One of God. The Trustee of God. The Best of God from the creation of God. The Choice of God from the innocent of God. The Confidant of God from the Prophets of God. The Handhold of God. The Modesty of God. The Blessing of God. The Key to the Mercy of God. The Chosen One from the Messengers of God. The Elected One from the Creation of God and the one who succeeds with his requests at times of fear and apprehension. The Sincere One in what he is given. The Most Honoured Envoy. The Most True Speaker. The most successful Intercessor.

The Best Intercessor, the one honest to his pledge and true to his mission. The one who complied with the orders of his Lord and the one who bore his responsibilities. And he is the Messenger of God with the Closest Access to God. And he is the one whose position and pre-eminence in the sight of God is greater than all other Prophets and Messengers. He is the Most Honoured of God's honourable Prophets and the Loved one of God, more in love with God than them and closer to God than them. He is the noblest Creation in the sight of God, more fortunate and more satisfied than them in the Presence of God.

وَأَعْلَى الناسِ قَدْراً، وَأَعْظَمِهِمْ مَحَلاً، وَأَكْمَلِهِمْ مَحاسِناً وفَضْلاً، وَأَفْضَلِ الأنبياءِ دَرجةً، وَأَكْمَلِهِمْ شَريعةً، وَأَشْرَفِ الأنبياءِ

نِصاباً، وَأَبْيَنِهِمْ بَياناً وَخِطاباً، وَأَفْضَلِهِمْ مَولِداً وَمُهاجِراً وَعِتْرةً وَأَصحاباً، وَأَكْرَمِ الناسِ أُرُومَةً وَأَشْرَفِهِمْ جُرْثُومَةً، وَخَيْرِهِمْ نَفْساً،

وَأَطْهَرِهِمْ قَلْباً، وَأَصْدَقِهِمْ قَوْلاً، وَأَزْكاهُمْ فِعْلاً، وَأَثْبَتِهِمْ أَصْلاً، وَأَوْفاهُمْ عَهْداً، وَأَمْكَنِهِمْ مَجْداً، وَأَكْرَمِهِمْ طَبْعاً، وَأَحْسَنِهِمْ

صُنْعاً، وَأَطْيَبِهِمْ فَرْعاً، وَأَكْثَرِهِمْ طاعةً وَسَمْعاً، وَأَعْلاهُمْ مَقاماً، وَأَحْلاهُمْ كَلاماً، وَأَزْكاهُمْ سَلاماً، وَأَجَلِّهِمْ قَدْراً، وَأَعْظَمِهِمْ

فَخْراً، وَأَسْناهُمْ فَخْراً، وَأَرْفَعُهُمْ في المَلإِ الأَعْلى ذِكْراً، وَأَوْفاهُمْ عَهْداً، وَأَصْدَقِهِمْ وَعْداً، وَأَكْثَرِهِمْ شُكْراً، وَأَعْلاهُمْ أَمْراً،

وَأَجْمَلِهِمْ صَبْراً، وَأَحْسَنِهِمْ خَيْراً، وَأَقْرَبِهِمْ يُسْراً، وَأَبْعَدِهِمْ مَكاناً، وَأَعْظَمِهم شاناً، وَأَثْبَتِهِمْ بُرْهاناً، وَأَرْجَحِهِمْ مِيزاناً، وَأَوَّلِهِمْ

إيماناً، وَأَوْضَحِهِمْ بَياناً، وَأَفْصَحِهِمْ لِساناً، وَأَظْهَرِهِمْ سُلْطاناً.

Wa 'alannasi qadran Wa 'aazamihim- mahallanw-wa 'akmālihim-mahasinan wa fadlanw-wa 'afdalil-ambiya'i darajatan Wa 'akmālihim shari'atan waashrafil-ambiyaaa'i nisaaban wa abyanihim bayaanan-wa khitaaban-wa afdhālihim-maulidan-wa muhajaran-wa 'itratan-wa ashaban-wa akraminnasi arumatan-wa ashrafihim jurthumatan-wa khairihim nafsan-wa atharihim qalban-wa asdaqihim Qaulan-wa azkaahum fi'lanw-wa athbatihim aslan-wa awfaahum ahdan-wa amkanihim majdan-wa akramihim tab'anw-wa ahsanihim sun'anw wa atyabihim far'anw wa aktharihim to'atanw-wa sam'anw- w'aelahum mqamaan, w'ahlahum klamaan, w'azkahum slamaan, w'ajallihim qdraan, w'aezamihim fkhraan, w'asnahum fakhraan, w'arfaeuhum fi alml'i al'aelaa dhkraan, w'awfahum ehdaan, w'asdaqihim wedaan, w'aktharihim shukraan, w'aelahum amraan, w'ajmālihim sbraan, w'ahsanihim khyraan, w'aqrabihim yusraan, w'abeadihim makanaan, w'aezamhm shanaan, w'athbatihim burhanaan, w'arjahihim mizanaan, w'awwālihim 'iymanaan, w'awdahihim bayanaan, w'afsahihim lisanaan, w'azharihim sultanaan.

The Highest Human Being, with a position more excellent than theirs, and kindness and favour more perfect than theirs, and a rank better than all the other Prophets, with laws more complete than theirs and who has the noblest lineage. Whose Proofs and Preaching are more comprehensive than theirs and whose birth, migration, perfumed descendants and companions are the most gracious. He is the most tender human being.

And his origin is the noblest; his soul is the best; his heart is the purest, with the most faithful words. His actions are the most refined, and he has the most solid descent. He is the most devoted to his pledge, and his distinction is the weightiest. His disposition is the most honoured, and his design is the most beautiful. His family tree is the purest, and his obedience and dutifulness are the most outstanding.

And his station is the highest, his speech is the most beautiful, his peace is the purest, and his rank is the most splendid. His glory is the most significant and resplendent, his remembrance in the Highest Host is the loftiest, and his promise is the sincerest. His gratitude is the most profuse, his authority is the most elevated, his patience is the most beautiful, and his goodness is the finest. He has the greatest ability to create ease for his followers, his position is the loftiest, his value is the most excellent, and his argument is the soundest. His judgement is the most balanced, his faith is the most advanced, his evidence is the most apparent, his tongue is the most eloquent, and his authority is the most evident.

بسمِ اللهِ الرحمنِ الرحيمِ

اللهمَّ صلِّ على سيدِنا محمدٍ عبدِكَ ورسولِكَ النبيِّ الأميِّ وعلى آلِ سيدِنا محمدٍ، اللهمَّ صلِّ على سيدِنا محمدٍ وعلى آلِ سيدِنا محمدٍ صلاةً تكونُ لَكَ رضاءً، ولَهُ جزاءً ولِحَقِّهِ أداءً، وأعطِهِ الوسيلَةَ والفضيلَةَ والمقامَ المحمودَ الذي وعدتَّهُ، واجزِهِ عنا ما هو أهلُهُ واجزِهِ أفضلَ ما جازيتَ بِهِ نبياً عَنْ قومِهِ ورسولاً عَنْ أمتِهِ، وصلِّ على جميع إخوانِهِ مِنَ النَّبِيِّينَ والصالحينَ يا أرحمَ الراحِمِينَ، اللهمَّ اجعلْ فضائلَ صلواتِكَ، وشرائفَ زكواتِكَ ونوامِيَ بركاتِكَ، وعواطفَ رأفتِكَ ورحمتِكَ وتحيتِكَ وفضائلَ آلائكَ على سيدِنا محمدٍ سيدِ المُرْسَلِينَ ورسولِ رَبِّ العالمينَ، قائِدِ الخيرِ وفاتِحِ البِرِّ، ونبيِّ الرحمةِ وسيدِ الأمةِ، اللهمَّ ابعثهُ مقاماً محموداً تُزْلِفُ بِهِ قُرْبَهُ وتُقِرُّ بِهِ عَيْنَهُ، يغبطهُ بِهِ الأولونَ والآخِرونَ، اللهمَّ أعطِهِ الفضلَ والفضيلَةَ والشرفَ والوسيلَةَ، والدرجَةَ الرفيعَةَ والمنزلَةَ الشامِخَةَ،

Allahumma salli āla sayyidina Muhammad-in 'abdika wa rasuulika-nabiyyil-ummiyi wa āla Āli sayyidina Muhammad Allahumma salli āla sayyidina Muhammad-iuw-wa āla Āli sayyidina Muhammad-in salaatan takunu laka rida'an-walahu jaza'an-walihaqqihi adaa'n wa atihil-wasilata walfadilata wal maqamal-mahmuuda n'illadhi wa 'adtahu wajzihi 'anna aa huwa āhluhu wajzihi 'afdala ma jazaita nabiyyan 'an qaumihii Wa rasuulan 'ann ummatihii wa salli āla jamii 'I ikhwaanihii minan-nabiyyiina was-sālihiina yaa arhamar-raahimiin Allahummaj 'al fadaaa'ila salawatika wa shara'ifa zakawatika wa nawamiya barakatika wa 'awatifa r'afatika wa rahmatika wa tahiyatika wa fada'ila 'aalaa'ika āla sayyidina Muhammad-in sayyidil-mursalina wa rasuuli rabbil-'alamina qaa'idil-khairi wa faatihil-birri wa nabiyyir-rahmati wa sayyidil-ummah Allahummab-'ath-hu maqaamam- mahmuudan tuzlifu bihi qurbahu wa Tuqirru-bihi 'ainahu yaghbituhu bihil-auwaaluna wal-aakhiruun Allahumma 'aatihil-fadla wafadilata washarafa walwasilata waddarajatal-rafiiata walmunzilatash-shaamikhah

Thursday - The Fourth Part

BISMILLA HIRRAHMAAN NIRRAHIM

Dear God! Bless and support our noble master Muhammad, Your servant and Messenger, the Prophet sent to all nations, and his family. Dear God! Bless and support our noble master Muhammad and his family, blessings that are pleasing to You, a reward for him that is his right, and grant him the Nearest Access, the Pre-eminence and the Most Praised Station You have promised him. And reward him for what he deserves on our behalf, and reward him more than You have rewarded any other Messenger for his nation. And bless all his brother Prophets and Righteous Ones, O the Most Merciful.

Dear God! Bestow Your blessings and virtues, increase Your benedictions, and the benevolence of Your Compassion, Mercy, Salutations and Bounties upon our noble master Muhammad. He is the master of the Messengers, the Messenger of the Lord of all the Worlds, the Guide to Righteousness, the Starter of Piety, the Prophet of Mercy and the noble master of his nation.

Dear God! Grant him the Most Praised Station, thereby advancing his closeness, pleasing his eyes, and making him the admiration of those who came first and those who will come last. Dear God! Grant him Your Divine Favour, Grace, Honour, the Nearest Access, the Loftiest Rank, and the Highest Standing.

اللهمَّ أعطِ سيدَنا محمداً الوسيلةَ وبَلِّغْهُ مأمولَهُ، واجعلهُ أولَ شافعٍ وأولَ مشفعٍ، اللهمَّ عَظِّمْ برهانَهُ وثَقِّلْ ميزانَهُ وأَبْلِجْ حُجَّتَهُ، وارفعْ في أهلِ عِلِّيِّينَ درجتَهُ وفي أعلى المُقَرَّبينَ منزلتَهُ، اللهمَّ أحْيِنا على سُنَّتِهِ وتَوَفَّنا على مِلَّتِهِ، واجعلنا مِنْ أهلِ شفاعتِهِ واحْشُرْنا في زُمْرَتِهِ، وأوْرِدْنا حَوْضَهُ واسقِنا مِنْ كأسِهِ غيرَ خزايا ولا نادمِينَ ولا شاكِّينَ، ولا مُبَدِّلينَ، ولا مُغَيِّرِينَ، ولا فاتِنِينَ ولا مفتونِينَ آمِينَ، يا رَبَّ العالمِينَ، اللهمَّ صلِّ على سيدِنا محمدٍ وعلى آلِ سيدِنا محمدٍ، وأعطِهِ الوسيلةَ والفضيلةَ والدرجةَ الرفيعَةِ، وابعثهُ المقامَ المحمودَ الذي وَعَدْتَهُ مَعَ إخوانِهِ النَّبِيِّينَ صلى اللهُ على سيدِنا محمدٍ نبيِّ الرحمةِ وسيدِ الأمةِ، وعلى أبينا سيدِنا آدمَ وأمنا سيدتنا حواءَ، ومَنْ ولدا مِنَ النَّبِيِّينَ والصَّدِّيقينَ والشُّهداءِ والصالحِينَ، وصلِّ على مَلائِكَتِكَ أجمعِينَ، مِنْ أهلِ السَّماواتِ والأراضِينَ، وعلينا معهم يا أرحمَ الراحِمِينَ،

Allahumma āati saiyidina Muhammada-nelwasilata waballighu maāmulahu wajālhu auwala shaafi-'in-wa-auwala mushaffa' Allahumma 'azzim burhanahu wathaqqil mizanahu wa ablij hujjatuhu warfa' fi ahli 'illiyiina darajatah Wafii 'aalal-muqarrabina manzelatah

Allahumma ahyina āla sunnatihi Watawaffanaa āla m'illatihi Waj'alna min 'ahli shafa'atih wah-shurna fi zumratihi wa-auridna hudaho wasqina min kaa'sihi ghaira khazaya wala nadimina wala shaaqina wala mubaddilina wala mughaiyirina wala-fatinina wala maftunina amina ya-rabbal-'aalamin

Allahumma salli āla sayyidina Muhammad-in wa-'ala Āli sayyidina muhammaddin wa'atihil wasilata walfadilata waddarajatar-rafiiata wab-ath-hul-maqamal-mahmudalladhi wa ad tahu ma'a ikhwaanihi-nabiyyiin sallallahu āla Sayyidina Muhammad in-nabiyyil-rahmati wa-sayyidil-ummati wa'ala abinaa sayyidina adama wa-ummina sayyidatina hauwa'a waman-walada minan-nabiyyina wassiddiqina wash-shuhada'ie was-salihina wasalli āla malaaikat'ika ajma'iina min 'aalis-samawati wal-aradina wa'alainaa ma'ahum ya-arhamarrahimiin

Dear God! Grant our noble master Muhammad the Closest Approach. And grant him what he hopes for, and make him the first intercessor and the first whose intercession is accepted. Dear God! Support his proof, make his wisdom sound, his argument shine, and raise his station among the residents of the Highest Heaven. And grant him the highest standing among the Heights of those who are closest.

Dear God! Make us follow his way and die following his faith. And make us among those for whom he will intercede. And resurrect us in his company and cause us to drink from his Pool with grace, no regrets, doubts, or temptations, Ameen, O the Lord of all the Worlds.

Dear God! Bless and support our noble master Muhammad and his family, and grant him the Closest Access, the Pre-eminence and Loftiest Status. And send him to the Best Praised Station You promised him, with his brother Prophets.

The blessings of God be upon our noble master Muhammad, the Prophet of Mercy and master of his nation. And blessings be upon our noble parents, master Adam and his wife Eve, and upon all the descendants of the Prophets, the truthful ones, the martyrs and the righteous ones. And bless all Your angels among those inhabiting the Heavens and the Earth, and upon us, O the Most Merciful of the Merciful.

اللهمَّ اغفر لي ذنوبي ولوالِديَّ، وارحمها كما رَبَّيَاني صغيراً، ولِجميع المؤمنينَ والمؤمناتِ والمسلمينَ والمسلماتِ، الأحياء منهم والأمواتِ، وتابعْ بيننا وبينهم بالخيراتِ، رَبِّ اغفر وارحم وأنتَ خيرُ الراحِمينَ، ولا حولَ ولا قوةَ إلا باللهِ العليِّ العظيم، اللهمَّ صلِّ على سيدنا محمدٍ نُورِ الأنوارِ وسرِّ الأسرارِ، وسيدِ الأبرارِ، وزَينِ المُرْسَلينَ الأخيارِ، وأكرم مَنْ أظلمَ عليهِ الليلُ وأشرقَ عليهِ النهارُ، وعددَ ما نزلَ مِنْ أولِ الدنيا إلى آخرها مِنْ قطرِ الأمطارِ، وعددَ ما نبتَ مِنْ أولِ الدنيا إلى آخرها مِنَ النباتِ والأشجارِ، صلاةً دائمةً بدوام ملكِ اللهِ الواحدِ القهار، اللهمَّ صلِّ على سيدنا محمدٍ صلاةً تُكرِمُ بها مَثواهُ وتُشَرِّفُ بها عقباهُ وتبلغُ بها يومَ القيامةِ مُنَاهُ ورِضَاهُ، هذهِ الصلاةُ تعظيماً لحَقّكَ يا سَيِّدَنا محمداً، اللهمَّ صلِّ على سيدنا محمدٍ حاءِ الرحمةِ وميما الملكِ ودالِ الدوام، السيدِ الكاملِ الفاتحِ الخاتم، عددَ ما في علمِكَ كائنٌ أو قد كانَ، كلما ذكركَ وذكرهُ الذاكِرونَ، وكلما غَفَلَ عَنْ ذكرِكَ وذكرِه الغافِلونَ، صلاةً دَائِمَةً بدوامِكَ باقيةً ببقائِكَ، لا مُنْتَهَى لها دونَ عِلْمِكَ إنَّكَ على كل شيءٍ قديرٌ،

Allahummagh-firli zunuubi waliwalidayya war-hamhumaa kama rabba-yaani saghiiran-walijami-il-mu'miniina wal'muminaati walmuslimiina walmuslimaatil-ahyaa'i minhum wal-amwaati wataabi' bainanaa Wa bainahum bil khairati rabbighfir warham wa 'anta khairur-rahimin wala haula wala quwwata 'illa b'illahil-aliyyil-azim Allahumma salli āla sayyidina Muhammad-in nuuril-anwari wasirril-asrari wa sayyidil-abrari wa zainil-mursalinal-akhyari wa akrami man azlama 'alaihil-lailu wa ashraqa 'alaihin-naharu 'adada ma nazala min auwalid-dunya ila aakhirihaa minn qatril-amtari wa 'adada ma nabata min auwaled-dunya ila ākhiriha minan-nabati wal ashjari salatan daa'imatan bidawami mulki Allahiel-wahidiel-qahhar

Allahumma salli āla sayyidina Muhammad-in salaatan tukrimu biha mathwaahu watusharrifu biha uqbaahu watuballighu biha yaumal-qiyamate munaahu waridhah Haazihis-salaatu ta'ziiman-lihaqqika ya sayyidina Muhammad Allahumma salli āla sayyidina Muhammadin h'au 'irrahmati wa mima-al-mulki wa dalid-dawaamis-sayyidil-kamilil-fatihil-khatimi 'adada maa fi 'ilmika ka'inun auqad kana kullama dhakaraka wadhakarahuz-zakiruna wa kullama ghafala 'an dhikrika wa dhikrihil-ghafiluun Salatan daa'imatam bidawaamika baaqiyatann bibaqaa 'ika la muntahalahaa duuna 'ilmika innaka āla kulli shai'in qadir

Dear God! Grant me forgiveness and my parents, and bestow Your mercy on them as they cherished me in childhood, and all the Muslim men and women, all the believing men and women, the living and the dead, and may Your blessings ensue upon us. Dear God! Forgive us and bestow Your mercy, for You are the Most Merciful of the merciful. And no power is there, nor strength, save with God, the Most High, the Great. Dear God! Bless and support our noble master Muhammad, the Essence of Lights, the Utmost Secret of the Secrets, Leader of the Pious, Ornament of the Messengers. He is the Chosen One, the noblest one the night has ever covered, the day has ever bathed in light, and in every drop of rain which has ever fallen, from the beginning of this world until its end. And in every plant and tree that has grown, from the beginning of this world to its end, eternal blessings that last forever in the Dominion of God, the One, the Ever-Subduing. Dear God! Bless and support our noble master Muhammad, blessings that ennoble his Place of Rest, honour his final destination, and bring his heart's desires and contentment on the Day of the Rising-Up. These great blessings are the right of our noble master Muhammad.

Dear God! Bless and support our noble master Muhammad, the 'Ha' (middle letter of Rahmah) of Mercy, the 'Mim' (first letter of Mulk) of Supremacy, and the 'Dal' (first letter of Daw'im) of Eternity, the perfect noble master, the Opener, the Seal One, as much as Your Omniscience, now and before. And whenever You are remembered, he is remembered by those who remember. Dear God! Bless and support our noble master Muhammed with eternal blessings that have no end, just as Your Omniscience is infinite. You are the Most Powerful over all things.

اللهمَّ صلِّ على سيدنا محمدٍ النبيِّ الأميِّ وعلى آلِ سيدنا محمدٍ الذي هو أبهى شموسِ الهُدى نوراً وأبهرُها، وأسيَرُ الأنبياءِ فخراً وأشهرُها، ونُورُهُ أزهرُ أنوارِ الأنبياءِ وأشرفُها وأوضحُها، وأزكى الخليقةِ أخلاقاً وأطهَرُها، وأكرَمُها خُلُقاً وأعدَلُها، اللهمَّ صلِّ على سيدنا محمدٍ النبيِّ الأميِّ وعلى آلِ سيدنا محمدٍ الذي هو أبهى مِنَ القمرِ التَّامِّ، وأكرَمُ مِنَ السحابِ المُرْسَلةِ والبحرِ الخِطَمِّ، اللهمَّ صلِّ على سيدنا محمدٍ النبيِّ الأميِّ وعلى آلِ سيدنا محمدٍ الذي قُرِنَتِ البَرَكةُ بذاتِهِ ومُحَيَّاهُ، وتَعَطَّرَتِ العوالِمُ بطيبِ ذكرِهِ ورَيَّاهُ، اللهمَّ صلِّ على سيدنا محمدٍ وعلى آلِهِ وسَلِّم، اللهمَّ صلِّ على سيدنا محمدٍ وعلى آلِ سيدنا محمدٍ، وباركْ على سيدنا محمدٍ وعلى آلِ سيدنا محمدٍ، وارحمْ سيدَنا محمداً وآلَ سيدنا محمدٍ كما صليتَ وباركتَ وترحمتَ على سيدنا إبراهيمَ وعلى آلِ سيدنا إبراهيمَ إنَّكَ حميدٌ مجيدٌ،

Allahumma salli āla sayyidina Muhammadi-nin-nabiyyil-ummiyi wa āla Āli sayyidina Muhammadin-alladhi huwa abha shumusil-huda nuuran-wa abharuha Wa asyarul-ambiya'i fakhran-wa ashharuha Wa nuuruhu azharu anwaril-ambiya'i wa ashrafuha wa 'audhahuha wa azkal-khaliqati akhlaaqan-wa athharuha wa ākramuha khalqaw-wa 'aadaluha

Allahumma salli āla Sayyidina Muhammadi- n'illazi huwa abhaa minal-qamarit-taa-ammi wa akramu minas-sahhabil-mursalati wal bahril-khidham

Allahumma salli āla sayyidina Muhammadi-nin-nabiyyil-ummiyyi wa āla Āli sayyidina Muhammadi-n'illazi qurinatil-barakatu b'idhatihii wa muhayyaahu wata 'attaratil-awaalimu bitiibi zikrihii warayya Allahumma salli āla sayyidina Muhammad-iuw-wa āla āalihi wa sallim

Allahumma salli āla sayyidina Muhammad-in-wa āla Āli sayyidina Muhammad-iuw-wa barik āla sayyidina Muhammad-iuw-wa āla Āli sayyidina Muhamamd-iuw-warham sayyidina Muhammad-an Kama sallaita wa baarakta watarahhamta āla sayyidina Ibraahima wa āla Āli sayyidina Ibraahima innaka hamidun-majid

Dear God! Bless and support our noble master Muhammad, the Prophet sent to all nations, and the family of our noble master Muhammad, whose light is the most beautiful and overwhelming of all the suns of guidance. And whose behaviour and glory are the best and most renowned of all the Prophets. And whose light is the most radiant and brilliant of the lights of the Prophets, who has the purest and most immaculate conduct in creation, and who is the most just and generous of all Your creatures. Dear God! Bless and support our noble master Muhammad, the Prophet sent to all nations, and the family of our noble master Muhammad, who is more beautiful than the full moon, and more dignified than the flowing clouds and raging seas.

Dear God! Bless and support our noble master Muhammad, the Prophet sent to all nations, and the family of our noble master Muhammad, whose face and essence are diffused with the benediction and remembrance of whom perfumes and lightens all the worlds. Dear God! Bless, support, and grant peace to our noble master Muhammad and his family. Dear God! Bless and support our noble master Muhammad and his family, and bestow grace upon our noble master Muhammad and his family. And bestow mercy upon our noble master Muhammad and his family, just as You blessed and bestowed grace and mercy upon our noble master Abraham and his family, for You are the Praiseworthy, the Mighty.

اللهمَّ صلِّ على سيدنا محمدٍ عبدِكَ ونبيِّكَ ورسولِكَ النبيِّ الأميِّ وعلى آلِ سيدنا محمدٍ، اللهمَّ صلِّ على سيدنا محمدٍ وعلى آلِ
سيدنا محمدٍ مِلءَ الدنيا ومِلءَ الآخرةِ، وبارِكْ على آلِ سيدنا محمدٍ وعلى آلِ سيدنا محمدٍ مِلءَ الدنيا ومِلءَ الآخرةِ، وارحم سيدنا
محمد و آل سيدنا محمد ملء الدنيا و ملء الآخره، واجزِ سيدَنا محمداً وآلَ سيدنا محمدٍ مِلءَ الدنيا ومِلءَ الآخرةِ، وسَلِّمْ على سيدنا
محمدٍ وعلى آلِ سيدنا محمدٍ مِلءَ الدنيا ومِلءَ الآخرةِ، اللهمَّ صلِّ على سيدنا محمدٍ كما أمرتنا أن نُصَلِّيَ عليهِ، وصلِّ على سيدنا
محمدٍ كما ينبغي أن يُصَلَّى عليهِ، اللهمَّ صلِّ على نبيكَ المصطفى ورسولكَ المرتضى، ووليِّكَ المجتبى وأمينِكَ على وحي السماءِ،
اللهمَّ صلِّ على سيدنا محمدٍ أكرَمِ الأسلافِ القائِمِ بالعدلِ والإنصافِ، المنعوتِ في سورَةِ الأعرافِ، المنتخَبِ مِنْ أصلابِ الشِّرافِ
والبطونِ الظرافِ، المصفى مِنْ مُصاصِ عبدِ المطَّلبِ بن عبدِ منافٍ، الذي هديتَ بِهِ مِنَ الخِلافِ، وبَيَّنْتَ سبيلَ العفافِ

Allahumma salli āla sayyidina Muhammad-in abdika wa nabiyyika wa rasuulikan-nabiyyil-ummiyyi wa āla Āli sayyidina Muhamamd Allahumma salli āla sayyidina Muhammad-in-wa āla Āli sayyidina Muhamamd-in mil'ad-dunya wamil'al aakhirat Wa barik āla sayyidina Muhamamd-in-wa 'aala Āli sayyidina Muhamamd-in mil'ad-dunya wamil'al aakhira

Warham sayidana Muhammad-aw-wa Āli sayyidina Muhammad-im-mil'ad-dunya wa Mil'al aakhira Wajzi sayidana Muhamamd-aw-wa aala sayyidina Muhammad-in-mil 'ad-dunyaa wamil 'al aakhira wasallim āla sayyidina Muhammad-in-wa āla Āli sayyidina Muhammad-in-mil 'ad-dunya wamil 'al aakhira

Allahumma salli āla sayyidina Muhamamd-in kama amartanaa 'an nusalliya 'alaih Wa salli āla sayyidina Muhamamd-in kama yambaghi ayyusallaa 'alaih Allahumma salli āla nabiyyikal-mustafaa warasuulikal-murtadhaa wa waliyikal-mujtabaa wa amiinika āla wahyis-sama

Allahumma salli āla sayyidina Muhammad-in akramil-aslaafil-qaa'imi bil 'adli wal inssafil-man'uuti fi suratil-a'arafil-muntakhabi min aslabish-shirafi wal butuniz-zhirafil-musaffa mim-musasi 'abdil-muttalibi-bni'abdi manafi n'illadhi hadaita bihi minal-khilafi wabayyanta bihi sabilal-afafi

Dear God! Bless and support our noble master Muhammad - Your Servant, Prophet and Messenger, the Prophet sent to all nations - and his family. Dear God! Bless and support our noble master Muhammad and his family to the fullness of this world and the Hereafter. Dear God! Bestow grace upon our noble master Muhammad and his family to the fullness of this world and the Hereafter.

Dear God! Bestow mercy upon our noble master Muhammad and his family to the fullness of this world and the Hereafter. Dear God! Reward our noble master Muhammad and his family to the fullness of this world and the Hereafter. Dear God! Grant peace upon our noble master Muhammad and his family to the fullness of this world and the Hereafter.

Dear God! Bless and support our noble master Muhammad as You ordered us to ask for blessings upon him. And bless our noble master Muhammad as he should be blessed. Dear God! Grant Your blessings upon Your Chosen Prophet and Messenger, the Contented One, Your Friend and Selected One, and Your Custodian of the Heavenly Revelation.

Dear God! Bless and support our noble master Muhammad, the noblest ancestor, the One in charge of Equity and Justice, the One described in Surah al-'Araf, the One Chosen from the noble loins and refined womb. And the One purified by suckling, from Abdul Muttalib, son of Abdul Manaf, through whom You guided and made the path of forgiveness clear.

اللهُمَّ إني أسأَلُكَ بأفضلِ مسألَتِكَ، وبأَحَبِّ أسمائِكَ إليكَ وأكرمِها عليكَ، وبما مننتَ علينا بسيدنا محمدٍ نَبِيّنا ﷺ فاستنقذتنا بهِ مِنَ الضلالَةِ، وأمرتنا بالصلاةِ عليهِ، وجعلتَ صلاتنا عليهِ درجَةً وكفارَةً ولُطفاً ومَنّاً مِنْ إعطائِكَ، فأدعوكَ تعظيماً لأمرِكَ، واتباعاً لوصيَّتِكَ، ومنتجزاً لموعودِكَ، لما يجب لنَبِيّنا سيدنا محمدٍ ﷺ في أداءِ حَقِّهِ قِبَلَنا، إذ آمنا بهِ وصدقناهُ واتبعنا النورَ الذي أنْزِلَ مَعَهُ، وقُلْتَ وقولُكَ الحَقُّ، (إنَّ اللهَ ومَلائِكَتَهُ يُصَلُّونَ على النَّبِيِّ يَأَيُّها الذينَ ءامنوا صَلُّوا عليهِ وسَلِّمُوا تَسْليماً)، وأَمَرْتَ العِبادَ بالصلاةِ على نَبِيِّهِمْ، فريضةً افترضتها وأمرتهم بها، فنسأَلُكَ بجلالِ وجهِكَ ونورِ عظمتِكَ، وبما أَوْجَبْتَ على نفسِكَ للمُحْسِنينَ، أن تُصَلِّيَ أنتَ ومَلائِكَتُكَ على سيدنا محمدٍ عبدِكَ ورسولِكَ، ونَبِيِّكَ وصفِيِّكَ وخيرَتِكَ مِنْ خلقِكَ، أفضلَ ما صليتَ على أحدٍ مِنْ خلقِكَ إنَّكَ حميدٌ مجيدٌ،

Allahumma inni as-aluka bi āfdali mas'alatika wabi 'ahabi 'asma'ika 'ilaika wa akramiha 'alaika wa bima mananta 'alaina bisayyidina Muhammad-in-nabiyyiinaa sallallahu 'alaihi wa sallama fastanqaztanaa bihi minad-dhalaalati wa amartana bissalaati Ālaihi waja ālta salatana Ālaihi darajatan-wa kaffaratan-wa lutfan-wa mannan min 'ita'ika F'ad'uuka ta'ziman-li'amrika wattiba'an-liwasiyyatika wa muntajizal-limu'udika lima yajibu linabiyyina sayyidina Muhamad-in sallallahu 'alaihi wasallama fi adaa'i haqqihi qibalana izz amanna bihi wasaddaqnahu wattaba'nan-nuuralladhi 'unzila maa'hu wa qulta wa qaulukal-haqqu innallah-ha wa mala'ikatahu yusalluuna 'alannabi Ya ayyuhalladhina aamanu sallu 'alaihi wa sallimu taslima

Wa amartal-'ibaada bissalah āla nabiyyihim Fariidhata niftaradhtahaa wa amratahum biha fanas-aluka bijalĀli wajhika wanuuri 'izmatika wabimaa aujabta āla nafsika lil-muhsiniina 'an tusalliya anta wamalaa'ikatuka āla saiyidina Muhamad-in 'abdika warasulika wa-nabiyika wa-safiyika wa-khiratika min khalqika afdala ma sallaita āla ahadin-min khalqika innaka hamiidun-majiid

Dear God! I ask You by the most superior asking, in the most loved of Your Names, in the noblest of Your Names, and because You blessed us with our noble master Muhammad, may Your blessings and peace be upon him, saving us through him from wrongdoing. And because You ordered us to ask for blessings upon him, and because You made our asking for blessings upon him a way of raising our station, an expiation of our sins, and a blessing and grace for us.

Out of submission to You, I call on You, exalting Your Command, following Your Instruction and Fulfilling Your Promise, to render to Your Prophet, our noble master Muhammad, the blessings and peace of God be upon him, what is due from us. We have faith in him, believe in him, and follow the Light that came with him. And You said, and Your Word is True, 'God and His angels bless the Prophet, O you who believe, ask God to bless and support him and grant him abundant peace.' (Q 33:56)

And because You made it obligatory for Your servants to ask for blessings upon Your Prophet, making it mandatory on them, I ask You by the Majesty of Your Face and the Light of Your Greatness. And because of that which You have made binding on Yourself, due to the virtuous, You and Your angels bless our noble master Muhammad. He is Your Servant, Messenger, Prophet, Pure One and Treasure from Your creation, the best blessings ever bestowed upon any of Your creation. You are the Praiseworthy, the Mighty.

اللهمَّ ارفعْ دَرَجَتَهُ وأكرِمْ مَقامَهُ، وثقِّلْ ميزانَهُ وأبلِغْ حُجَّتَهُ وأظهِرْ مِلَّتَهُ، وأجزِلْ ثوابَهُ وأضِئْ نورَهُ وأدِمْ كرامَتَهُ، وألْحِقْ بِهِ مِنْ
ذُرِّيَّتَهُ وأهلِ بَيْتِهِ ما تُقِرُّ بِهِ عينَهُ، وعَظِّمْهُ في النَّبِيِّينَ الذينَ خَلَوْا قَبْلَهُ، اللهمَّ اجعلْ سيدَنا محمداً أكثرَ النَّبِيِّينَ تبعاً، وأكثَرَهم أُزَراءَ
وأفْضَلَهُمْ كرامَةً ونوراً، وأعلاهم درجةً وأفْسَحَهُمْ في الجنةِ منزلاً، اللهمَّ اجعل في السابقينَ غايَتَهُ وفي المنتخبينَ منزلَتَهُ، وفي المقرَّبينَ
دارَهُ وفي المصطَفَيْنَ منزلَهُ، اللهمَّ اجعلهُ أكرمَ الأكرمينَ عندَكَ منزلاً وأفضَلَهُم ثواباً، وأقرَبَهُم مجلِساً وأثبتَهُم مَقاماً، وأصوبَهُم كلاماً
وأنجَحَهُم مَسألةً، وأفضَلَهُم لديكَ نصيباً وأعظَمَهُم فيما عندَكَ رغبةً، وأنزِلْهُ في غُرُفاتِ الفِرْدَوْس مِنَ الدرجاتِ العُلى التي لا دَرَجَةَ
فوقَها، اللهمَّ اجعلْ سيدَنا محمداً أصدَقَ قائِلٍ وأنْجَحَ سائِلٍ، وأولَ شافِعٍ وأفضَلَ مُشَفَّعٍ، وشَفِّعْهُ في أمتِهِ بشفاعةٍ يغبطُهُ بها الأولونَ
والآخرونَ، وإذا مَيَّزْتَ عبادَكَ بفصلِ قضائِكَ، فاجعل سيدَنا محمداً في الأصدقينَ قيلاً، والأحسنينَ عملاً، وفي المهدِيِّينَ سبيلاً،

Allahumma arfa' darajatahu wa 'akrim maqamahuu wathaqqil mizanahu wa ablij hujjatahu wa azhir m'illatahu wa ajzil thawabahu wa adi' nurahu wa adim karamatahu wa alhiq bihi Min zurriyyatihii wa ahli baitehi ma toqerru bihi āinuhu wa āzzimhu finnabiyyinaal-lazina khalau qablahu

Allahummaj 'al sayidana Muhammad-an aktharan-nabiyyina taba'an wa aktharahum 'uzara'a wa afdalahum karamatan-wanura Wa 'aalahum darajatn Wa afsahahum fil jannati manzila

Allahummaaj'al fissabiqina ghayatahu wafil-muntakhabina manzila Wafil muqarrabina darahu wafil mustafaina manzilahu Allahummaj'alhu akramal akramina 'indaka manzilan -wa afdalahum thawaban-wa aqrabahum Majilisan-wa athbatahum-maqaman-wa asswabahum kalaaman-wa anjahahum mas'aslatan wa afdalahum ladaika nasiban-wa 'azamahum fima 'indaka raghbatan-wa anzilhu fi ghuruufatil-fildausi minad-darajatil-'ullal-lati la darajata fauqaha

Allahummaj'al sayidana Muhammad-an ashdaqa qaa'ilin-wa anjaha saa'ilin-wa auwala shaafi'iw-wa afdala mushaffa'in-wa shaffi'u fi ummatihi bi-shafaa'atin-yaghbituhu bihal-auwalunawal-akhiruna wa idha mayyazta 'ibadaka bifasli qada'ika faj'al sayidana Muhammad-an fi Asdaqiina qiilaw-wa fil-ahsaniina 'amalaw-wa fil-mahdiyina sabila

Dear God! Raise his rank, ennoble his station, grant him sound judgement, refine his testimony, cause his religion to triumph, increase his reward, make his light radiant, and extend his nobility. Join his descendants and the People of his Household with him to comfort his eyes. And exalt him among all the Prophets. Dear God! Of all the Prophets, cause our noble master Muhammad to have the most significant number of followers, increase their strength, and give them perfect nobility and light. And raise their ranks, and widen their dwellings in the Garden.

Dear God! Make their goal to be among the foremost in faith, their dwelling place among those close to You, and their abode among the elite and chosen ones. Dear God! Make their residence the Noblest in Your Presence and grant them favour with Your reward. Make them close to You, strengthen their rank, reward them with Your Word, give success to their request, favour their allocation in Your Presence, strengthen their longing for what is with You and allow them entry into the chambers of Firdaus in the highest ranks, above which there is no other rank.

Dear God! Grant our noble master Muhammad the most exact word, the most successful petitioning, the first and most perfect intercession, and intercede for his nation, an intercession that will be the longing of those who came first and who will come last. And distinguish Your servant in the discharge of Your Decree, and make our noble master Muhammad the best Speaker of the Truth, Doer of Good, and Guide to the Path.

اللهمَّ اجعل نَبيَّنا لنا فرطاً، واجعل حوضَهُ لنا موعداً لأوَّلِنَا وآخِرِنا، اللهمَّ احشُرْنا في زُمْرَتِهِ، واستعمِلْنا في سُنَّتِهِ وتَوَفَّنَا على مِلَّتِهِ، وعَرِّفْنا وجهَهُ، واجعلنا في زُمْرَتِهِ وحِزْبِهِ، اللهمَّ اجمعْ بيننا وبينَهُ كما آمَنَّا بِهِ ولم نَرَهُ، ولا تُفَرِّقْ بيننا وبينَهُ حتى تُدْخِلَنَا مَدْخَلَهُ، وتُورِدَنا حوضَهُ، وتجعلنا مِنْ رُفَقائِهِ، مَعَ المُنْعَمِ عليهم مِنَ النَّبيِّينَ والصِّدِّيقِينَ والشُّهَداءِ والصَّالِحِينَ، وحَسُنَ أولئكَ رفيقاً، والحمدُ للهِ رَبِّ العالَمِينَ.

Allahummaj‘al nabiyyana lana faratan waj’al haudahu lana mau’idan-li auwalina wa akhirina Allahummah-shurna fi zumratihi wasta’milna fi sunnatihi watawaffana āla m’illatihi wa ‘arifnaa wajhahu waj‘alnaa fi zumratihi wahizbihi

Allahummajma’ bainanaa wa bainahuu kama ‘amanna bihi walam narahu wala tufarriq bainana wa bainahu hatta tudkhilana madkhalahu waturidana haudahu wataj‘alana min-rufaqa‘ihi ma‘al-mun‘ami ‘alaihim-minan-nabiyyina wassiddiqina wash-shuhada‘i Wassālihina wahasuna ula‘ika rafiiqa Walhamdu l’illahi rabbil-‘alamin

Dear God! Grant our Prophet plenty and make his Pool a promise for the first and last of us.

Dear God! Raise us up in his company, establish us on his way, make us die following his message, acquaint us with his face, and make us among his company and party.

Dear God! Unite us with him because we have believed in him without seeing him. Do not separate us from him, and make us enter from his entrance, water us at his Pool, and grant us his company with those favoured from the Prophets, the Truthful Ones, the Pious Ones, and the Martyrs. And what a wonderful company that is.

And the totality of Grace belongs to God, the Lord of all the Worlds.

<h1 style="text-align:center">ابتداء الربع الثالث</h1>

اللهمَّ صلِّ على سيدنا محمدٍ نُورِ الهُدَى والقائِدِ إلى الخيرِ والداعِي إلى الرُّشْدِ، نَبِيِّ الرحمةِ وإمامِ المُتَّقِينَ ورسولِ رَبِّ العالَمِينَ

لا نَبِيَّ بعدَهُ كما بَلَّغَ رِسالَتَكَ ونَصَحَ لِعِبادِكَ، وتلا آياتِكَ وأقامَ حُدُودَكَ، ووَفَّى بعهدِكَ وأَنْفَذَ حُكْمَكَ، وأَمَرَ بِطاعَتِكَ ونهى عَنْ

معصِيَتِكَ، ووالى وَلِيَّكَ الذي تُحِبُّ أن تواليَهُ، وعادى عَدُوَّكَ الذي تُحِبُّ أن تُعادِيَهُ، وصلى اللهُ على سيدنا محمدٍ، اللهمَّ صلِّ على

جَسَدِهِ في الأجسادِ، وعلى رُوحِهِ في الأرواح، وعلى مَوْقِفِهِ في المواقِفِ، وعلى مَشْهَدِهِ في المشاهِدِ، وعلى ذكرِهِ إذا ذُكِرَ، صلاةً مِنّا

على نَبِيِّنا، اللهمَّ أَبْلِغْهُ مِنّا السلامَ كما ذُكِرَ السلامُ، والسلامُ على النَّبِيِّ ورحمةُ اللهِ تعالى وبركاتُهُ، اللهمَّ صلِّ على مَلائِكَتِكَ المُقَرَّبِينَ،

وعلى أنبيائِكَ المُطَهَّرِينَ وعلى رُسُلِكَ المُرْسَلِينَ، وعلى حملةِ عرشِكَ وعلى سيدنا جبريلَ، وسيدنا ميكائِيلَ وسيدنا إسرافِيلَ،

وسيدنا مَلَكِ الموتِ وسيدنا رِضْوانَ خازِنِ جَنَّتَكَ وسيدنا مالِكٍ، وصلِّ على الكِرامِ الكاتِبِينَ، وصلِّ على أهلِ طاعَتِكَ أجمعِينَ

مِنْ أهلِ السماواتِ والأرَضِينَ،

Allahumma salli āla sayyidina Muhamad-in nuril-huda wal qa'idi ilal-khairi wadda'ii 'ila-rrushdi nabiyir-rahmati wa imaamil-mutaqina warasuli rabbil-'alamina la nabiyya ba'dahu kama ballagha-risalataka wanasaha li'ibadika watala āyatika wa 'aqama hududaka wawaffa bi'ahdika wa 'anfaza hukmaka wa 'amara Bi ta'atika wanaha 'ann ma'asiyatika wawala waliyaka alladhi tuhibbu 'an tuwaliyahu wa 'āada 'aduwwaka-alladhi tuhibbu 'an tu'a,diyahu wasalla-allahu āla sayyidina Muhammad-in Allahumma salli āla jasadihii fil ajsaadi wa āla ruuhihi fil arwaahii wa āla qabrihi fil qubuuri wa āla mauqifihi fil mawaaqifii wa āla mashhadihii fil mashaahidi wa āla zikrihii iza zukira salaatan minna āla nabiyyinaaa Allahumma abligh hu minas-salaama kama zukiras-salaamu wassalaamu 'alan-nabiyyi warahmatullahi ta'la wabarkaatu

Allahumma salli āla malaa 'ikatikal-muqarrabiina wa āla anbiyaa 'ikal-mutohhariina wa āla rusulikal-mursalina wa āla hamalati arshika wa āla sayyidina jibriila wasayyidina mikaa āla wa sayyidina israfiila wasaiyidina malakil-mauti wasayyidina ridh waana khaazini jannatika wasayyidina maalikin-wasalli'alal-kiraamil-kaatibiina wa salli āla ahli to 'atika ajma 'iina min ahlis-samaawaati wal aradiin

Beginning of the Third Quarter

Dear God! Bless and support our noble master Muhammad, the Guiding Light, the Guide to Goodness, the Inviter to Spiritual Direction, the Prophet of Mercy, Leader of the Pious, Messenger of the Lord of all the Worlds, and Seal of the Prophets. He conveyed Your Message, advised Your servants, recited Your Verses, sustained Your Divine Statutes, faithfully discharged Your Covenant, and carried out Your rulings. And he enjoined obedience to You, forbade disobedience to You, befriended Your Friends whom You chose to befriend, and opposed Your enemies whom You opposed. And abundant peace of God be upon him. Dear God! Of all the bodies You have created, bless his body. Of all the souls You have made, bless his soul. Of all the places You have created, bless his home. Of all the tombs that exist, bless his tomb, and bless his memory whenever he is remembered, and blessings from us on our Prophet.

Dear God! Send him peace from us, just as he invoked peace. May peace, mercy and the benediction of God be upon the Prophet. Dear God! Bless Your nearest angels, Your Purest Prophets, Your Divine Messengers, the Bearers of Your Throne, our noble master Gabriel, our noble master Mika'il, our noble master Israfil, our noble master the Angel of Death, our noble master Ridwan - the Guardian of Your Garden, our noble master Malek, and bless the honourable recording angels, and all the people obedient to You, those on the Earths and those inhabiting the Heavens.

اللهمَّ آتِ أهلَ بيتِ نَبِيِّكَ أفضلَ ما آتيتَ أحداً مِنْ أهلِ بُيُوتِ المُرْسَلِينَ واجزِ أصحابَ نَبِيِّكَ أفضلَ ما جازيتَ أحداً مِنْ أصحابِ المُرْسَلِينَ، اللهمَّ اغفِرْ للمؤمنينَ والمؤمناتِ، والمُسْلِمِينَ والمُسْلِماتِ، الأحياء منهم والأمواتِ، واغْفِرْ لنا ولإخْوانِنَا الذينَ سَبَقُونَا بالإيمانِ ولا تجعلْ في قلوبِنَا غِلاً للذينَ آمنوا، رَبَّنا إنَّكَ رَؤُوفٌ رَحِيمٌ، اللهمَّ صلِّ على النَّبِيِّ الهاشِمِيِّ سيدنا محمدٍ وعلى آلِهِ وصحبِهِ وسَلِّمْ تَسْلِيماً، اللهمَّ صلِّ على سيدنا محمدٍ خيرِ البَرِيَّةِ، صلاةً تُرْضِيكَ وتُرْضِيهِ وتَرْضى بها عَنَّا يا أرحَمَ الراحِمِينَ، اللهمَّ صلِّ على سيدنا محمدٍ وعلى آلِهِ وصحبِهِ وسَلِّمْ تَسْلِيماً كثيراً طَيِّباً مُبارَكاً فيهِ جَزِيلاً جَمِيلاً دائماً بدوامِ مُلْكِ اللهِ، اللهمَّ صلِّ على سيدنا محمدٍ وعلى آلِهِ مِلْءَ الفضاءِ وعددَ النُّجُومِ في السَّماءِ، صلاةً تُوازِنُ السماواتِ والأرضَ، وعددَ ما خلقتَ وما أنتَ خَالِقُهُ إلى يومِ القِيامَةِ،

Allahumma āti ahle baiti nabiyyika afdala maa aataita ahadan min ahli buyuti-Lmursalina wajzi as-haba nabiyyika 'afdala ma jazaita ahadan-min as-habil-mursalina

Allahummaghfir lil-mu'minina wal-mu'minati wal-muslimina wal-muslimatil-'ahyaa'i minhum wal-amwati Waghfirlana wali 'ikhwaninal-ladhina sabaquna bil 'imani wala taj'al fi-quluubina gh'illan-l'illadhina aamanu rabbana innaka ra 'ufur-rahiim

Allahummasalli'alan-nabiyyil-haashimyii sayyidina Muhammad-in-wa āla āalihii wasahbihi wasallim tasliima Allahumma salli āla sayyidina Muhammad-in khairil-bariyyati salaatan turdhiika Waturdhiihi watardaa biha 'anna yaa arhamar-rahimiin

Allahumma salli āla sayyidina Muhammad-in-wa āla āalihii wasahbihi wasallim tasliiman kathiiran taiyiban mubaarakan fiihi jaziilan jamiilan daa 'iman bidawaami mulk'illah Allahumma salli āla sayyidina Muhammad-in wa āla 'āalihi mil'al fadaa'i wa 'adadan-nujuumi fissama'i salatan tuwazinus-samawati wal 'arda wa 'adada ma khalaqta wama 'anta khaliquhu ila yaumil-qiyama

Dear God! Give the People of the Household of Your noble Prophet the best given to any of the People of the Households of the Messengers. And give the Companions of Your noble Prophet the best reward delivered to any of the Companions of the Messengers. Dear God! Grant Your forgiveness to the submitting men and women, the believing men and women, the living and the dead.

And forgive us and our brothers and sisters who came before us in faith. "And leave not in our hearts any resentment against those who believe. Our Lord! You are full of Kindness, the Most Merciful." (Q 59:10) Dear God! Bless, support, and grant abundant peace to the Hashimi Prophet - our noble master Muhammad, and his family and Companions. Dear God! Bless and support our noble master Muhammad, the Best of all Creation, blessings that content You, content him, and by which You are contented with us. And You are the Most Merciful of the Merciful.

Dear God! Bless and grant peace to our noble master Muhammad, his Household, and his Companions, abundantly, profusely, agreeably, graciously, generously, and beautifully for all eternity.

Dear God! Bless and support our noble master Muhammad and his family to the fullness of the cosmic space and stars in the night sky, blessings that outweigh the heavens and the earth, what You have created, and will create until the Day of the Rising-Up.

اللهمَّ صلِّ على سيدنا محمدٍ وعلى آلِ سيدنا محمدٍ كما صليتَ على سيدنا إبراهيمَ، وباركْ على سيدنا محمدٍ وعلى آلِ سيدنا محمدٍ كما باركْتَ على سيدنا إبراهيمَ وعلى آلِ سيدنا إبراهيمَ في العـالَمِينَ إنَّكَ حميدٌ مجيدٌ، اللهمَّ إنِّي أسألُكَ العَفْوَ والعَافِيَةِ في الدِّين والدُّنيا والآخِرَةِ، اللهمَّ اسْتُرْنا بِسِتْرِكَ الجميل (ثلاثاً) اللهمَّ إنِّي أسألُكَ بِحَقِّكَ العظيم، وبِحَقِّ نُورِ وجهِكَ الكريم، وبِحَقِّ عرشِكَ العظيم، وبما حَمَلَ كُرْسِيُّكَ مِنْ عَظَمَتِكَ وجَلالِكَ وجَمَالِكَ، وبَهَائِكَ وقُدْرَتِكَ وسُلْطانِكَ، وبِحَقِّ أسمائِكَ المخزونةِ المكنونةِ التي لم يَطَّلِعْ عليها أحدٌ مِنْ خلقِكَ، اللهمَّ وأسألُكَ بالاسم الذي وضعتَهُ على الليل فأظلمَ وعلى النهار فاستنارَ، وعلى السماواتِ فاستَقَلَّتْ وعلى الأرضِ فاستَقَرَّتْ، وعلى الجبالِ فأرْسَتْ وعلى البِحَارِ والأوْدِيَةِ فَجَرَتْ، وعلى العُيونِ فَنَبَعَتْ وعلى السَّحابِ فأمطَرَتْ، وأسألُكَ اللهمَّ بالأسماءِ المكتوبةِ في جبهةِ سيدنا إسرافيلَ عليه السَّلامُ وبالأسماءِ المكتوبةِ في جبهةِ سيدنا جبريلَ عليهِ السلامُ وعلى المَلائِكَةِ المُقَرَّبينَ، وأسألُكَ اللهمَّ بالأسماءِ المَكْتُوبةِ حولَ العرش، وأسألُكَ بالأسماءِ المَكْتُوبةِ حولَ الكُرْسِيِّ، وأسألُكَ اللهمَّ بالاسمِ المَكْتُوبِ على وَرَقِ الزَّيْتُونِ، وأسألُكَ اللَّهُمَّ بالأسْمَاءِ الْعِظَامِ الْتي سَمَّيْتَ بِها نَفْسَكَ مَا عَلِمْتُ مِنْهَا وَمَا لَمْ أَعْلَمْ.

Allahumma salli āla sayyidina Muhammad-in-wa āla Āli sayyidina Muhammad-in kama sallaita āla sayyidina Ibraahima Wa barik āla sayyidina Muhammad-iuw-wa āla Āli sayyidina Muhammad-in kama baarakta āla sayyidina Ibraahima wa āla Āli sayyidina Ibraahima fil 'alamiina innaka hamiidun-majiid Allahumma inni as-alukal-'afwa wal 'aafiata fideen waldunya wal akhirati Allahumma austurna bisatrika aljamil Thalaatha

Allahumma ini 'as-'aluka bihaqikal-'azimi wabihaqi nuri wajhikal-karimi wabihaqi arshikal-azimi wabima hamala kursiyuka min 'adhmatika wa-jalalika wa-jamalika wa-baha'ika wa-qudratika Wasultoonika wabihaqqi asmaa 'ikal-makhzuunatil-maknuuna-t'illati lam yattali 'alaihaa ahadun-min khalqi Allahumma wa 'ass'aluka bil-'ism'illadhi wad'atahu 'alal-laili fa'azlama wa 'alan-nahari fastanara wa 'alas-samawati fa-staqallat Wa 'alal-'ardi fastaqarrat wa 'alal-jibĀli fa arsat wa 'alal-bihari wal audiyati fajarat Wa 'alal-uyuuni fanaba'at Wa 'alas-sohaabi fa amtarat

Wa as-alukallahumma bil asmaa 'il-maktuubati fi jabhati sayyidina israafiila 'alaihis-salaamu Wabil asmaa 'il-maktuubati fi jabhati sayyidina jibrila 'alaihis-salamu wa 'alal-mala'ikatil-muqarrabina Wa as-aluka-allahumma bil 'asmail-maktubati haula-larshi wa bil asma'il-maktubati-haulal-kursiyi Wa as-'alukallahumma bil 'ismil-maktubi āla waraqiz-zaitun

Dear God! Bless and support our noble master Muhammad and his family, just as You blessed our noble master Abraham. And favour our noble master Muhammad and his family, just as You favoured our noble master Abraham and his family in all the worlds, for You are the Praiseworthy, the Mighty.

Dear God! I beg You for pardon and good health in my religion, in this world and the Hereafter. Dear God, cover my faults with a beautiful covering (three times). Dear God! I ask You by Your Great Truth of the Light of Your Munificent Face and by the Truth of Your Great Throne. And I ask You by that which bears Your Great Throne from Your Oceans of Strength and Glory, Your Oceans of Beauty and Light, Your Oceans of Might and Power, and by the Truth of Your Hidden and Preserved Names which no one of Your Creation will ever come to know.

Dear God! I ask You in the Name which makes the night dark and the day light. And when laid upon the Heavens, they became high. And when laid upon the Earth, it was made stable. And when laid upon the mountains and valleys, they became fixed, and when laid upon the seas and streams, they began to flow, and when laid upon the springs, they burst forth. And when laid upon the clouds, they sent down rain. And I ask You, dear God, in the Names written upon the forehead of Israfil, peace be upon him, and the Names written upon the forehead of Gabriel, peace be upon him, and upon all the angels of Intimacy.

And I ask You, dear God, in the Names written around the Throne and the Names written around the Footstool. And I ask You, dear God, in the name written on the olive leaf, And I ask You, O Allah, by the Greatest Names that You have named Yourself – those I know and those I do not know.

الحزبُ الخامسُ وِرد يومِ الجمعةِ

بسمِ اللهِ الرحمنِ الرحيم

أسألُكَ اللهمَّ بالاسماءِ العظام التي سميتَ بِها نَفْسَكَ ما عَلِمْتُ مِنها وما لم أعلم. وأسألُكَ اللهمَّ بالأسماءِ التي دعاكَ بها

آدمُ عليهِ السَّلامُ، وبالأسماءِ التي دعاكَ بها نُوحٌ عليهِ السَّلامُ، وبالأسماءِ التي دعاكَ بها هُودٌ عليهِ السَّلامُ، وبالأسماءِ التي دعاكَ

بها إبراهيمُ عليهِ السَّلامُ، وبالأسماءِ التي دعاكَ بها صالحٌ عليهِ السَّلامُ، وبالأسماءِ التي دعاكَ بها يُونُسُ عليهِ السَّلامُ، وبالأسماءِ

التي دعاكَ بها أيُّوبُ عليهِ السَّلامُ، وبالأسماءِ التي دعاكَ بها يعقُوبُ عليهِ السَّلامُ، وبالأسماءِ التي دعاكَ بها يُوسُفُ عليهِ السَّلامُ،

وبالأسماءِ التي دعاكَ بها مُوسى عليهِ السَّلامُ، وبالأسماءِ التي دعاكَ بها هارُونُ عليهِ السَّلامُ، وبالأسماءِ التي دعاكَ بها شُعَيْبٌ

عليهِ السَّلامُ، وبالأسماءِ التي دعاكَ بها إسماعيلُ عليهِ السَّلامُ، وبالأسماءِ التي دعاكَ بها داودُ عليهِ السَّلامُ،

As-alukalla-humma bil-asmaa'il-'idham'illati samaita biha nafsaka ma 'alimta minha wama lam 'alam Wa 'as-alukall-ahumma bil -asmaa-''illati daāka biha sayyidunaa 'adamu 'alaihis-salaam Wabel āsmaa ''illati daāka beha sayidunaa nuhun alaihis-salaam

Wabel āsmaa ''illati daāka beha sayidunaa hudun 'alaihis-salaam Wabel āsmaa ''illati daāka beha sayidunaa Ibraahimu 'alaihis-salaam Wabil-asmaa''illati daāka biha Sayyidunaa saalihun Alaihis-salaam Wabel āsmaa ''illati daāka beha sayidunaa yunusu Alaihis-salaam

Wabel āsmaa ''illati daāka beha sayidunaa ayyubu Alaihis-salaam Wabel āsmaa ''illati daāka beha sayidunaa ya'aqubu Alaihis-salam Wabil-asmaa''illati da'aka biha Sayyidunaa yusufu Alaihis-salam Wabel āsmaa ''illati daāka beha sayidunaa musa Alaihis-salaam

Wabel āsmaa ''illati daāka beha sayidunaa haruuna Alaihis-salaam Wabel āsmaa ''illati daāka beha sayidunaa Shua'ibunn 'alaihis-salaam Wabil asmaa''illati daāka biha sayyidunaa Isma 'iilu 'alaihis-salaam Wabil asmaa''illati daāka biha sayyidunaa Daudu 'alaihis-salaam

---

Friday - The Fifth Part

BISMILLA HIRRAHMAAN NIRRAHIM

Dear God! I ask You in the most beautiful and greatest names You have named Yourself, those of which I am aware and unaware. And I ask You, dear God, in the name our noble master Adam, peace be upon him, called You. And I ask You, dear God, in the name our noble master Noah, peace be upon him, called You. And I ask You, dear God, in the name our noble master Hud, peace be upon him, called You. And I ask You, dear God, in the name our noble master Abraham, peace be upon him, called You. And I ask You, dear God, in the name our noble master Salih, peace be upon him, called You. And I ask You, dear God, in the name our noble master Jonah, peace be upon him, called You. And I ask You, dear God, in the name our noble master Job, peace be upon him, called You. And I ask You, dear God, in the name our noble master Jacob, peace be upon him, called You. And I ask You, dear God, in the name our noble master Joseph, peace be upon him, called You. And I ask You, dear God, in the name our noble master Moses, peace be upon him, called You. And I ask You, dear God, in the name our noble master Aaron, peace be upon him, called You. And I ask You, dear God, in the name our noble master Shuayb, peace be upon him, called You. And I ask You, dear God, in the name our noble master Ishmael, peace be upon him, called You. And I ask You, dear God, in the name our noble master David, peace be upon him, called You.

وبالأسماءِ التي دعاكَ بها سُلَيْمانُ عليهِ السَّلامُ، وبالأسماءِ التي دعاكَ بها زَكَرِيَّا عليهِ السَّلامُ، وبالأسماءِ التي دعاكَ بها يَحْيَى عليهِ السَّلامُ، وبالأسماءِ التي دعاكَ بها أُرْمِيا عليهِ السَّلامُ، وبالأسماءِ التي دعاكَ بها شَعْيا عليهِ السَّلامُ، وبالأسماءِ التي دعاكَ بها إلِيَاسَ عليهِ السَّلامُ، وبالأسماءِ التي دعاكَ بها الْيَسَعُ عليهِ السَّلامُ، وبالأسماءِ التي دعاكَ بها ذُو الكِفْلِ عليهِ السَّلامُ، وبالأسماءِ التي دعاكَ بها يُوشَعُ عليهِ السَّلامُ، وبالأسماءِ التي دعاكَ بها عِيسَى عليهِ السَّلامُ، وبالأسماءِ التي دعاكَ بها محمدٌ ﷺ وعلى جميع النَّبِيِّينَ والمُرْسَلِينَ، أَن تُصَلِّيَ على محمدٍ نَبِيِّكَ، عددَ ما خلقتَهُ مِنْ قبلِ أَن تكونَ السَّماءُ مَبْنِيَّةً، والأرضُ مَدْحِيَّةً والجبالُ مُرْسِيةً، والبحارُ مُجْراةً والعُيونُ مُنْفَجِرَةً، والأنهارُ مُنْهَمِرَةً والشمسُ مُضْحِيَّةً والقَمَرُ مُضِيئاً والكَواكِبُ مُسْتَنِيرَةً، كُنْتَ حَيْثُ كُنْتَ، لا يعلَمُ أحدٌ حَيْثُ كُنْتَ إلا أنتَ وَحْدَكَ لا شَرِيكَ لَكَ،

Wabel āsmaa ''illati daāka beha sayidunaa Sulaimanu 'alaihis-salam Wabel āsmaa ''illati daāka beha sayiduna Zakariyya alaihis-salam Wabel āsmaa ''illati daāka beha sayiduna Yahya alaihis-salam Wabel āsmaa ''illati daāka beha sayiduna armiya āalaihis-salam

Wabil asma''illati da'aka biha sayyiduna shaya'u 'alaihis-salam Wabil asmaa ''illati daāka biha sayyidunaa Ilyaasu 'alaihis-salaam Wabil asmaa ''illati daāka biha sayyidunaa-yasa'u 'alaihis-salaam Wabil asmaa''illati daāka biha sayyidunaa Zulkifli 'alaihis-salaam

Wabil asmaa ''illati daāka biha sayyidunaa Yusha'u 'alaihis-salaam Wabil asmaa ''illati daāka biha sayyidunaa iisabnu maryama 'alaihis-salaam Wabil asma ''illati daāka biha sayyidunaa Muhammad-un sallallahu alaihis-salaam Wa āla jami'il nabiyina walmursalina antusalliyya 'ala sayyidina Muhammad-in nabiyyika

'adada ma khalaqtahu min qabli 'an takunas-sama'u mabniyatan wal-jibalu mursytan walbibaru mujratan-wal 'uyunu munfajiratan wal-'anharu munhamiratan wash-shamsu mud-hiyatan wal-qamaru mudi'an wal-kawakibu mustaniratan kunta haithu kunta la ya'lamu ahadun haithun kunta ''illa 'anta wahdaka la sharika laka

And I ask You, dear God, in the name our noble master Solomon, peace be upon him, called You. And I ask You, dear God, in the name our noble master Zachariah, peace be upon him, called You. And I ask You, dear God, in the name our noble master John, peace be upon him, called You. And I ask You, dear God, in the name our noble master Jeremiah, peace be upon him, called You. And I ask You, dear God, in the name our noble master Shaaya, peace be upon him, called You. And I ask You, dear God, in the name our noble master Elias, peace be upon him, called You. And I ask You, dear God, in the name our noble master Esau, peace be upon him, called You. And I ask You, dear God, in the name our noble master Dhul-Kifl, peace be upon him, called You. And I ask You, dear God, in the name our noble master Joshua, peace be upon him, called You. And I ask You, dear God, in the name our noble master Jesus, son of Mary, peace be upon him, called You. And I ask You, dear God, in the name our noble master Muhammad, peace and blessings be upon him and the other Prophets and Messengers called You. Dear God! Bless and support our noble master Muhammad, Your Prophet, as much as what You created before the sky was raised, the Earth was spread out, the mountains were made stable, the seas made to flow, the springs burst forth, the rivers began streaming, the sun shone, the moon beamed and the planets were lit up. There You were, and no one knows where You were except You Alone, You Who have no partner.

اللهمَّ صلِّ على محمدٍ عددَ حِلْمِكَ، وصلِّ على محمدٍ عددَ عِلْمِكَ، وصلِّ على محمدٍ عددَ كَلِمَاتِكَ، وصلِّ على محمدٍ عددَ نِعْمَتِكَ، وصلِّ على محمدٍ مِلْءَ سماواتِكَ، وصلِّ على محمدٍ مِلْءَ أرْضِكَ، وصلِّ على محمدٍ مِلْءَ عَرْشِكَ، وصلِّ على محمدٍ زِنَةَ عَرْشِكَ، وصلِّ على محمدٍ عددَ ما جَرَى بهِ القلمُ في أمِّ الكِتاب، وصلِّ على محمدٍ عددَ ما خَلَقْتَ في سَبْع سماواتِكَ وصلِّ على محمدٍ عددَ ما أنتَ خالِقٌ فيهنَّ إلى يوم القيامَةِ، في كُلِّ يوم ألفَ مَرَّةٍ، اللهمَّ صلِّ على محمدٍ عددَ كلِّ قَطْرَةٍ قَطَرَتْ من سماواتِكَ إلى أرْضِكَ من يوم خلقتَ الدنيا إلى يوم القيامةِ في كلِّ يوم ألفَ مرةٍ، اللهمَّ صلِّ على محمدٍ عددَ مَنْ يُسَبِّحُكَ ويُهَلِّلُكَ، ويُكَبِّرُكَ ويُعَظِّمُكَ، منْ يوم خلقتَ الدنيا إلى يوم القيامةِ، في كُلِّ يوم ألفَ مَرَّةٍ، اللهمَّ صلِّ على محمدٍ عددَ أنفاسِهِمْ وألفَاظِهِمْ، وصلِّ على محمدٍ عددَ كُلِّ نَسَمَةٍ خلقتَها فيهِمْ، مِنْ يَوْم خلقتَ الدُّنيا إلى يَوْم القِيَامَةِ، في كُلِّ يوم ألفَ مَرَّةٍ،

Allahumma salli āla sayyidina Muhammad-in 'adada ilmi Wa salli āla sayyidina Muhammad-in 'adada 'ilmikai Wa salli āla sayyidina Muhammad-in 'adadaka lima tika Wa salli āla sayyidina Muhammad-in 'Adada ni'mati Wa salli āla sayyidina Muhammad-in mil 'asamawaati Wa salli āla sayyidina Muhammad-in mil'a ardeka

Wa salli āla sayyidina Muhamamd-in mil'a arshi Wa salli āla sayyidina Muhammad-in zinata arshi Wa salli āla sayyidina Muhammad-in 'adada ma jaraa bihil-qalamu fi ummil-kitaab Wa salli āla sayidina Muhammad-in 'adada ma khalaqta fi sab'ie samawat Wa salli āla sayyidina Muhammad-in 'adaad maa anta khaaliqun fiihinna ila yaumil-qiyamate fi kulli yaumin alfa marra

Allahumma salli āla sayyidina Muhammad-in 'Adada kulli qatratin qatarat min samawatika ila ardika min-yaumi khalaqtad-dunyaa ila yaumil-qiyamate fi kulli yaumin alfa marra Allahumma salli āla sayyidina Muhammad-in 'adada man yusabbihuka wa-yuhaliluka wa-yukabbiruka wa-yu 'azimuka min-yaumi khalaqtad-dunya ila yaumil-qiyamate fi kulli yaumin alfa marra Allahumma salli āla sayyidina Muhammad-in 'adada anfaasihim wa alfaazihim Wa salli āla sayyidina Muhammad-in 'adada kulli nasamatin khalaqtaha fiihim min-yaumi khalaqtad-dunyaa ila yaumil-qiyaama Fi kulli yaumin alfa marra

Dear God! Bless and support our noble master Muhammad to the extent of Your Forbearance. Dear God! Bless and support our noble master Muhammad to the extent of Your Omniscience. Dear God! Bless and support our noble master Muhammad as many times as Your words are. Dear God! Bless and support our noble master Muhammad to the extent of Your Favour. Dear God! Bless and support our noble master Muhammad to the fullness of Your Skies. Dear God! Bless and support our noble master Muhammad to the fullness of Your Earth. Dear God! Bless and support our noble master Muhammad to the fullness of Your Throne. Dear God! Bless and support our noble master Muhammad in the weight of Your Throne. Dear God! Bless and support our noble master Muhammad as much as all that Your Pen has written in the Mother of the Book. Dear God! Bless and support our noble master Muhammad as much as You have created in Your Seven Heavens. Dear God!

Bless and support our noble master Muhammad as much as You will create in them until the Day of the Rising-Up. And every day a thousand times. Dear God! Bless and support our noble master Muhammad in every drop of rain that has fallen from the Heavens to Earth from the day You created the world to the Day of the Rising-Up. And every day a thousand times. Dear God! Bless and support our noble master Muhammad as often as those who have glorified You, declared Your Unity, exalted and extolled Your Name from when You created the world to the Day of the Rising-Up. And every day a thousand times. Dear God! Bless and support our noble master Muhammad in every one of their inhalations and utterances. Dear God! Bless and support our noble master Muhammad in every one of their fragrant exhalations from the Day You created this world to the Day of the Rising-Up, and every day a thousand times.

اللهمَّ صلِّ على محمدٍ عددَ السَّحابِ الجارِيَةِ، وصلِّ على محمدٍ عددَ الرِّياح الذارِيَةِ مِنْ يَوْم خلقتَ الدُّنيا إلى يَوْم القِيَامَةِ، في

كُلِّ يَوْمٍ ألفَ مَرَّةٍ، اللهمَّ صلِّ على محمدٍ عددَ ما هَبَّتْ عليهِ الرِّيَاحُ وَحَرَّكَتْهُ مِنَ الأغْصَانِ والأشْجَارِ والأوْراقِ والثَّمارِ، وجميعِ ما

خلقتَ على أرضِكَ وما بينَ سماواتِكَ، مِنْ يَوْمَ خلقتَ الدُّنيا إلى يَوْم القيامَةِ، في كُلِّ يَوْمٍ ألفَ مَرَّةٍ، اللهمَّ صلِّ على محمدٍ عددَ

نُجُومِ السَّماءِ، مِنْ يوم خلقتَ الدُّنيا إلى يوم القيَامَةِ، في كُلِّ يوم ألفَ مرةٍ، اللهمَّ صلِّ على محمدٍ مِلْءَ أرضِكَ مِما حملتْ وأقلَّتْ مِنْ

قُدْرَتِكَ، اللهمَّ صلِّ على محمدٍ عددَ ما خلقتَ في سَبْعِ بِحَارِكَ، مِما لا يعلمُ عِلْمَهُ إلا أنتَ، وما أنتَ خَالِقُهُ فيها إلى يوم القِيَامَةِ، في

كُلِّ يومٍ ألفَ مَرَّةٍ، اللهمَّ صلِّ على محمدٍ عددَ مِلْءٍ سَبْعٍ بِحَارِكَ، وصلِّ على محمدٍ زِنَةَ سَبْعٍ بِحَارِكَ، مِما حملتَ وأقلَّتْ مِنْ قُدْرَتِكَ،

Allahumma salli āla sayyidina Muhammad-in 'adadas-sahaabil-jaariyati wa salli āla sayyidina Muhammad-in 'adadar-riyaahiz-zaariyati min-yaumin khalaqtad-dunyaa ila yaumil-qiyamate fi kulli yaumin alfa marra

Allahumma salli āla sayyidina Muhammad-in 'adad ma habbat 'alaihir-riyahu wa-harrakat-hu minal-aghsani wal ashjari wal 'auraqi wath-thimari wajami'i ma khalaqta āla ardika wabaina samawatika min-yaumin khalaqtad-dunyaa ila yaumil-qiyamate fi kulli yaumin alfa marra

Allahumma salli āla Sayyidina Muhammad-in 'adada najuumis-samaa'i min yaumi khalaqtad-dunyaa ila yaumil-qiyamate fi kulli yaumin alfa marra Allahumma salli āla sayyidina Muhammad-in mil'a ardika mimma hamalat wa aqallat min qudratika

Allahumma salli āla sayyidina Muhammad-in 'adada ma khalaqta fi sab'i biharika mima la ya'lamu ilmahu 'illa anta wama anta khaliquhu fiha ila yaumil-qiyamate fi kulliyau mil alfa marra

Allahumma salli āla sayyidina Muhamamd-in 'adada mil 'a sab'i biharika Wasalli āla sayyidina Muhammad-in zinata sab'i biharika mimma hamalat Wa aqqalat minn qudratika

Dear God! Bless and support our noble master Muhammad in every rolling cloud and every wind, from the Day You created this world to the Day of the Rising-Up, and every day a thousand times. Dear God! Bless and support our noble master Muhammad in the movement of every leaf, branch, tree, and fruit moved by the wind. And in every wind-caused movement of all You have created on Earth and in the Heavens from the day You created this world to the Day of the Rising-Up, and every day a thousand times.

Dear God! Bless and support our noble master Muhammad in every star in the night sky, from the Day You created this world to the Day of the Rising-Up, and every day a thousand times. Dear God! Bless and support our noble master Muhammad as much as the entire Earth and what it holds and bears of Your Power.

Dear God! Bless our noble master Muhammad in all You have created in Your Seven Seas, knowledge of which is Yours alone, and in all that You will create in them until the Day of the Rising-Up, and every day a thousand times.

Dear God! Bless and support our noble master Muhammad to the fullness of Your Seven Seas. Dear God! Bless and support our noble master Muhammad in the adornment of Your Seven Seas, and in that which they bear and hold of Your Creation.

اللهمَّ وصلِّ على محمدٍ عددَ أمواجٍ بِحَارِكَ، مِنْ يوم خلقتَ الدُّنيا إلى يوم القِيَامَةِ، في كُلِّ يوم ألفَ مَرَّةٍ، وصلِّ على محمدٍ عددَ

الرملِ والحصى، في مُسْتَقَرِّ الأرضينَ وسهلِها وجبالِها، مِنْ يوم خلقتَ الدُّنيا إلى يوم القِيَامَةِ، في كُلِّ يوم ألفَ مَرَّةٍ، اللهمَّ وصلِّ

على محمدٍ عددَ اضطرابِ المِياهِ العَذْبَةِ والمِلْحَةِ، مِنْ يوم خلقتَ الدُّنيا إلى يوم القِيَامَةِ، في كُلِّ يوم ألفَ مَرَّةٍ، وصلِّ على محمدٍ عددَ

ما خلقتَهُ على جديدِ أرضِكَ في مُسْتَقَرِّ الأرضينَ شرقِها وغربِها، سهلِها وجبالِها وأوديَتِها وطَرِيقِها وعامِرِها وغامِرِها، إلى سائرِ

ما خلقتَهُ عليها، وما فيها مِنْ حَصاةٍ ومَدَرٍ وحَجَرٍ، مِنْ يوم خلقتَ الدُّنيا إلى يوم القِيَامَةِ، في كُلِّ يوم ألفَ مَرَّةٍ،

Allahumma wasalli āla sayyidina Muhammad-in 'adada amwaaja biharika min yaumi khalaqtaa-dunya ila yaumil-kiyamati fi kulli yaumin alfa marra

Allahumma wasalli āla sayyidina Muhammad-in 'adadar-ramli wal hasaa fi mustaqarril-ardhaini wasahliha wajibaaliha minn-yaumi khalaqtad-dunyaa ila yaumil-qiyamate fi kulli alfa marra

Allahumma wa salli āla sayyidina Muhammad-in 'adada idhtiraabil-miyaahil-azbati wal milhati min-yaumi khalaqtad-dunyaa ila yaumil-qiyamate fi kulli yaumi alfa marra

Wasalli āla sayyidina Muhammad-in 'adada ma khalaqtahu āla jadiidi ardika fi mustaqarril-'ardiina sharqiha wagharbiha wasahliha wajibaaliha wa audiyatiha watariiqiha wa'aamiriha wa ghaamirihaa ila saa'iri ma khalaqtahu 'alaiha wama fiiha minn hasatin-wamadaren-wahajaren-min yaumin khalaqtaa dunya ila yaumil kiyamati fi kulliyaumen alfa marra

Dear God! Bless and support our noble master Muhammad in every wave on Your Seven Seas from the Day You created this world to the Day of the Rising-Up, and every day a thousand times.

Dear God! Bless and support our noble master Muhammad in every grain of sand, every pebble on the fixed abode of settlement on the Earth. And in every mountain on the Earth from the day You created the world to the Day of the Rising-Up, and every day a thousand times.

Dear God! Bless and support our noble master Muhammad in the turbulence between salt water and fresh water from the creation of this world to the Day of the Rising-Up, and every day a thousand times.

Dear God! Bless and support our noble master Muhammad in everything You have created on the face of Your Earths, the fixed abode of settlement, in the East and the West, on the plains and on the mountains, in the streets and the by-ways, in populated areas and wastelands. And also what is in the creation and elsewhere in every pebble, lump of mud, and stone from the Day You created this world to the Day of the Rising-Up, and every day a thousand times.

اللهمَّ صلِّ على محمدٍ النّبيِّ الأمي عددَ نباتِ الأرضِ مِنْ قِبْلَتِها وشَرْقِها وغَرْبِها، وسَهْلِها وجِبَالِها وأوديَتِها وأشْجَارِها وثِمَارِها وأوْرَاقِها وزُرُوعِها، وجميع ما يخرُجُ مِنْ نَبَاتِها وبَرَكاتِها، مِنْ يوم خلقتَ الدُّنيا إلى يوم القيَامَةِ، في كُلِّ يوم ألفَ مَرَّةٍ، اللهمَّ وصلِّ على محمدٍ عددَ ما خلقتَ مِنَ الجنِّ والإنسِ والشّياطِينِ وما أنتَ خالِقُهُ منهم إلى يوم القيَامَةِ، في كُلِّ يوم ألفَ مَرَّةٍ، اللهمَّ وصلِّ على محمدٍ عددَ كُلِّ شَعْرَةٍ في أبدانِهم وفي وُجُوهِهم وعلى رُؤُوسِهم، مُنْذُ خلقتَ الدُّنيا إلى يوم القيَامَةِ، في كُلِّ يوم ألفَ مَرَّةٍ، اللهمَّ وصلِّ على محمدٍ عددَ خفقانِ الطّيْرِ وطَيَرانِ الجنِّ والشّياطِينِ، مِنْ يوم خلقتَ الدُّنيا إلى يوم القيَامَةِ، في كُلِّ يوم ألفَ مَرَّةٍ، اللهمَّ وصلِّ على محمدٍ عددَ كُلِّ بَهيمَةٍ خَلَقْتَها على جديدِ أرضِكَ، مِنْ صَغيرٍ أو كَبيرٍ في مَشارقِ الأرضِ ومغاربِها، مِنْ إنْسِها وجِنِّها ومما لا يعلمُ عِلْمَهُ إلا أنتَ مِنْ يوم خلقتَ الدُّنيا إلى يوم القيَامَةِ، في كُلِّ يوم ألفَ مَرَّةٍ، اللهمَّ وصلِّ على محمدٍ عددَ خُطَاهُم على وَجْهِ الأرضِ، مِنْ يوم خلقتَ الدُّنيا إلى يوم القيَامَةِ، في كُلِّ يوم ألفَ مَرَّةٍ،

Allahumma salli āla sayyidina Muhammad-ini-nabiyyi 'adada nabaa til-'ardi min qiblatiha wa-sharqiha wa-gharbiha wa-sahliha wa-jibaliha wa-audiyatiha wa ashjariha wa-thimariha wa-auraqiha Wa-zuru'iha wa-jami'i ma yakhruju min-nabatiha wa-barakatiha min-yaumi khalaqtaad-dunya ila yaumil-qiyamate fi kulli yaumin alfa marra Allahumma wa salli āla sayyidina Muhammaden 'adada ma khalaqta minal-jinni wal-inse wash-shayatini wama anta khaliquhu menhum ila yaumil-qiyamate fi kulli yaumin alfa marra Allahumma wa salli āla sayyidina Muhammad-in 'adada kulli sha'ratin fi abdaanihim wa fi wujuuhihim wa āla ru 'sihim munzu khalaqtad-dunyaa ila yaumil-qiyamate fi kulli alfa marra

Allahumma Wa salli āla sayyidina Muhammad-in 'adada khafaqaaniht-tairi wa tairaanil-jinni wash-shayatiini min-yaumi khalaqtad-dunyaa ila yaumil-qiyamate fi kulli yaumi alfa marra Allahumma wa salli āla sayyidina Muhammad-in 'adada kulli bahiimatin khalaqtaha āla jadiidi ardika min saghirin 'au-kabirin fi mashariqil-'ardi wa magharibiha min insiha wa jinniha wa mimma la ya'lamu 'ilmahu ''illa anta min yaumi khalaqtaa-dunya ila yaumil-kiyamati fi kulli yaumen alfa marra Allahumma wa salli āla sayyidina Muhammad-in 'adada khutaahum āla wajhi 'ardi min-yaumi khalaqtad-dunyaa ila yaumil-qiyamate fi kulli yaumin alfa marra

Dear God! Bless and support our noble master Muhammad, the Prophet sent to all nations, in every plant on the Earth, in the East and the West, on the plains, mountains and valleys. And in every tree, every fruit, every leaf, every plant, and other vegetation or foliage that grows from the Day You created this world to the Day of the Rising-Up, and every day a thousand times.

Dear God! Bless and support our noble master Muhammad by the number of every jinn, human and devil You have created and will create until the Day of the Rising-Up, and every day a thousand times.

Dear God! Bless and support our noble master Muhammad in every hair follicle on their bodies, faces, and heads, from the creation of the world to the Day of the Rising-Up, and every day a thousand times. Dear God! Bless and support our noble master Muhammad by the number of flappings of every flying bird's wings, and the number of jinn and devils from the Day You created this world to the Day of the Rising-Up, and every day a thousand times. Dear God! Bless and support our noble master Muhammad by the number of all the cattle You have created on the surface of the Earth, large and small, in the East and West, all humanity and jinn. And in all of that which there is no knowledge except Yours, from the Day You created this world to the Day of the Rising-Up, and every day a thousand times. Dear God! Bless and support our noble master Muhammad by the number of every steppe on the face of this earth from the Day You created the world to the Day of the Rising-Up, and every day a thousand times.

اللهمَّ وصلِّ على محمدٍ عددَ مَنْ يُصَلِّي عليهِ، وصلِّ على محمدٍ عددَ مَنْ لم يُصَلِّ عليهِ، وصلِّ على محمدٍ عددَ القَطْرِ والمَطَرِ والنَّباتِ، وصلِّ على محمدٍ عددَ كُلِّ شيءٍ، اللهمَّ وصلِّ على محمدٍ في الليل إذا يَغْشَى، وصلِّ على محمدٍ في النَّهارِ إذا تَجَلَّى، وصلِّ على محمدٍ في الآخِرةِ والأُولى، وصلِّ على محمدٍ شابّاً زَكِيّاً، وصلِّ على محمدٍ كَهْلاً مَرْضِيّاً، وصلِّ على محمدٍ مُنْذُ كانَ في المَهْدِ صَبِيّاً، وصلِّ على محمدٍ حتى لا يبقى مِنَ الصَّلاةِ شيءٌ، اللهمَّ وأعطِ محمداً المقامَ المحمودَ الذي وَعَدْتَهُ، الذي إذا قالَ صَدَّقْتَهُ وإذا سَأَلَ أعطَيْتَهُ، اللهمَّ وأعْظِمْ بُرْهَانَهُ وشَرِّفْ بُنْيَانَهُ، وأَبْلِجْ حُجَّتَهُ وبَيِّنْ فَضِيلَتَهُ، واستعملْنا بِسُنَّتِهِ وتَوَفَّنا على مِلَّتِهِ، واحشُرْنا في زُمْرَتِهِ وتحتَ لِوائهِ واجعلنا مِنْ رُفَقائهِ، وأوردْنا حَوْضَهُ واسْقِنا بِكَأْسِهِ وانْفَعْنا بِمَحَبَّتِهِ، اللهمَّ آمينَ، وأسأَلُكَ بِأسمائِكَ التي دَعَوْتُكَ بِها أن تُصَلِّيَ على محمدٍ عددَ ما وَصَفْتَ، ومما لا يعلمُ عِلْمَهُ إلا أنتَ، أن تَرْحَمَني وتَتُوبَ عَلَيَّ، وتُعافِيَني مِنْ جميعِ البَلاءِ والبَلْواءِ،

Allahumma wa salli āla sayyidina Muhammad-in 'adada man-yusalli 'alaih Wa salli āla sayyidina Muhamamd-in 'adadal-qatri wal matari wannabaat Wa salli āla sayyidina Muhammad-in 'adada kulli sha'in Allahumma wa salli āla sayyidina Muhamamd-in fil-laili 'idha yaghsha Wa salli āla sayyidina Muhammad-in finnahaari 'idha tajallaa Wa salli āla sayyidina Muhamamd-in fil aakhirati Wal uula Wa salli āla sayyidina Muhammad-in shaa'abban zakiyya Wa salli āla sayyidina Muhamamd-in khalan-m'ardiyya Wa salli āla sayyidina Muhammad-in munzu kaana fil-mahdi sabiyya Wa salli āla sayyidina Muhammad-in hatta la yabqaa minas-salaati sha'i Allahumma wa 'aati sayyidina Muhammadan-il-maqamal-mahmudalladhi wa'dtahu-alladhi 'idha qala saddaqtahu wa 'idha sa'ala 'aataitahu Allahumma wa 'aazim burhanahu wa sharrif bunyanahu wa 'ablij hujjatahu wa bayyin fadilatahu

Allahumma wa-taqabbal shafa'atahu fi ummatihi Wasta'milna bisunnatihi watawaffana āla m'illatihi wa-hshurna fi zumratihi wa tahta liwaa'ihi waj'alna min-rufaqa'ihi wa auridna haudahu wasqina bik'asihi wanfa'na bimahabbathi Allahumma 'amiin

Wa as-'aluka bi'asma'ika-allati da'utuka biha 'an tusalliya āla sayyidina Muhammad-in 'adada ma wasafta wa mimma la ya'lamu 'ilmahu 'illa anta 'ana tarhamani watatuuba 'alaiya watua'afiyani min jami'i'il-bala'i wal balwa'i

Dear God! Bless and support our noble master Muhammad as often as those who ask for blessings upon him and as often as those who do not ask for blessings upon him. Dear God! Bless our noble master Muhammad in every raindrop, rainfall and plant. And bless our noble master Muhammad in everything that exists. And bless our noble master Muhammad at night when it grows dark and in the day when it produces light. And bless our noble master Muhammad in the Hereafter and at the beginning and end of the world. And bless our noble master Muhammad in his youth and his purity.

And bless our noble master Muhammad in his middle age. And bless our noble master Muhammad even in the cradle. And bless our noble master Muhammad until there remain no more blessings.

Dear God! Grant to our noble master Muhammad the Most Praised Rank that You promised him, the place where he speaks, You vindicate him, and when he asks, You give him. Dear God, approve his intercession for his nation. And keep us on his way, and let us die in his way, raise us in his company, under his banner. And make us among his company, to drink from his Pool, and enjoy his love. Dear God! Ameen.

And I ask You, in the Names I have called upon You, to bless our noble master Muhammad, as much as I have described and as much as Your knowledge, to have mercy on me, accept my repentance, and absolve me of all trials and tribulations.

وأن تَغْفِرَ لي وتَرْحَمَ الْمُؤمِنِينَ والْمُؤمِناتِ، والْمُسلِمِينَ والْمُسلِماتِ، الأحْياءِ منهم والأمْواتِ، وأن تَغْفِرَ لِعَبْدِكَ فلان بن فلان، الْمُذنِبِ الْخَاطِئِ الضَّعِيفِ، وأن تَتُوبَ عليهِ، إنّكَ غَفُورٌ رَحِيمٌ، اللهمَّ آمِينَ، يا رَبَّ العالمِينَ. قال رسول الله صلى الله عليه وسلم من قرأ هذه الصلاة مرة واحدة كتب الله له ثواب حجة مقبولة وثواب من أعتق رقبة من ولد إسماعيل عليه السلام، فيقول الله تبارك وتعالى يا ملائكتي هذا عبد من عبادي أكثر الصلاة على حبيبي محمد فوعزتي وجلالي وجودي ومجدي وارتفاعي لأعطينه بكل حرف صلى قصراً في الجنة، وليأتيني يوم القيامة تحت لواء الحمد، ونور وجهه كالقمر ليلة البدر وكفه في كف حبيبي محمد هذا لمن قالها كل يوم جمعة له هذا الفضل والله ذو الفضل العظيم. وفي رواية أخرى: اللهمَّ إنِّي أسألُكَ بحَقِّ ما حَمَلَ كُرسِيَّكَ، مِنْ عَظَمَتِكَ وقُدْرَتِكَ وجَلالِكَ وبَهائِكَ وسُلْطانِكَ، وبحَقِّ اسمِكَ الْمَخْزُونِ الْمَكْنُونِ الذي سَمَّيْتَ بِهِ نَفْسَكَ، و أنْزَلْتَهُ في كِتابِكَ و اسْتَأْثَرْتَ بِهِ في عِلْمِ الغَيْبِ عِنْدَكَ، أن تُصَلِّيَ على محمدٍ عَبْدِكَ ورَسُولِكَ، وأسألُكَ باسمِكَ الذي إذا دُعِيتَ بِهِ أجَبْتَ، وإذا سُئِلْتَ بِهِ أعْطَيْتَ، وأسألُكَ باسمِكَ الذي وَضَعْتَهُ على الليلِ فأظلمَ وعلى النَّهارِ فاستنارَ، وعلى السماواتِ فاستقلتْ، وعلى الأرضِ فاستقرت وعلى الجِبالِ فَرَسَتْ وعلى الصَّعْبَةِ فَذَلَّتْ، وعلى ماءِ السَّماءِ فَسَكَبَتْ وعلى السَّحابِ فأمْطَرَتْ، وأسألُكَ بِهِ محمدٍ نَبِيَّكَ، وأسألُكَ بِها سألَكَ بِهِ آدمُ نَبِيَّكَ، وأسألُكَ بِما سألَكَ بِهِ أنْبِياؤُكَ ورُسُلُكَ، ومَلائكَتُكَ الْمُقَرَّبُونَ، صلى اللهُ عليهم أجمعينَ

وَأَسْأَلُكَ بِمَا سَأَلَكَ بِهِ أَهْلُ طَاعَتِكَ أَجْمَعِينَ، أَنْ تُصَلِّيَ على محمدٍ وعلى آلِ محمدٍ عدَدَ ما خلقتَ مِنْ قَبْلِ أَنْ تكونَ السماءُ مَبْنِيَّةً والأرضُ مَطْحِيَّةً والجبالُ مُرْسِيَةً والعُيُونُ مُنْفَجِرَةً والأنهارُ مُنْهَمِرَةً، والشَّمْسُ مُضْحِيَةً والقَمَرُ مُضِيئاً والكَواكِبُ مُنِيرَةً، اللهمَّ صلِّ على محمدٍ وعلى آلِ محمدٍ عدَدَ عِلْمِكَ، وصلِّ على محمدٍ وعلى آلِ محمدٍ عدَدَ حِلْمِكَ، وصلِّ على محمدٍ وعلى آلِ محمدٍ عدَدَ ما أحصاهُ اللوحُ المحفوظُ مِنْ عِلْمِكَ، اللهمَّ صلِّ على محمدٍ وعلى آلِ محمدٍ عدَدَ ما جَرَى بِهِ القَلَمُ في أُمِّ الكِتَابِ عِنْدَكَ، وصلِّ على محمدٍ وعلى آلِ محمدٍ مِلْءَ سماواتِكَ، وصلِّ على محمدٍ وعلى آلِ محمدٍ مِلْءَ أَرْضِكَ، وصلِّ على محمدٍ وعلى آلِ محمدٍ مِلْءَ ما أنتَ خالِقُهُ مِنْ يوم خلقتَ الدُّنيا إلى يوم القِيَامَةِ، اللهمَّ صلِّ على محمدٍ وعلى آلِ محمدٍ عدَدَ صُفُوفِ المَلائِكَةِ، وتَسْبِيحِهِم وتَقْدِيسِهِم وتَحْمِيدِهِم، وتَمْجِيدِهِم وتَكْبِيرِهِم وتَهْلِيلِهِم، مِنْ يوم خلقتَ الدُّنيا إلى يوم القِيَامَةِ،

Wa as-aluka bima sa'alaka bihi ahlu ta'atika ajmaiinAnn tusalliya āla sayyidina Muhammad-in-wa āla Āli sayyidina Muhammad-in 'adada ma khalaqta min qabli 'an takunas-sama'u mabniyatan-wal ardu mat-hiyyatan-wal jibalu marsiyatan-wa aluyunu munfajiratan-wal 'anharu munhamiratan Wash-shamsu mudhhiyatan-wal qamaru mudhii'an wal kawaakibu muniira Allahumma salli āla sayyidina Muhammad-in-wa āla Āli sayyidina Muhammad-in 'adada 'ilmika Wa salli āla sayyidina Muhammad-in-wa āla Āli sayyidina Muhammad-in 'adada hilmika Wa salli āla sayyidina Muhamamd-in-wa āla Āli sayyidina Muhammad-in 'adada maa ahsaahul-lauhul-mahfuuzu min ilmika Allahumma salli āla sayyidina Muhamamd-in-wa āla Āli sayyidina Muhamamd-in 'adada ma jaraa bihil-qalamu fi ummil-kitaabi inda Wa salli āla sayyidina Muhamamd-in-wa āla Āli sayyidina Muhamamd-in-mil'a Samawatika Wa salli āla sayyidina Muhammad-in-wa āla Āli sayyidina Muhammad-in mil'a ardika Wa salli āla sayyidina Muhammad-in-wa āla Āli sayyidina Muhammad-in-mil'a maa anta khaaliquhu min-yaumi khalaqtad-dunyaa ila yaumil-qiyaama Allahumma salli āla sayyidina Muhammad-in-wa āla Āli sayyidina Muhammad-in 'adada sufuufil-malaaikati wa tasbihihim wa taqdisihim wa tamjidihim wa takbirihim wa tahlihim-min-yaumi-khalaqtad-dunyaa ila yaumil-qeyama

And I ask You, by what all your obedient servants have asked You, to bless and support our noble master Muhammad and his family in all that You created before building the sky and spreading out the Earth. And before You made the mountains stable, the seas and rivers to flow, the springs to burst forth, the sun to shine, the moon to beam, and the plants to illuminate.

Dear God! Bless and support our noble master Muhammad and his family as much as Your Omniscience and Forbearance. Dear God! Bless and support our noble master Muhammad and his family as much as Your Omniscience is registered on the Preserved Tablets. Dear God! Bless and support our noble master Muhammad and his family as much as Your Pen has written in the Mother of the Book.

Dear God! Bless and support our noble master Muhammad and his family to the fullness of Your Heavens and Your Earth. Dear God! Bless and support our noble master Muhammad and his family in everything You have created from the Day You created the world until the Day of the Rising-Up.

Dear God! Bless and support our noble master Muhammad and his family as many times as Your angels have glorified, praised, and magnified You. And as many times as Your angels have declared Your Greatness and Unity, from the Day You created the world until the Day of the Rising-Up.

اللهمَّ صلِّ على محمدٍ وعلى آلِ محمدٍ عددَ السَّحابِ الجاريةِ والرِّياحِ الذَّارِيةِ، مِنْ يوم خلقتَ الدُّنيا إلى يوم القِيَامَةِ، اللهمَّ صلِّ على محمدٍ وعلى آلِ محمدٍ عددَ كُلِّ قطرةٍ تَقْطُرُ مِنْ سماواتِكَ إلى أَرْضِكَ وما تَقْطُرُ إلى يوم القِيَامَةِ، اللهمَّ صلِّ على محمدٍ وعلى آلِ محمدٍ عددَ ما هَبَّتِ الرِّيَاحُ، وعددَ ما تَحَرَّكَتِ الأَشْجَارُ والأَوْرَاقُ والزُّرُوعُ، وجميع ما خلقتَ في قَرَارِ الحِفْظِ، مِنْ يوم خلقتَ الدُّنيا إلى يوم القِيَامَةِ، اللهمَّ صلِّ على محمدٍ وعلى آلِ محمدٍ عددَ القَطْرِ والمَطَرِ والنَّباتِ، مِنْ يوم خلقتَ الدُّنيا إلى يوم القِيَامَةِ، اللهمَّ صلِّ على محمدٍ وعلى آلِ محمدٍ عددَ النُّجُوم في السَّماءِ، مِنْ يوم خلقتَ الدُّنيا إلى يوم القِيَامَةِ، اللهمَّ صلِّ على محمدٍ وعلى آلِ محمدٍ عددَ ما خلقتَ في بِحَارِكَ السَّبْعَةِ مما لا يعلمُ عِلْمَهُ إلا أنتَ، وما أنتَ خالِقُهُ إلى يوم القِيَامَةِ،

Allahumma salli āla sayyidina Muhammad-wa āla Āli sayyidina Muhammad-in Adadas-sahaabil-jaariyati warriyaahiz-zaariyati min-yaumi khalaqtad-dunyaa ila yaumil- qeyama

Allahumma salli āla sayyidina Muhammad-in-wa āla Āli sayyidina Muhammad-in ʻadada kulli qatratin taqturu min samawatika ila ardika wama taqturu ila yaumil-qiyaama

Allahumma salli āla sayyidina Muhammad-in-wa āla Āli sayyidina Muhammad-in ʻadada ma habbatir-riyahu wa ʻadada ma taharrakatil-ʻashjaru wal ʻauraqu wazzuruʻu wa jamiʻi ma khalaqta fi qararil-hifzi min yaumi khalaqtad-dunya ila yaumil-qiyama Allahumma salli āla sayyidina Muhammad-in wa āla Āli sayyidina Muhammad-in ʻadadal-qatri wal matari wannabaati min-yaumi khalaqtad-dunyaa yaumil-qiyaama

Allahumma salli āla sayyidina Muhammad-in-wa āla Āli sayyidina Muhammad-in ʻadadan-najuumu fissamaaʻi min-yaumi khalaqtad-dunyaa ila yaumil-qiyaama Allahumma salli āla sayyidina Muhammad-in-wa āla Āli sayyidina Muhammad-in ʻadada ma khalaqta fi biharikas-sabʻati mimma la yaʼlamu ilmahuu ʼilla anta wamaa anta khaaliquhuu ila yaumil-qiyaama

Dear God! Bless and support our noble master Muhammad and his family by the number of every moving cloud and flowing wind from the beginning of the creation of this world until the Day of the Rising-Up. Dear God! Bless and support our noble master Muhammad and his family by the number of every raindrop that falls from the Heavens to the Earth and in all the rain that will fall until the Day of the Rising-Up.

Dear God! Bless and support our noble master Muhammad in the movement of every tree, branch, leaf and plant moved by the wind and the wind-stirred movement of everything else You have created in the Abode of Preservation from the creation of this world to the Day of the Rising-Up. Dear God! Bless and support our noble master Muhammad and his family in every dewdrop, raindrop, and plant from the Day You created this world to the Day of the Rising-Up.

Dear God! Bless and support our noble master Muhammad and his family by the number of all the stars in the sky from the day You created this world until the Day of the Rising-Up. Dear God! Bless and support our noble master Muhammad and his family, as much as You have created in Your Seven Seas, knowledge of which is Yours alone, and as much as You will create until the Day of the Rising-Up.

اللهمَّ صلِّ على محمدٍ وعلى آلِ محمدٍ عددَ الرَّمْلِ والحَصَى، في مَشَارِقِ الأرضِ ومغارِبِها، اللهمَّ صلِّ على محمدٍ وعلى آلِ محمدٍ عددَ ما خلقتَ مِنَ الجِنِّ والإِنْسِ، وما أنتَ خالِقُهُ إلى يوم القِيَامَةِ، اللهمَّ صلِّ على محمدٍ وعلى آلِ محمدٍ عددَ أَنْفَاسِهِم وأَلْفَاظِهِم وأَلْحَاظِهِم، مِنْ يوم خلقتَ الدُّنيا إلى يوم القِيَامَةِ، اللهمَّ صلِّ على محمدٍ وعلى آلِ محمدٍ عددَ طَيَرانِ الجِنِّ والمَلائِكَةِ، مِنْ يوم خلقتَ الدُّنيا إلى يوم القِيَامَةِ، اللهمَّ صلِّ على محمدٍ وعلى آلِ محمدٍ عددَ الطُّيُورِ والهَوَامِّ، وعددَ الوُحُوشِ والآكامِ، في مَشَارِقِ الأرضِ ومغارِبِها، اللهمَّ صلِّ على محمدٍ وعلى آلِ محمدٍ عددَ الأحياءِ والأمواتِ، اللهمَّ صلِّ على محمدٍ وعلى آلِ محمدٍ عددَ ما أَظْلَمَ عليهِ الليلُ و أَشْرَقَ عليهِ النَّهارُ، مِنْ يوم خلقتَ الدُّنيا إلى يوم القِيَامَةِ،

Allahumma salli āla sayyidina Muhammad-in-wa āla Āli sayyidina Muhammad-in 'adadar-ramli wal hasaa fi Mashaariqil-'ardi wa magharibiha Allahumma salli āla sayyidina Muhammad-in-wa āla Āli sayyidina Muhammad-in 'adada ma khlaqta minal-jinni wal insi wamaa anta khaaliquhuu ila yaumil-qiyaama

Allahumma salli āla sayyidina Muhammad-in-wa āla Āli sayyidina Muhammad-in 'adada anfasihem wa alfazihem wa alhazihem min-yaumi khalaqtad-dunya ila yaumil-qiyaama

Allahumma salli āla sayyidina Muhammad-in-wa āla Āli sayyidina Muhammad-in 'adada tairaanil-jinni wal malaaikati min-yaumi khalaqtad-dunyaa ila yaumil-qiyaama

Allahumma salli āla sayyidina Muhammad-in-wa āla Āli sayyidina Muhamamd-in 'adadat-tuyuri wal hawammi wa 'adadal-wuhushi wal ākami fi mashariqil-'ardi wa magharibi Allahumma salli āla sayidina Muhammad-in-wa āla Āli sayidina Muhamamd-in 'adadal-ahyaa'i wal amwaat

Allahumma salli āla sayyidina Muhammad-in-wa āla Āli sayyidina Muhammad-in 'adada ma 'azlama 'alaihil-lailu wa-ashraqa 'alaihin-naharu min-yaumi khalaqtad-duya ila yaumil-qiyaama

Dear God! Bless and support our noble master Muhammad and his family in every grain of sand and every pebble on the Earth, in the East and the West. Dear God! Bless and support our noble master Muhammad and his family by the number of every jinn and human being You created and will create of them until the Day of the Rising-Up.

Dear God! Bless and support our noble master Muhammad and his family in every one of their breaths, glances and utterances from the Day You created this world until the Day of the Rising-Up. Dear God! Bless and support our noble master Muhammad and his family by the number of Your angels and flying jinn from the day You created them until the Day of the Rising-Up.

Dear God! Bless and support our noble master Muhammad and his family in every bird, insect, wild beast and hill on the Earth, in the East and the West. Dear God! Bless and support our noble master Muhammad and his family in the living and the dead. Dear God! Bless and support our noble master Muhammad and his family by the number of all the nights and all the days You have illuminated since You created this world until the Day of the Rising-Up.

اللهمَّ صلِّ على محمدٍ وعلى آلِ محمدٍ عددَ مَنْ يَمْشِي على رِجْلَينِ ومَنْ يَمْشِي على أرْبَعٍ، مِنْ يوم خلقتَ الدُّنيا إلى يوم القِيَامَةِ اللهمَّ صلِّ على محمدٍ وعلى آلِ محمدٍ عددَ مَنْ صَلَّى عليهِ مِنَ الجنِّ والإنْسِ والمَلائِكَةِ، مِنْ يوم خلقتَ الدُّنيا إلى يوم القِيَامَةِ، اللهمَّ صلِّ على محمدٍ وعلى آلِ محمدٍ عددَ مَنْ لم يُصَلِّ عليهِ، اللهمَّ صلِّ على محمدٍ وعلى آلِ محمدٍ كما يَجِبُ أنْ يُصَلَّى عليهِ، اللهمَّ صلِّ على محمدٍ وعلى آلِ محمدٍ كما يَنْبَغِي أنْ يُصَلَّى عليهِ، اللهمَّ صلِّ على محمدٍ وعلى آلِ محمدٍ حتى لا يبقى شيءٌ مِنَ الصَّلاةِ عليهِ، اللهمَّ صلِّ على محمدٍ في الأوَّلِينَ، وصلِّ على محمدٍ في الآخِرِينَ، اللهمَّ صلِّ على محمدٍ في المَلإِ الأعلى إلى يوم الدِّينِ ما شاءَ اللهُ، لا قُوَّةَ إلا باللهِ العَلِيِّ العَظِيمِ.

Allahumma salli āla sayyidina Muhammad-in-wa āla Āli sayyidina Muhammad-in 'adada man-yamshi āla rijlaini waman-yamshi āla araba'in min-yaumi khalaqtad-dunyaa ila yaumil-qiyaama

Allahumma salli āla sayyidina Muhammad-iuw-wa āla Āli sayyidina Muhammad-in 'adada man salla 'alaihi minal-jinni wal insi wal mala'ikati min-yaumi khalaqtad-dunya ila yaumil-qiyama

Allahumma salli āla sayyidina Muhammad-iuw-wa āla Āli sayyidina Muhammad-in 'adada man-yusalli 'alaih Allahuma salli āla sayyidina Muhammad-iuw-wa āla Āli sayyidina Muhamamd-in 'adada man-lam yusalli 'alaih Allahumma salli āla sayyidina Muhammad-iuw-wa āla Āli sayyidina Muhammad-in kama yajibu 'an Yusalla 'alaih

Allahumma salli āla sayyidina Muhammad-iuw-wa āla Āli sayyidina Muhammad-in kama yambaghii an-yusalla 'alaih Allahumma salli āla sayyidina Muhammad-iuw-wa āla Āli sayyidina Muhammad-in hatta la yabqa shia'un-minas-solaata 'alaih

Allahumma salli āla sayyidina Muhammad-in fil-awwaliin Wa salli āla sayyidina Muhammad-in fil-aakhiriin Allahumma salli āla sayyidina Muhammad-in fil-mala'il-aala ila yaumid-diin Ma shaa'allahu la quwwata 'illa b'illahil-aliyyil-aziim

Dear God! Bless and support our noble master Muhammad and his family by the number of every two-legged and four-legged creature You have created from the Day You created this world until the Day of the Rising-Up. Dear God! Bless and support our noble master Muhammad and his family as often as the angels, jinn, and human beings have asked You to bless him from the Day You created this world until the Day of the Rising-Up.

Dear God! Bless and support our noble master Muhammad and his family as often as those who have asked for blessings upon him and those who have not asked for blessings upon him. Dear God! Bless and support our noble master Muhammad and his family as it is incumbent upon us to ask You to bless him. Dear God! Bless and support our noble master Muhammad and his family, as it is fitting for him to be blessed.

Dear God! Bless and support our noble master Muhammad and his family until all blessings are exhausted. Dear God! Bless and support our noble master Muhammad among the First and the Last. Dear God! Bless and support our noble master Muhammad in the Highest Host until the Day of the Rising-Up. And what God wills. There is no power nor ability save through God, the Most High, the Great.

الحزبُ السادسُ وِرد يومِ السبتِ

بسم اللهِ الرحمنِ الرحيم

اللهمَّ صلِّ على سيدنا محمدٍ وعلى آلِ سيدنا محمدٍ، وأعطِهِ الوَسِيلَةَ والفَضِيلَةَ والدَّرَجَةَ الرَّفِيعَةَ، وابعثهُ مقاماً محموداً الذي وَعَدْتَهُ، إنَّكَ لا تُخْلِفُ الميعادَ، اللهمَّ عَظِّم شَأْنَهُ وبَيِّنْ بُرْهانَهُ، وأَبْلِجْ حُجَّتَهُ وبَيِّنْ فَضِيلَتَهُ، وتَقَبَّلْ شَفاعَتَهُ في أُمَّتِهِ واستعملنا بِسُنَّتِهِ، يا رَبَّ العَالَمِينَ ويا رَبَّ العَرْشِ العَظِيم، اللهمَّ يا رَبّ احْشُرْنَا في زُمْرَتِهِ وتحتَ لِوائِهِ، واسْقِنا بِكَأْسِهِ وانْفَعْنا بِمَحَبَّتِهِ آمِينَ، يا رَبّ العَالَمِينَ، اللهمَّ يا رَبّ بَلِّغْهُ عَنَّا أفضَلَ السَّلام، واجزِهِ عَنَّا أفضَلَ ما جَازَيْتَ بهِ النَّبِيَّ عَنْ أُمَّتِهِ، يا رَبّ العَالَمِينَ، اللهمَّ يا رَبّ إنِّي أسأَلُكَ أن تغفرَ لي وترحَمَني وتتوبَ عَلَيَّ، وتُعَافِيَني مِنْ جميعِ البلاءِ والبلواءِ، الخارِج مِنَ الأرضِ والنَّازِل مِنَ السَّماءِ، إنَّكَ على كُلِّ شيءٍ قديرٌ بِرَحْمَتِكَ وأن تغفرَ للمُؤمِنينَ والمُؤمناتِ، والمُسْلِمينَ والمُسْلِماتِ، الأحْيَاءِ منهم والأمْواتِ، ورَضِيَ اللهُ عَنْ أزواجِهِ الطَّاهِراتِ أُمَّهاتِ المُؤمِنينَ، ورَضِيَ اللهُ عَنْ أصْحَابِهِ الأعلامِ، أئِمَّةِ الهُدى ومَصابِيحِ الدُّنْيَا، وعَنِ التَّابِعِينَ وتابِع التَّابِعِينَ لهم بإحْسَانٍ إلى يوم الدِّينِ، والحمدُ لله رّبّ العَالَمِينَ.

Allahumma salli āla sayyidina Muhammad-iuw-wa āla Āli sayyidina Muhammaden- wa āatihil-wasilata walfadilata waddarajatarrafiāta walmaqam almhmod alladhi waādtahu innaka la tukhleful-miāad Allahumma 'azzim shaānahu wa bayyin burhanahu wa āblej hujjatuhu wa bayyin fadhilatahu wataqabbal shafaātuhu fi ummatihi wastaāmilna bisunnatehi ya rabbal-ālamiin Wa ya rabbal-arshil-'azim Allahumma ya rabbia-hshurna fi zumratihi watahta liwa'ihi wasqina bika'asihi Wanfa'na bima-habbatihi aamiina ya rabbal-'alamiin Allahumma ya rabbi ballighu ānna afdalassalami wajzihi ānna afdala ma jazaita bihi nabiyyan ān ummatihi ya rabbal-'alamina Allahumma yaa rabbi inni as-aluka 'an taghfirali watarhamani wa tatuba 'alayya watu'afiyani min jamii'il-balaa'i walbalwaa'il khaariji minal 'ardi wannazili minas-samaa'i innaka āla kulli sha'in qadiir Birahmatika wa antaghfira lilmu'miniina wal-mauminaati wal muslimiina wal muslimaatil-ahyaa'i minhum wal amwaati wradia allh āan azwajihea alttahirati ummahatil-mu'minina wradia allh āan as-habihil 'aalami aāimmatil huda wama sabihiad-dunya wa-anittabi'ina watabi'ittabi-ina lahum bi-ihsanin ila yaumiddini walhamdu l'illahi rabil-'alalimin

Saturday - The Sixth Part

BISMILLA HIRRAHMAAN NIRRAHIM

Dear God! Bless and support our noble master Muhammad and his family. Grant him the Closest Access, Pre-eminence, Highest Rank, and Most Praised Station You have promised him, for You do not break Your promise. Dear God! Increase his value, clarify his argument, embellish his proof, make evident his excellence, approve his intercession for his Nation, and keep us on his way, Dear Lord of all the Worlds and Lord of the Mighty Throne. Dear God! Dear Lord! Gather us with his company, under his banner, to drink from his cup and avail us of his love: Ameen, dear Lord of all the Worlds. Dear God! Dear Lord! Bestow upon him the best peace and a better reward than any other Prophet for what he has done for his Nation and us, dear Lord of all the Worlds. Dear God! Dear Lord, I implore You for forgiveness. Grant me forgiveness, accept my repentance, and remove all trials and tribulations from me that come from the Earth and those sent down from the Heavens. You are the Most Powerful over everything. Through Your Mercy, forgive the submitting men and women, the believers, the living and the dead. And the Contentment of God be with his pure wives - the Mothers of the Believers - and his Companions, Eminent Leaders of Guidance and Lamps of this world. And with the Followers and the Followers of the Followers. Salutations be upon them all until the Day of the Rising-Up, and the totality of Grace belongs to God, the Lord of all the Worlds.

ابتداء الثلث الثالث

اللهمَّ رَبَّ الأرْواحِ والأجْسادِ البَالِيَةِ، أسألُكَ بِطاعَةِ الأرْواحِ الرَّاجِعَةِ إلى أجْسادِهَا وبِطاعَةِ الأجْسادِ المُلْتَئِمَةِ بِعُرُوقِهَا،

وبِكَلِمَاتِكَ النَّافِذَةِ فيهم، وأخْذِكَ الحَقَّ منهم والخَلائِقُ بَيْنَ يَدَيْكَ ينتظرونَ فَصلَ قَضَائِكَ ويَرْجُونَ رَحْمَتَكَ ويَخَافُونَ عِقَابَكَ، أن

تجعلَ النُّورَ في بَصَري، وذِكْرَكَ بالليلِ والنَّهارِ على لِسَاني وعَمَلاً صَالِحاً فارْزُقْني، اللهمَّ صلِّ على سيدنا محمدٍ كما صليتَ على

سيدنا إبراهيمَ، وبَارِكْ على سيدنا محمدٍ كما بارَكْتَ على سيدنا إبراهيمَ، اللهمَّ اجعلْ صَلَوَاتِكَ وبَرَكَاتِكَ على سيدنا محمدٍ و آلِ

سيدنا محمدٍ، كما جعلتها على سيدنا إبراهيمَ و آلِ سيدنا إبراهيمَ إنَّكَ حميدٌ مجيدٌ،

Allahumma rabbal-arwaahi wal-ajsaadil baliyyati as-aluka bita‘atil-arwaahir-raji‘ati ila ajsaadiha wabita‘atil ajsaadil-multa‘imati bi-uruuqiha bikalimaatika- naafizati fiihim wa ‘akhzika Alhaqqa minhum wal-khala‘iqu baina yadaika yantadhiruna fasla qada‘ika wa yarjuna rahmataka wa yakhafuna ‘iqabaka ‘an taj‘ala-anura fi basari wazikraka b’illaili wannahari āla lisaani wa ‘amalan saalihan farzuqni

Allahumma salli āla sayyidina Muhammad-in kama sallaita āla sayyidina Ibrahiima wabarik’ala sayyidina Muhammad-in kamma baarakta āla sayyidina Ibraahiim Allahummaj-al salawaatika wabarakaatika āla sayyidina Muhammad-in-wa āla Āli sayyidina Muhammad-in kama ja-al’taha āla sayyidina Ibraahima wa’ala Āli sayyidina Ibraahima innaka hamiidun majiid

Beginning of the Final Third

Dear God! Dear Lord of all souls and mortal flesh. I ask You for the obedience of souls returning to their bodies, for the compliance of bodies becoming whole again, for Your Words which will order this, and for Your extracting the rights. And for Your creatures waiting for Your Decree, hoping for Mercy and fearing punishment. I ask You to bestow light in my eyes, remembrance of You day and night with my tongue, and help me to do good deeds.

Dear God! Bless and support our noble master Muhammad just as You blessed our noble master Abraham and sanctify our noble master Muhammad just as You sanctified our noble master Abraham.

Dear God! Grant Your blessings and favours upon our noble master Muhammad and his family, just as You granted them to our noble master Abraham and his family. You are the Praiseworthy, the Mighty.

وبارِكْ على سيدِنا محمدٍ و آلِ سيدِنا محمدٍ، كما بارَكْتَ على سيدِنا إبراهيمَ و آلِ سيدِنا إبراهيمَ إنَّكَ حميدٌ مجيدٌ، اللهمَّ صلِّ على سيدِنا محمدٍ عَبْدِكَ ورَسُولِكَ، وصلِّ على المؤمِنينَ والمؤمِناتِ، والمُسلِمينَ والمُسلِماتِ، اللهمَّ صلِّ على سيدِنا محمدٍ وعلى آلِهِ عدَدَ ما أَحاطَ بهِ عِلْمُكَ، وأحصاهُ كِتابُكَ، وشَهِدَتْ بهِ مَلائِكَتُكَ، صلاةً دائمةً تدومُ بدوامِ مُلْكِ اللهِ، اللهمَّ إنِّي أسألُكَ بأسْمائِكَ العِظامِ، ما عَلِمْتُ منها وما لم أعلمْ، وبالأسْماءِ التي سَمَّيْتَ بها نَفْسَكَ، ما عَلِمْتُ منها وما لم أعلمْ، أن تُصَلِّيَ على سيدِنا محمدٍ عَبْدِكَ ونَبِيِّكَ ورَسُولِكَ، عدَدَ ما خلقتَ مِنْ قبلِ أن تكونَ السَّماءُ مَبْنِيَّةً والأرضُ مَدْحِيَّةً والجبالُ مَرْسِيَّةً، والعُيونُ مُنْفَجِرَةً والأنْهارُ مُنْهَمِرَةً، والشمسُ مُشْرِقَةً والقمرُ مُضِيئاً والكواكبُ مُسْتَنِيرَةً، والبِحارُ مجريةً والأشْجارُ مُثْمِرَةً، اللهمَّ صلِّ على سيدِنا محمدٍ عدَدَ عِلْمِكَ، وصلِّ على سيدِنا محمدٍ عدَدَ حِلْمِكَ، وصلِّ على سيدِنا محمدٍ عدَدَ كَلِماتِكَ، وصلِّ على سيدِنا محمدٍ عدَدَ نِعْمَتِكَ، وصلِّ على سيدِنا محمدٍ عدَدَ فَضْلِكَ،

Wabarik āla sayyidina Muhammad-in-wa Āli sayyidina Muhammad-in kama baarakta 'ala sayyidina Ibrahiima wa Āli sayyidina ibrahiima innaka hamiidun majiid Allahumma salli āla sayyidina Muhammad-in abdika warasuulika wasalli 'alal-mu'minina walmu'minaati walmuslimiina walmuslimaat Allahumma salli āla sayyidina Muhammad-iuw-wa āla āalihi 'adada ma 'ahata bihi 'ilmuka wa 'ahsahu kitabuka washahidat bihi mala'ikatuka salatan daa'imatan tadumu bidawami mulk'illah

Allahumma 'inni As-'aluka bi-'asmaikal-'idhami ma 'alimtu minha wama lam 'alam wa bil-asma'illati sammaita bihaa nafsaka ma 'alimtu minha wa-ma lam 'aālam 'an tusalliya āla sayyidina Muhammad-in abdika wanabiyyika wa rasuuleka 'adada ma khalaqta min qabla ānn takunas-samaa'u mabniyyatan-walardu madhiyyatan-waljibaalu marsiyatan walāuyyunu munfajiratan-walānharu munhamiratan wash-shamsu mushreqatan walqamaru mudiān wal kawakebu mustaniratan walbiharu mujriyatan walashjaru Muthmiratan

Allahumma salli āla sayyidina Muhamamd-in 'adaada 'Ilmi Wa salli āla sayyidina Muhammad-in 'adada hilmika Wa salli āla sayyidina Muhammad-in 'adada kalimaatika Wa salli āla sayyidina Muhammad-in 'adada ni'matika Wa salli āla sayyidina Muhammad-in 'adada fadleka

And sanctify our noble master Muhammad and his family, just as You blessed our noble master Abraham and his family. You are the Praiseworthy, the Mighty. Dear God! Bless and support our noble master Muhammad, Your Servant and Messenger, and bless the submitting men and women, and the believing men and women. Dear God! Bless and support our noble master Muhammad and his family as much as all that is encompassed by Your Omniscience, all that Your Book has enumerated, and all that is witnessed by Your angels. Bless our noble master Muhammad with blessings that last for all eternity.

Dear God! I pray to You with Your Greatest Names, those that I know and those that I do not, and in the Names You have named Yourself, names I know not and names I shall never know.

Dear God! Bless and support our noble master Muhammad, Your Servant, Prophet and Messenger, by the number of what You created before the sky was raised, the Earth was extended, the mountains made firm, the springs burst forth, the rivers flowed, the sun blazed, the moon shone, the stars illuminated the night sky, the seas flowed, and the trees gave of their fruit. Dear God! Bless and support our noble master Muhammad to the extent of Your Omniscience. Dear God! Bless and support our noble master Muhammad to the extent of Your Forbearance. Dear God! Bless and support our noble master Muhammad to the number of Your Words. Dear God! Bless and support our noble master Muhammad to the number of Your Favours. Dear God! Bless and support our noble master Muhammad to the extent of Your Grace.

وصلِّ على سيدنا محمدٍ عددَ جُودِكَ، وصلِّ على سيدنا محمدٍ عددَ سَمَاواتِكَ، وصلِّ على سيدنا محمدٍ عددَ أَرْضِكَ، وصلِّ على سيدنا محمدٍ عددَ ما خلقتَ في سبعِ سَمَاواتِكَ مِنْ مَلائِكَتِكَ، وصلِّ على سيدنا محمدٍ عددَ ما خلقتَ في أَرْضِكَ مِنَ الجِنّ والإِنْسِ وغيرِهِما، ومِنَ الوَحْشِ والطيرِ وغيرِهِما، وصلِّ على سيدنا محمدٍ عددَ ما جَرَى بِهِ القَلَمُ في عِلْمِ غَيْبِكَ وما يجري بِهِ إلى يوم القِيَامَةِ، وصلِّ على سيدنا محمدٍ عددَ القَطْرِ والمَطَرِ، وصلِّ على سيدنا محمدٍ عددَ مَنْ يَحْمَدُكَ ويَشْكُرُكَ، ويُهَلّلُكَ ويُمَجِّدُكَ، ويَشْهَدُ أَنّكَ أنتَ اللهُ، وصلِّ على سيدنا محمدٍ عددَ ما صليتَ عليهِ أنتَ ومَلائِكَتُكَ، وصلِّ على سيدنا محمدٍ عددَ مَنْ صلى عليهِ مِنْ خَلْقِكَ، وصلِّ على سيدنا محمدٍ عددَ مَنْ لم يُصَلِّ عليهِ مِنْ خَلْقِكَ وصلِّ على سيدنا محمدٍ عددَ الجِبالِ والرِّمَالِ والحَصَى،

Wa salli āla sayyidina Muhammad-in 'adada judika Wa salli āla sayyidina Muhammad-in 'adada samawatika Wa salli āla sayyidina Muhammad-in 'adada 'ardika Wa salli āla sayyidina Muhammad-in 'adada ma khalaqta fi sab'I samawatika min-mala'ikati Wa salli āla sayyidina Muhammad-in 'adada ma khalaqta fi ardika minal-Jinni wal insi wa ghairi hima minal-wahshi wattoiri wa ghairi hima

Wa salli āla sayyidina Muhammad-in 'adada ma jara bihil-qalamu fi 'ilmi ghaibika wama yajri bihi ila yaumil-qiyamate wa salli āla sayyidina Muhammad-in 'adadal-qatri wal matari wa salli āla sayyidina Muhammad-in 'adada man yahmaduka wayashkuruka wayuhalliluka wayumajjiduka wayashhadu ānnaka ānta allahu

wasalli āla sayyidina Muhammad-in 'adada ma sallaita 'alaihi anta wamalaa 'ikatu Wa salli āla sayyidina Muhammad-in 'adada man salla 'alaihi min-khalqika wa-salli āla sayyidina Muhammad-in 'Adada man lam yusalli 'alaihi min khalqi Wa salli āla sayyidina Muhammad-in 'adadal-jibĀli warrimali wal hasaa

Dear God! Bless and support our noble master Muhammad to the extent of Your Generosity. Dear God! Bless and support our noble master Muhammad to the extent of Your Heavens. Dear God! Bless and support our noble master Muhammad to the size of Your Earth. And bless and support our noble master Muhammad as many times as all the angels You have created in Your Seven Heavens.

And bless and support our noble master Muhammad as many times as all the jinn, human beings and others than them, and the beasts and birds and beings other than them, that You have created on Your Earth.

And bless and support our noble master Muhammad in all that the Pen has written about the Knowledge of the Unwitnessed, and in all that the Pen will write until the Day of the Rising-Up. And bless and support our noble master Muhammad in every dewdrop and raindrop.

And bless and support our noble master Muhammad as often as You are praised and thanked, as repeatedly as Your Unity is acknowledged, as often as You are magnified, and as often as it is witnessed that You are indeed God. And bless and support our noble master Muhammad as many times as You and Your angels have already blessed him.

And bless and support our noble master Muhammad as many times as all Your creation who have asked for blessings on him, and as many times as all those of Your creation who have not asked for blessings on him. And bless and support our noble master Muhammad in every mountain, grain of sand, and stone.

وصلِّ على سيدنا محمدٍ عددَ الشَّجَرِ وأوراقِها والمَدَرِ وأثقالِها، وصلِّ على سيدنا محمدٍ عددَ كُلِّ سَنةٍ وما تَخْلُقُ فيها وما يَمُوتُ فيها، وصلِّ على سيدنا محمدٍ عددَ ما تَخْلُقُ كُلَّ يوم وما يموتُ فيه إلى يوم القِيَامَةِ، اللهمَّ وصلِّ على سيدنا محمد عددَ السَّحاب الجارِيَةِ ما بَيْنَ السَّمَاءِ والأرضِ وما تُمْطِرُ مِنَ المِيَاهِ، وصلِّ على سيدنا محمدٍ عددَ الرِّياح المُسَخَّرَاتِ في مَشَارِقِ الأرض ومغارِبها وجَوْفِها وقِبْلَتِها، وصلِّ على سيدنا محمدٍ عددَ نُجُوم السَّمَاءِ، وصلِّ على سيدنا محمدٍ عددَ ما خلقتَ في بِحَارِكَ مِنْ الحِيتَانِ والدَّوابِّ والمِيَاهِ والرَّمَالِ وغيرِ ذَلِكَ، وصلِّ على سيدنا محمدٍ عددَ النَّباتِ والحَصَى، وصلِّ على سيدنا محمدٍ عددَ النَّمْلِ، وصلِّ على سيدنا محمدٍ عددَ المِيَاهِ العَذْبَةِ، وصلِّ على سيدنا محمدٍ عددَ المِيَاهِ المِلْحَةِ، وصلِّ على سيدنا محمدٍ عددَ نِعْمَتِكَ على جميع خَلْقِكَ، وصلِّ على سيدنا محمدٍ عددَ نِقْمَتِكَ وعَذَابِكَ على مَنْ كَفَرَ بسيدنا محمدٍ ﷺ، وصلِّ على سيدنا محمدٍ عددَ ما دامَتِ الدُّنْيَا والآخِرَةِ، وصلِّ على سيدنا محمدٍ عددَ ما دامَتِ الخَلَائِقُ في الجَنَّةِ،

Wsalli āla sayyidina Muhammad-in 'adadash-shajari wa auraaqiha wal madari wa athqaaliha Wa salli āla sayyidina Muhammad-in 'adada kulli sanatin-wama takhluku fiha wama yamutu fiha Wa salli āla sayyidina Muhammad-in 'adada matakhluku kulla yaumin wama yamutu fihi ila yaumel-qiyamah

Allahumma wa salli āla sayyidina Muhammad-in 'adadas-sahaabil-jaariyati ma bainas-samaa'i wal-'ardi wama tamturu minal-miyah Wa salli āla sayyidina Muhammad-in 'adada 'ir-riyaahil-musakh-kharaati fi mashaariqil-'ardi wa maghaaribiha wa jaufiha wa qiblatiha Wa salli āla sayyidina Muhammad-in 'adada najuumis-samaa Wa salli āla sayyidina Muhammad-in 'adada ma khalaqta fi biharika minal-hiitaani waddawaa'abi wal miyaahi warrimĀli wa ghairi zaalika Wa salli āla sayyidina Muhammad-in 'adadan-nabaati wal-hasaa Wa salli āla sayyidina Muhammad-in 'adadan-namli Wa salli āla sayyidina Muhamamd-in 'adadal-miyaahil-azbate Wa salli āla sayyidina Muhammad-in 'adadal-miyahil-milhate

Wa salli āla sayyidina Muhammad-in 'adada ni'matika āla jamii 'i khalqi Wa salli āla sayyidina Muhammad-In 'adada niqmatika wa azaabika āla man kafara bisayyidina Muhammad-in wa salli 'alaa sayyidinaa Muhammadin 'adada ma daamatid-dunya wal aakhirah Wa salli āla sayyidina Muhammad-in 'adada ma daamatil-khalaa 'iqu fil-janna

And bless and support our noble master Muhammad in every tree, every one of its leaves, and the soil and its weight. And bless and support our noble master Muhammad as many times as the years have created in them and all that dies in them. And bless and support our noble master Muhammad by the number of all Your creation and all those who die every day until the Day of the Rising-Up. Dear God! Bless and support our noble master Muhammad in every cloud that sails between the Heavens and the Earth, and in every drop of its rain. And bless and support our noble master Muhammad in every swirling wind in the East and West of the Earth and the North and South.

And bless and support our noble master Muhammad as often as there are stars in the night sky. And bless and support our noble master Muhammad as often as all the fish and sea creatures, all the water, all the grains of sand, and whatever else there is. And bless and support our noble master Muhammad in every plant and every stone. And bless and support our noble master Muhammad as many times as there are ants. And bless and support our noble master Muhammad as abundantly as there is fresh water and salty water. And bless and support our noble master Muhammad as much as all Your Grace is shown to the whole of Your creation.

And bless and support our noble master Muhammad as much as Your vengeance and punishment are on those who deny our noble master Muhammad, God's blessings and peace be upon him. And bless and support our noble master Muhammad for as long as the duration of this world and the Hereafter. And bless and support our noble master Muhammad for as long as Your creatures will stay in The Garden.

وصلِّ على سيـدِنا محمدٍ عددَ ما دامَتِ الخَلائِقُ في النَّارِ، وصلِّ على سيدِنا محمدٍ على قَدْرِ ما تُحِبُّهُ وتَرْضَاهُ، وصلِّ على سيدِنا محمدٍ على قَدْرِ ما تُحِبُّكَ ويَرْضَاكَ، وصلِّ على سيدِنا محمدٍ أَبَدَ الآبِدينَ، وأَنْزِلْهُ المُنَزَّلَ المُقَرَّبَ عِنْـدَكَ، وأَعْطِهِ الوَسِيلَةَ والفَضِيلَةَ، والشَّفَاعَةَ والدَّرَجَةَ الرَّفِيعَةَ، والمَقامَ المحمودَ الذي وَعَدْتَهُ، إِنَّكَ لا تُخْلِفُ المِيعَادَ، اللهمَّ إِنِّي أَسْأَلُكَ بِأَنَّكَ مالِكِي وسَيِّدِي ومَوْلايَ وثِقَتِي ورَجَائِي، أَسْأَلُكَ بِحُرْمَةِ الشَّهْرِ الحَرامِ والبَلَدِ الحَرامِ، والمَشْعَرِ الحَرامِ وقَبْرِ نَبِيِّكَ عليهِ السَّلامُ، أن تَهَبَ لِي مِنَ الخَيْرِ ما لا يَعْلَمُ عِلْمَهُ إلا أنتَ، وتَصْرِفَ عَنِّي مِنَ السُّوءِ ما لا يَعْلَمُ عِلْمَهُ إلا أنتَ، اللهمَّ يا مَنْ وَهَبَ لِسيدِنا آدَمَ سيدَنا شِيثاً، ولسيدِنا إبراهيمَ سيدَنا إسمـاعِيلَ وسيدَنا إسْحاقَ، ورَدَّ سيدَنا يُوسُفَ على سيدِنا يَعْقُوبَ، ويا مَنْ كَشَفَ البَـلاءَ عَنْ سيدِنا أَيُّوبَ، ويا مَنْ رَدَّ سيدَنا مُوسَى إلى أُمِّهِ، ويا زَائِدَ سيدِنا الخَضِرِ في عِلْمِهِ، ويا مَنْ وَهَبَ لِسيدِنا دَاوُدَ سيدَنا سُلَيْمَانَ، ولسيدِنا زَكَرِيَّاءَ سيدَنا يَحْيَى، ولسيدتِنا مريمَ سيدَنا عِيسَى، ويا حافِظَ ابنةِ سيدِنا شُعَيْبٍ،

Wa salli āla sayyidina Muhammad-in 'adada ma daamatil-khalaa 'iqu finnar Wa salli āla sayyidina Muhammad-in āla qadri ma tuhibbuhu wa tardhaahu Wa salli āla sayyidina Muhammad-in āla qadri ma yuhibbuka wa yardhaaka wasalli āla Sayyidina Muhammaden ābadal-āabidina waānzilhul manzelal-muqarraba indaka wa āatihil-wasilata walfadilata wash-shafaāta waddarajatarrafiāta walmaqam almhmod alladhi waādtahu innaka la tukhleful-miāad Allahumma inni assāluka beānnaka maliki wasayyidi wamaulaya watheqati warajaā'i assāluka behurmatiesh-shahril-harami walbaladielharami walmashārilharami waqabri nabiyyeka ālaihiessalaamu an tahaba li minaal-khairi ma la yaālamu ilmahu 'illa anta watasrefa ānni minassuuāi mala yaālamu ilmahu 'illa Anta

Allahumma yaaman-wahaba lisaiyidinaa aadama sayyidina shiitha Wali sayyidina Ibraahima saiyidanaa Isma 'iila wa sayyidina Ishaaq Wa radda sayyidina yusufa āla sayyidina ya'quuba wayaa man kashafal-balaa'a 'an sayyidina ayyub Wayaa man radda Musa ila ummihi wayaa zaa'ida sayyidinal-kadhiri fi 'ilmi Wayaa man-wahaba lisayyidina da'uda saiyidina sulaimaana wali sayyidina zakariyya sayyidina yahya Wali sayyidatina maryama sayyidana 'iisa waya hafiz abnat sayidina shueaybin,

And bless and support our noble master Muhammad for as long as Your creatures will stay in The Hellfire. And bless and support our noble master Muhammad equal to Your love for him and Your contentment with him. And bless and support our noble master Muhammad equal to his love for You and his contentment with You. And bless and support our master Muhammad forever and ever and grant him the Closest Access to Your Presence and grant him the Closest Entrance, Pre-eminence, Intercession and Highest Rank. And give him the Most Praised Station You have promised him, for You do not break Your promise.

Dear God! I ask You for the fact that You are my King, Lord, Noble Master, Trust and Hope. I ask You for the honour of the Holy Month, The Holy Sanctuary, the Holy Land, and the grave of Your Prophet (peace be upon him). Bestow upon me goodness, knowledge of which is Yours alone, and that You remove evil from me, knowledge of which You alone know.

Dear God! You gave to our noble master Adam our noble master Seth. And You gave to our noble master Abraham our noble masters Ismail and Isaac. And You returned our noble master Joseph to our noble master Jacob and removed the trials from our noble master Job.

And You returned our noble master Moses to his mother and increased our noble master Khidr in knowledge. And You gave our noble master David our noble master Solomon and to our noble master Zachariah our noble master John the Baptist. And You gave to our Lady Maryam our noble master Jesus, and You preserved the daughter of Shua'ib.

أَسْأَلُكَ أَنْ تُصَلِّيَ على سيدنا محمدٍ وعلى جميع النَّبِيِّينَ والمُرْسَلِينَ، ويا مَنْ وَهَبَ لسيدنا محمدٍ ﷺ الشَّفَاعَةَ والدَّرَجَةَ الرَّفِيعَةَ، أَنْ تَغْفِرَ لِي ذُنُوبِي وتَسْتُرَ لِي عُيُوبِي كُلَّها، وتُجِيرَنِي مِنَ النَّارِ وتُوجِبَ لِي رِضوانَكَ وأَمَانَكَ، وغُفْرانَكَ وإِحْسَانَكَ، وتُمَتِّعَنِي في جَنَّتِكَ مَعَ الذين أَنْعَمْتَ عليهم مِنَ النَّبِيِّينَ والصِّدِّيقِينَ والشُّهَدَاءِ والصَّالِحِينَ، إِنَّكَ على كُلِّ شيءٍ قَدِيرٌ، وصلى اللهُ على سيدنا محمدٍ وعلى آلِهِ ما أَزْعَجَتِ الرِّيَاحُ سَحَاباً رُكَاماً، وذَاقَ كُلُّ ذِي رُوحٍ حِمَاماً، وأَوْصِلِ السَّلامَ لأَهْلِ السَّلامِ في دَارِ السَّلامِ تَحِيَّةً وسَلاماً، "اللهمَّ أَفْرِدْنِي لِمَا خَلَقْتَنِي لَهُ ولا تَشْغَلْنِي بِمَا تَكَفَّلْتَ لِي بِهِ، ولا تَحْرِمْنِي وأَنَا أَسْأَلُكَ ولا تُعَذِّبْنِي وأَنَا أَسْتَغْفِرُكَ" (ثلاثاً)، اللهمَّ صَلِّ على سيدنا محمدٍ وعلى آلِهِ وسَلِّمْ، اللهمَّ إِنِّي أَسْأَلُكَ وأَتَوَجَّهُ إِليكَ بِحَبِيبِكَ المُصْطَفَى عِنْدَكَ، يا حَبِيبَنا يا سيدَنا محمداً، إِنا نَتَوَسَّلُ بِكَ إلى رَبِّكَ، فاشْفَعْ لنا عِنْدَ المَوْلَى العَظِيمِ يا نِعْمَ الرَّسُولُ الطَّاهِرُ،

as'aluka an tusalli 'aala sayyidina Muhammad-in-wa āla jamii'I Nabiyyiina wal mursalina wayaa man-wahaba lisayyidina Muhammad-in sallallahu 'alaihi wa sallama-ashafa'ata waddarajatar-rafi'ata an taghfira li dhunubi watastura-li 'uyubi kullaha watujirani minan-nari watujiba li ridwanaka wa amanaka wa ghufranaka wa ihsanaka wa tumati'aniya fi jannatika ma'alladhina an'amta 'alaihim minan-nabiyyina wassiddiqina wash-shuhada'i wassālihina 'innaka āla kulli sha'in qadir

Wa sallallahu āla sayyidina Muhammad-in-wa āla āalihi ma azāajatir-riyahu sahaban rukaaman wazaqa kulla zie ruuhin himaman waāusil alsalama liāhli essalami fi darissalami tahiyyatan wa salama

Alalhumma āfridni lima khalaqtani lahu wala tushghalni bima takaffalta le bihi wala tahrimni wa āna assāluka wala tu-āzzibni wa āna astaghferuka (Thalaatha) Allahumma salli āla sayyidina Muhammad-iuw-wa āla āalihi wa sallim Allahumma inni as-aluka wa aatawajjahu ilayka bihabiibikal-mustafa indaka ya habiibana ya sayyidina Muhammadu inna natawassalu bika ila rabbika fashfa' lana indal-maulal-aziimi ya ni'mar-rasulut-tahir

I ask You to bless our noble master Muhammad and all the Prophets and Messengers. And You gave to our noble master Muhammad (God's blessings and peace be upon him) the Great Intercession and Lofty Rank. I pray that You forgive all my sins, conceal all my failings, grant me sanctuary from the Fire, and grant me Your Contentment, Safety, and Beneficence. Admit me to Your Garden with those You have favoured, the Prophets, the true ones, the martyrs and the righteous. You are the All-Powerful of all existence.

And the blessings of God be upon our noble master Muhammad and his family as often as the wind has moved and the clouds gathered, and as often as the soul has tasted death. And send peace and salutations to the People of Peace in the House of Peace.

Dear God! Keep me focused on what You created me for, and let me not be occupied with what You are going to provide me, and do not deprive me or punish me, and I seek Your Forgiveness. (repeat three times)

Dear God! Bless and grant peace to our noble master Muhammad and his family. Dear God! I turn my face to You for the sake of Your Beloved Mustafa in Your Presence. O our Beloved, our noble master Muhammad, I seek your mediation to intercede for us with the Great and Noble Lord of all the Worlds. Oh, what a Pure Messenger.

"اللهمَّ شَفِّعْهُ فِينَا بِجَاهِهِ عِنْدَكَ" (ثلاثاً)، واجعلنا مِنْ خيرِ المُصَلِّينَ والمُسَلِّمِينَ عليهِ، ومِنْ خيرِ المُقَرَّبِينَ مِنْهُ والوَارِدِينَ عليهِ، ومِنْ أخْيَارِ المُحِبِّينَ فِيهِ والمَحْبُوبِينَ لَدَيْهِ، وفَرِّحْنَا بِهِ في عَرَصَاتِ القِيَامَةِ، واجعلهُ لَنَا دليلاً إلى جَنَّةِ النَّعِيمِ، بلا مَؤْنَةٍ ولا مَشَقَّةٍ ولا مُنَاقَشَةِ الحِسَابِ واجعلهُ مُقْبِلاً علينا، ولا تجعلهُ غَاضِباً علينا واغفرْ لنَا ولِوالِدِينا، ولِجميع المُسْلِمِينَ الأَحْيَاءِ منهم والمَيِّتِينَ، وآخِرُ دَعْوانَا أَنِ الحمدُ للهِ رَبِّ العَالَمِينَ [يونس: 10].

Allahumma shaffi' hu fiina bijaahihi Indaka Thalaatha Wal 'alna mi khairil-mussalliina wal-musallimmina 'alaih Wa min khairil-muqarrabiina minhu walwaaridiina 'alaihi wa min akhyaaril-muhibbina fiihi wal mahbubiina ladahi Wa farrihna bihi fi ārasatil-qiyama Wajālhu lana dalilan ila jannaten-na'imi bila muānatin wala mashaqqaten wala munaqashatel-hisabi wajālhu muqbelan ālaina wala tajālhu ghadiban ālaina Waghfir lana waliwalidaina wali jami'iel-muslimina al-āhyaāi minhum wal maiyitina wa āakheru daāwana anil-hamdu l'illahi rabbil-āalamin

Dear God! Grant us his intercession for his honour with You. (repeat three times) And let us be the best among those who ask blessings and peace upon him. And make us the best among those near him and who are received by him. And make us the best among those who love him and are loved in his presence. And grant us mercy because of him in the courtyards of the Day of the Rising-Up. And make him a guide for us to the Garden of Bliss, burdenless, trouble-free, and unopposed. And make him welcome us and not be angry with us. And forgive our parents and us and all the submitting ones, living and dead. Our final prayer is, "Praise be to God, Lord of all the Worlds." [Q 10:10]

ابتداء الربع الرابع

فأسألكَ يا اللهُ، يا اللهُ، يا اللهُ، يا حيُّ يا قيومُ، يا ذا الجلالِ والإكرام، لا إلهَ إلا أنتَ سبحانكَ إني كنتُ منَ الظالمينَ، أسألكَ بما حملَ كرسيكَ مِنْ عظمتِكَ وجلالِكَ، وبهائكَ وقدرتِكَ وسلطانِكَ، وبحقِّ أسمائكَ المخزونةِ المكنونةِ المطهرةِ التي لم يطلعْ عليها أحدٌ مِنْ خلقِكَ، وبحقِّ الاسم الذي وضعتَهُ على الليل فأظلمَ وعلى النهار فاستنارَ، وعلى السماواتِ فاستقلتْ وعلى الأرضِ فاستقرتْ، وعلى البحارِ فانفجرتْ وعلى العيونِ فنبعتْ وعلى السحابِ فأمطرتْ، وأسألكَ بالأسماءِ المكتوبةِ في جبهةِ سيدنا جبريلَ عليهِ السلامُ، وبالأسماءِ المكتوبةِ في جبهةِ سيدنا إسرافيلَ عليهِ السلامُ وعلى جميع الملائكةِ، وأسألكَ بالأسماءِ المكتوبةِ حولَ العرشِ، وبالأسماءِ المكتوبةِ حولَ الكرسيِّ، وأسألكَ باسمكَ العظيم الأعظم الذي سميتَ بهِ نفسكَ، وأسألكَ بحقِّ أسمائكَ كلها ما علمتُ منها وما لم أعلمْ، وأسألكَ بالأسماءِ التي دعاكَ بها سيدنا آدمُ عليهِ السلامُ،

Fa āss-āluka ya-Allahu ya-Allahu ya-Allahu ya hayu ya qayumu ya-zaljalali wal-'ikrami la 'ilaha 'illa 'anta subhaanaka 'inni kuntu mina-dhalimin

asāluka bema hamla kursyika men āzmtika wajalalika, wabhāyika waqudrtika wasultanika, wabehqqi asmaāyika almakhzuunatil almaknuwnati almutahrati allty lam yatli' lyha ahdu men khalqika, wbehqi alāsmi alzy wadātahu ly allyli faāzlma wāla alnnhari fastnara, wala alsmawati fastqlat wāla alārdi fastaqarrt, wāla albehari fanfajrat wala aloywni fanabāt wala alssahabi faāmtrt,

Wa as-aluka bil asmaa 'il-maktuubati fi jabhati sayyidina jibriila 'alaihis-salaam Wa bil-asmaa'il-maktuubati fī jabhati sayyidina Israfiila 'alaihis-salaam Wa āla jamii 'il- malaa 'ikati wa as-aluka bil-āsmaāe il-maktuubati haulal-arshi wa bil-asama'il-maktuubati haulal-kursiyyi

Wa as-aluka bismikal-azzmil-aazam'illazi Samaita bihi nafsaka wa as-'aluka bihaqi asma'ika kuliha ma alimtu minha wa-ma lam 'aalam Wa as-'aluka bil-āsmāe'illati daāka biha sayiduna adamu 'alaihis-salam

Beginning of the Fourth Quarter

"So I ask You, dear God, dear God, dear God, O Life, O Everlasting, O Noble Master of Majesty and Honour. There is no deity but You, and Exalted are You. I am one lost in the darkness." [Q 21:87]

I ask You for the sake of those who shoulder Your Throne from Your Might, Majesty, Beauty, Power, and Strength. And by the reality of Your pure, guarded and hidden Names, which no created being can know. And by the truth of Your Name which, when applied to the night, it darkens; when applied to the day, it lightens; when applied to the Heavens, they rise; when applied to the Earth, it becomes firm; when applied to the seas, they flow; when applied to the springs, they burst forth; and when applied to the clouds, they pour down rain.

I ask You by the Names written on the forehead of our noble master Gabriel, peace be upon him. And the Names written on the forehead of our noble master Israfil, peace be upon him. And upon all the angels, I ask You in the Names written around Your Throne and Footstool.

Dear God! I ask You by the most majestic Names You have named Yourself, and by the reality of all Your Names, those I am aware of, and those of which I am unaware. And I ask You, dear God, in the name our noble master Adam, peace be upon him, called You.

وبالأسماءِ التي دعاكَ بها سيدنا نوحٌ عليهِ السلامُ، وبالأسماءِ التي دعاكَ بها سيدنا صالحٌ عليهِ السلامُ، وبالأسماءِ التي دعاكَ بها سيدنا يونسُ عليهِ السلامُ، وبالأسماءِ التي دعاكَ بها سيدنا موسى عليهِ السلامُ، وبالأسماءِ التي دعاكَ بها سيدنا هارونُ عليهِ السلامُ، وبالأسماءِ التي دعاكَ بها سيدنا شعيبٌ عليهِ السلامُ، وبالأسماءِ التي دعاكَ بها سيدنا إبراهيمُ عليهِ السلامُ، وبالأسماءِ التي دعاكَ بها سيدنا إسماعيلُ عليهِ السلامُ، وبالأسماءِ التي دعاكَ بها سيدنا داودُ عليهِ السلامُ، وبالأسماءِ التي دعاكَ بها سيدنا سليمانُ عليهِ السلامُ، وبالأسماءِ التي دعاكَ بها سيدنا زكرياءُ عليهِ السلامُ، وبالأسماءِ التي دعاكَ بها سيدنا يحيى عليهِ السلامُ، وبالأسماءِ التي دعاكَ بها سيدنا يوشعُ عليهِ السلامُ، وبالأسماءِ التي دعاكَ بها سيدنا الخِضرُ عليهِ السلامُ، وبالأسماءِ التي دعاكَ بها سيدنا إلياسُ عليهِ السلامُ،

bil-āsmaāe ''illati daāka biha sayyiduna nuhun 'Alaihis-salam Wa bil-āsmaāe ''illati daāka biha sayyiduna salihun 'Alaihis-salaam Wa bil-āsmaāe ''illati da'aka biha sayyiduna yunus 'Alaihis-salaam Wa bil-āsmaāe ''illati Daāka biha sayyiduna Musa 'Alaihis-salaam

Wa bil-āsmaāe ''illati da 'aka biha sayyiduna haaruuna 'Alaihis-salaam Wa bil-āsmaāe ''illati da'aka biha sayyiduna sha'ibun 'Alaihis-salaam Wa bil-āsmaāe ''illati da'aka biha sayyiduna Ibraahima 'Alaihis-salaam

Wa bil-āsmaāe ''illati da'aka biha sayyiduna Ismaiilu 'Alaihis-salaam Wa bil-asmaa'illati da 'aka biha sayyiduna da uudu 'Alahis-salaam Wa bil-āsmaāe ''illati da'aka biha sayyiduna Sulaimaanu 'Alahis-salaam Wa bil-āsmaāe ''illati da'aka biha sayyiduna Zakariyya 'Alahis-salaam

Wa bil-āsmaāe ''illati Da 'aka biha sayyiduna yahya 'Alaihis-salaam Wa bil-āsmaāe ''illati da 'aka biha sayyiduna yuusha'u 'Alaihis-salaam Wa bil-āsmaāe ''illati da 'aka biha sayyidunal -khadhiru 'Alaihis-salaam Wa bil-āsmaāe ''illati da 'aka biha sayyiduna ilyaasu 'Alahis-salaam

And I ask You, dear God, in the name our noble master Noah, peace be upon him, called You. And I ask You, dear God, in the name our noble master Salih, peace be upon him, called You. And I ask You, dear God, in the name our noble master Jonah, peace be upon him, called You. And I ask You, dear God, in the name our noble master Joseph, peace be upon him, called You.

And I ask You, dear God, in the name our noble master Moses, peace be upon him, called You. And I ask You, dear God, in the name our noble master Aaron, peace be upon him, called You. And I ask You, dear God, in the name our noble master Shuayb, peace be upon him, called You. And I ask You, dear God, in the name our noble master Abraham, peace be upon him, called You.

And I ask You, dear God, in the name our noble master Ishmael, peace be upon him, called You. And I ask You, dear God, in the name our noble master David, peace be upon him, called You. And I ask You, dear God, in the name our noble master Solomon, peace be upon him, called You. And I ask You, dear God, in the name our noble master Zachariah, peace be upon him, called You.

And I ask You, dear God, in the name our noble master John the Baptist, peace be upon him, called You. And I ask You, dear God, in the name our noble master Joshua, peace be upon him, called You. And I ask You, dear God, in the name our noble master Khidr, peace be upon him, called You. And I ask You, dear God, in the name our noble master Elias, peace be upon him, called You.

وبالأسماءِ التي دعاكَ بها سيدنا اليسعُ عليهِ السلامُ، وبالأسماءِ التي دعاكَ بها سيدنا ذو الكفلِ عليهِ السلامُ، وبالأسماءِ التي دعاكَ بها سيدنا عيسى عليهِ السلامُ، وبالأسماءِ التي دعاكَ بها سيدنا محمدٌ ﷺ نبيكَ ورسولكَ، وحبيبكَ وصَفِيُّكَ، يا مَنْ قالَ وقولُهُ الحقُّ، (واللهُ خَلَقَكُمْ وَمَا تَعْمَلُونَ)، ولا يصدرُ عَنْ أحدٍ مِنْ عبيدهِ قولٌ ولا فعلٌ ولا حركةٌ ولا سكونٌ، إلا وقد سبقَ في علمهِ وقضائهِ وقدرهِ كيفَ يكونُ، كما ألهمتني وقضيتَ لي بجمع هذا الكتابِ، ويَسَّرْتَ عَلَيَّ فيه الطريقَ والأسبابَ، ونفيتَ عَنْ قلبي في هذا النبيِّ الكريمِ الشكَّ والارتيابَ، وغَلَّبْتَ حبهُ عندي على حبِّ جميع الأقرباءِ والأحباءِ، أسألُكَ يا اللهُ، يا اللهُ، يا اللهُ، أنْ ترزقني وكلَّ مَنْ أحبهُ واتبعهُ شفاعتهُ ومرافقتهُ يومَ الحسابِ، مِنْ غيرِ مناقشةٍ ولا عذابٍ ولا توبيخٍ ولا عتابٍ، وأنْ تغفرَ لي ذنوبي وتسترَ لي عيوبي يا وهاب يا غفار، وأنْ تنعمني بالنظرِ إلى وجهكَ الكريمِ في جملةِ الأحبابِ يومَ المزيدِ والثوابِ، وأنْ تتقبلَ مني عملي،

Wa bil-āsmaāe ''illati da 'aka biha sayyidunal -yasa'u 'Alaihis-salaam Wa bil-āsmaāe ''illati da'aka biha sayyiduna zul-kifli 'Alaihis-slaam Wa bil-āsmaāe ''illati da'aka biha sayyiduna 'isa 'Alaihis-salaam Wa bil-āsmaāe ''illati da'aka biha sayyiduna Muhammad-un sallallahu 'alahi wa sallama nabiyyuka Wa rasuuluka wa habiibuka wa safiyyuka

yaa man qala wa qauluhulhaqqu wallahu khalaqakum wama taāmaluuna wala yasduru ānn ahaden min ābidihi qaulun wala fi'lun wala harakatun wala sukuunun Ella waqad sabaqa fi ilmihi wa qadaāihi waqadrihi kaifa yakunu

kma ālhmtny wqadyta ly bejmi hdha alktabi, wyasarta alaya fehe altryqa walasbaba, wnfyta n qlby fy hdha alnbyi alkrymi alshka walartyaba, wghalabta hbhu ndy ly hbi jmyi alaqrbai walahbai,

asāluka ya allhu, ya allhu, ya allhu, an trzqny wakla man ahbahu wattbhu shfāthu wamrafqthu yaoma alhesabi, men ghayri munaqshtin wla azabin wla twbykhin wla Etabin, wān taghfera ly zunwby watstura ly āywbi ya wahab ya gahffar,

Wa ān tuneāmuni binnazri ila wajhikal-karimi fi jumlatil-ahbabi yaumal-mazidi wath-thawab Wa ān taqabbala minni āmali

And I ask You, dear God, in the name our noble master Esau, peace be upon him, called You. And I ask You, dear God, in the name our noble master Dhul Kifl, peace be upon him, called You. And I ask You, dear God, in the name our noble master Jesus, son of Mary, peace be upon him, called You. And I ask You, dear God, in the name our noble master Muhammad, Your Prophet, Messenger and Selected One, the blessings and peace of God be upon him, called You. O He Who says, and His word is true, "God created you and what you do" [Q 37:96]. No word, action, movement or inactivity originates from His servants, but it has already been pre-ordained in His knowledge, Destiny and Decree.

I was inspired and destined to compile this book. And the means and method were facilitated for me. All doubts and misgivings about Your munificent Prophet, peace be upon him, were removed from my heart. And love for him overcame the love for all my loved ones and relatives.

I ask You, dear God, dear God, dear God, that You grant me, and all who love him and follow him, his intercession and his company on the Day of Judgment, without any dispute, punishment, reproach or censure. And forgive my sins and conceal my failings, dear Granter, dear Forgiver.

Dear God! Favour me with a glance at Your munificent Face among the dear ones on the Day of Reward and More Reward. And accept my actions.

وَأَنْ تَعفو عَمَّا أحاطَ عِلمكَ بِهِ مِنْ خطيئتي ونِسياني وزَلَلي، وأَنْ تبلغني مِنْ زيارةِ قبرِهِ والتسليم عليهِ وعلى صاحِبيهِ غايةَ أمَلي، بِمِنكَ وفضلِكَ وجودِكَ وكرمِكَ، يا رؤوفُ، يا رحيمُ، يا وليُّ، وأَنْ تُجازيهُ عني وعَنْ كُلِّ مَنْ آمَنَ بِهِ واتبعهُ مِنْ المُسلمينَ والمسلماتِ، الأحياءِ مِنهمْ والأمواتِ، أفضلَ وأتمَّ وأعَمَّ ما جازيتَ بِهِ أحداً مِنْ خلقِكَ، يا قويُّ، يا عزيزُ، يا عَليُّ، وأسألُكَ اللهمَّ بِحقِّ ما أقسمتُ بِهِ عليكَ، أنْ تُصَلِّيَ على سيدِنا محمدٍ وعلى آلِ سيدِنا محمدٍ عَدَدَ ما خلقتَ مِنْ قبلِ أنْ تكونَ السماءُ مبنيةً والأرضُ مدحيةً، والجبالُ علويةً والعيونُ منفجرةً، والبحارُ مسخرةً والأنهارُ منهمرةً، والشمسُ مضحيةً والقمرُ مضيئاً والنجمُ منيراً ولا يعلمُ أحدٌ حيثُ تكونُ إلا أنتَ، وأنْ تُصَلِّيَ عليهِ وعلى آلِهِ عَدَدَ كلامكَ، وأنْ تُصَلِّيَ عليهِ وعلى آلِهِ عَدَدَ آياتِ القرآنِ وحروفِهِ وأنْ تُصَلِّيَ عليهِ وعلى آلِهِ عَدَدَ مَنْ يُصَلِّي عليهِ، وأنْ تُصَلِّيَ عليهِ وعلى آلِهِ عَدَدَ مَنْ لم يصلِّ عليهِ،

wa 'an ta'afuwa amma ahata ilmuka bihi min khati'ati wanisyani wazalali wa 'an tuballighani min ziyarati qabrihi wattaslimi 'Alaihi wa āla sahibaihi ghayata 'amali bimannika wa fadlika wa judika wa karamika ya ra'ufu ya rahimu ya waliy

wa ān tujazyhi āny wān kuli man amana behi wattbāhu men alumslemyna walmuslemati, alahyāi menhum walāmwati, āfdla wātma wāmma ma jazayta behi ahdan men khalqeka, ya qawyu, ya āzyzu, ya āliu,

wa as'aluka allahumma bihaqqi ma 'aqsamtu bihi 'alaika 'an tusalliya āla sayyidina Muhammad-iuw-wa āla Āli sayyidina Muhammad-in 'adada maa khalaqta min qabli 'an takuunas-samaa'u Mabniyatan-wa ardu madhhiyyatan-wal jibaalu 'ulwiyyataw-wal 'uyuunu munfajirataw wal beharu musakharatan wal ānharu munhamiratan wash-shamsu mudhiyatan wal qamaru mudii'an wannajmu muniran wala yāālamu āhadun haithu takunu 'illa anta

wa 'an tusalliya 'alaihi wa āla āalihi 'adada kalaamika Wa 'an tusalliya 'alaihi wa āla āalihi 'adada 'aayatil-qur'ani wahurufihi wa 'an tusalliya 'alaihi wa āla āalihi 'adada man yusalli 'alaihi wa 'an tusalliya 'alaihi wa āla āalihi 'adada man-lam-yusalli 'alaihi

And annul all my failings, lapses and mistakes which You have encompassed with Your Omniscience. And grant me a visit to the tomb of our noble master Muhammad, peace be upon him, and the tombs of his Companions, to the limit of my hope for Your Favour, Grace, Generosity and Nobility, O Gracious, O Merciful, O Sovereign.

And reward him, dear God, on my behalf, and on behalf of every submitting man and woman, living or dead, who believe in him and follow him. Reward him better than, more perfect than, and more extensively than You have rewarded any other one from Your creation, O Most Powerful, O Mighty, O Sublime.

And I ask You, dear God, by the reality of my swearing by You, that You bless our noble master Muhammad and his family in all You created before the sky was built, the Earth spread out, the mountains raised, the springs burst forth, the seas flowed, the rivers streamed, the sun shone, the moon beamed, and the stars twinkled. And no one knew where You were but You.

And bless and support him and his family as many times as is the number of Your words. And bless and support him and his family as many times as there are letters and verses in Your Holy Quran. And bless and support him and his family as many times as those who ask You to bless him and his family, and as many times as those who do not ask You to bless him.

وأَنْ تُصَلِّيَ عليهِ وعلى آلِهِ ملءَ أرضكَ، وأَنْ تُصَلِّيَ عليهِ وعلى آلِهِ عَدَدَ ما جرى بهِ القلمُ في أمِّ الكتابِ، وأَنْ تُصَلِّيَ عليهِ وعلى آلِهِ عَدَدَ ما خلقتَ في سبعِ سماواتِكَ، وأَنْ تُصَلِّيَ عليهِ وعلى آلِهِ عَدَدَ ما أنتَ خالقهُ فيهنَّ إلى يومِ القيامةِ، في كلِّ يومٍ ألفَ مرةٍ. وأَنْ تُصَلِّيَ عليهِ وعلى آلِهِ عَدَدَ قطرِ المطرِ، وكلِّ قطرةٍ قطرتْ منْ سمائكَ إلى أرضكَ، منْ يومِ خلقتَ الدنيا إلى يومِ القيامةِ، في كلِّ يومٍ ألفَ مرةٍ.

wa 'an tusalliya 'alaihi wa āla āalihi mil'a ardika wa 'an Tusalliya 'alaihi wa āla āalihi 'adada ma jara bihil-qalamu fi 'umil-kitabi Wa 'an tusalliya 'alaihi wa āla āalihi 'adada ma khalaqta fi-sab'i samawatika Wa 'an tusalliya 'alaihi wa āla āalihi 'adada ma anta khaaliquhu fihinna ila yaumil-qiyamate fi kulli yaumin alfa marrah Wa 'an tusalliya 'alaihi wa āla āalihi 'adada qatril-matari wa kulli qatratin qatarat mi sama'ika ila ardika min-yaumi khalaqtad-dunya ila yaumil-qiyamate fi kulli yaumin alfa marrah

And bless and support him and his family as much as the Earth contains, and bless him and his family by the number of words Your Pen has written in the Mother of the Book.

And bless and support him and his family as much as You have created in Your Seven Heavens, and as much as You will create in them until the Day of the Rising-Up, and every day a thousand times.

And bless and support him and his family in every single drop of rain and in all the rain that has ever fallen from Your sky to Your Earth from the Day You created this world until the Day of the Rising-Up, and every day a thousand times.

الحِزبُ السابعُ ورد يومِ الأحدِ

بسمِ اللهِ الرحمنِ الرحيمِ

وأنْ تُصَلِّي عليهِ وعلى آلهِ عَدَدَ مِنْ سبحكَ وقدسكَ، وسجدَ لكَ وعظمكَ، مِنْ يوم خلقتَ الدنيا إلى يوم القيامةِ، في كلِّ يوم ألفَ مرةٍ، وأنْ تُصَلِّي عليهِ وعلى آلهِ عَدَدَ كل سنةٍ خلقتهمْ فيها، مِنْ يوم خلقتَ الدنيا إلى يوم القيامةِ، في كلِّ يوم ألفَ مرةٍ، وأنْ تُصَلِّي عليهِ وعلى آلهِ عَدَدَ السحاب الجاريةِ، وأنْ تُصَلِّي عليهِ وعلى آلهِ عَدَدَ الرياح الذاريةِ، مِنْ يوم خلقتَ الدنيا إلى يوم القيامةِ، في كلِّ يوم ألفَ مرةٍ، وأنْ تُصَلِّي عليهِ وعلى آلهِ عَدَدَ ما هبتِ الرياحُ عليهِ، وحركتهُ مِنَ الأغصانِ والأشجارِ، وأوراقِ الثمارِ والأزهارِ، عَدَدَ ما خلقتَ على قرارِ أرضكَ وما بينَ سماواتكَ، مِنْ يوم خلقتَ الدنيا إلى يوم القيامةِ، في كلِّ يوم ألفَ مرةٍ، وأنْ تُصَلِّي عليهِ وعلى آلهِ عَدَدَ أمواج بحاركَ، مِنْ يوم خلقتَ الدنيا إلى يوم القيامةِ، في كلِّ يوم ألفَ مرةٍ،

wa 'an tusalliya 'alaihi wa āla āālihii 'adada man sabbahaka waqaddasaka wasajada laka 'azzamaka min-yaumi khalaqtad-dunya ila yaumil-qiyaamati fi kulli yaumin alfa marrah Wa 'an tusalliya 'alaihi wa āla āalihi 'adada kulli sanaten khalaqtahum fiha min yaumi khalaqtad-dunya ila yaumil-qiyaamati fi kulli yaumin alfa marrah

wa 'an tusalliya 'alaihi wa āla 'ālihi 'adadas-sahabil-jaariya wa 'an tusalliya 'alaihi wa āla āalihi 'adada Arriyaahiz-zaariyati min-yaumi khalaqtad-dunyaa ila yaumil-qiyaamati fi kulli yaumin alfa marrah

wa 'an tusalliya 'alaihi wa āla āalihi 'adada maa habbatir-riyaahu 'alaihi waharraq kathu minal-aghsaani wal-ashjaari wa-auraaqith-thimari wal-azhaari wa 'adada maa khalaqta āla qaraari ardika wama baina samawatika min-yaumi khalaqtad-dunya ila yaumil-qiyaamati fi kulli yaumin alfa marrah

wa 'an tusalliya 'alaihi wa āla āalihi 'adada amwaaji beharka min-yaumi khalaqtad-dunya ila yaumil-qiyaamati fi kulli yaumin alfa marrah

Sunday - The Seventh Part

BISMILLA HIRRAHMAAN NIRRAHIM

And bless and support him and his family as many times as You are glorified by Your worshippers and prostrating servants who exalt You, from the time You created this world until the Day of the Rising-Up, and every day a thousand times. And bless and support him and his family as many times as the years in which You created those who glorify You, from the time You created this world until the Day of the Rising-Up, and every day a thousand times.

And bless and support him and his family in every gusting wind and sweeping cloud from the Day of creating this world until the Day of the Rising-Up, and every day a thousand times.

And bless and support him and his family in every tree's movements and every branch, leaf, fruit and flower stirred by the wind. And in every wind-stirred action of all those created on the Earth and within Your Heavens from the time of creating this world until the Day of the Rising-Up, and every day a thousand times.

And bless and support him and his family in every ocean wave from the time You created this world until the Day of the Rising-Up, and every day a thousand times.

وأنْ تُصَلِّيَ عليهِ وعلى آلِهِ عَدَدَ الرملِ والحصى وكلِّ حجرٍ ومدرٍ خلقتهُ في مشارقِ الأرضِ ومغاربِها، سهلِها وجبالِها وأودِيَتِها، منْ يومِ خلقتَ الدنيا إلى يومِ القيامةِ، في كلِّ يومٍ ألفَ مرةٍ، وأنْ تُصَلِّيَ عليهِ وعلى آلِهِ عَدَدَ نباتِ الأرضِ في قِبلَتِها وجوفِها، وشرقِها وغربِها، وسهلِها وجبالِها، منْ شَجَرٍ وثَمَرٍ وأوراقٍ وزَرعٍ، وجميعِ ما أخرجتْ وما يُخرجُ منها منْ نباتِها وبركاتِها، منْ يومِ خلقتَ الدنيا إلى يومِ القيامةِ، وأنْ تُصَلِّيَ عليهِ وعلى آلِهِ عَدَدَ ما خلقتَ منَ الإنسِ والجنِّ والشياطينِ، وما أنتَ خالقهُ منهمْ إلى يومِ القيامةِ، في كلِّ يومٍ ألفَ مرةٍ، وأنْ تُصَلِّيَ عليهِ وعلى آلِهِ عَدَدَ كلِّ شعرةٍ في أبدانِهمْ ووجوهِهمْ وعلى رؤوسِهمْ، منذُ خلقتَ الدنيا إلى يومِ القيامةِ، في كلِّ يومٍ ألفَ مرةٍ، وأنْ تُصَلِّيَ عليهِ وعلى آلِهِ عَدَدَ أنفاسِهمْ وألفاظِهمْ وألحاظِهمْ، منْ يومِ خلقتَ الدنيا إلى يومِ القيامةِ، في كلِّ يومٍ ألفَ مرةٍ، وأنْ تُصَلِّيَ عليهِ وعلى آلِهِ عَدَدَ طيرانِ الجنِّ وخفقانِ الإنسِ، منْ يومِ خلقتَ الدنيا إلى يومِ القيامةِ، في كلِّ يومٍ ألفَ مرةٍ،

wa 'an tusalliya 'alaihi Wa āla āalihi 'adadar-ramli wal-hasaa waqulli hajrin-wamadarin khalaqtahu fi mashaariqil-'ardi wamaghaaribiha sahliha wajibaaliha wa-audiyatiha min-yaumi khalaqtad-dunyaa ila yaumil-qiyaamati fi kulli yaumin alfa marrah

Wa 'an tusalliya 'alaihi wa āla āalihi 'adada nabatil-'ardi fi qiblatiha wajaufiha washarqiha wagharbiha wasahliha wajibaliha min shajarin wa thamarin wa auraqin wa zar'in wa jami'i ma akhrajat wa ma yakhruju minha min-nabatiha wabarakatiha min yaumi khlaqtad-dunya ila yaumil-qiyaamati fi kulli yaumin alfa marrah

Wa 'an tusalliya 'alaihi Wa āla āalihi 'adada maa khalaqta minal-insi wal-jinni wash-shayaatini wamaa anta khaaliquhu minhum ila yaumil-qiyaamati fi kulli yaumin alfa marrah Wa 'an tusalliya 'alaihi wa āla āalihi 'adada kulli sha'ratin fi abdaanihim wa ujuunihim wa āla ru- 'usihim munzu khalaqtad-dunyaa ila yaumil-qiyaamati fi kulli yaumin alfa marrah

Wa 'an tusloliya 'alaihi wa āla āalihi 'adada an-faasihim waal-faazihim waal-hazihim min-yaumi khalaqtad-dunyaa ila yaumi-lqiyamati fi kulli yaumin alfa marrah Wa 'an tusalliya 'alaihi wa āla āalihi 'adada tairaanil-jinni wakhafaqaani All-inssi miw-yaumin khalaqtaddunya ila yaumil-qiyamati fi kulli yaumin alfa marrah.

And bless and support him and his family as many as the number of grains of sand, every stone, rock and cloud You have created in the East and the West, on the lowlands and the highlands and in the valleys from the Day You created this world until the Day of the Rising-Up, every day a thousand times.

And bless and support him and his family in every tree, fruit, leaf and plant of the Earth, in the North and South, in the East and West, on the plains, on the mountains, and in everything You have produced from it. And bless him in everything You will cause to grow from the time You created this world until the Day of the Rising-Up, every day a thousand times.

And bless and support him and his family as many times as the number of human beings, jinn and devils You had created from when You created this world until the Day of the Rising-Up, every day a thousand times. And bless and support him and his family as many as the number of hairs on their bodies, faces, and heads since the time You created this world until the Day of the Rising-Up, every day a thousand times. And bless and support him and his family as many as the number of their breaths, utterances and every one of their glances, from when You created this world until the Day of the Rising-Up, every day a thousand times. And bless and support him and his family as many as the number of flights of the jinn and number of human heartbeats from when You created this world until the Day of the Rising-Up, every day a thousand times.

وأنْ تُصَلِّي عليهِ وعلى آلهِ عَدَدَ كلِّ بهيمةٍ خلقتها على أرضِكَ صغيرةً أو كبيرةً، في مشارقِ الأرضِ ومغاربِها، مما عُلِمَ وما لا يَعْلَمُ علمهُ إلا أنتَ، مِنْ يوم خلقتَ الدنيا إلى يوم القيامةِ، في كلِّ يوم ألفَ مرةٍ، وأنْ تُصَلِّي عليهِ وعلى آلهِ عَدَدَ مَنْ صلى عليهِ، وعَدَدَ مَنْ لم يُصَلِّ عليهِ، وعَدَدَ مَنْ يُصَلِّي عليهِ إلى يوم القيامةِ، في كلِّ يوم ألفَ مرةٍ، وأنْ تُصَلِّي عليهِ وعلى آلهِ عَدَدَ الأحياءِ والأمواتِ، وعَدَدَ ما خلقتَ مِنْ حيتانٍ وطيرٍ ونملٍ ونحلٍ وحشراتٍ، وأنْ تُصَلِّي عليهِ وعلى آلهِ في الليل إذا يغشى والنهارِ إذا تجلى، وأنْ تُصَلِّي عليهِ وعلى آلهِ في الآخرةِ والأولى، وأنْ تُصَلِّي عليهِ وعلى آلهِ منذُ كانَ في المهدِ صبياً، إلى أنْ صارَ كهلاً مهدياً، فقبضتهُ إليكَ مرضياً لتبعثهُ شفيعاً، وأنْ تُصَلِّي عليهِ وعلى آلهِ عَدَدَ خلقكَ ورضاءَ نفسكَ، وزنةَ عرشكَ ومدادَ كلماتِكَ، وأنْ تُعْطِيهُ الوسيلةَ والفضيلةَ، والدرجةَ الرفيعةَ والحوضَ المورودَ، والمقامَ المحمودَ والعزَّ الممدودَ، وأنْ تُعَظِّمَ برهانهُ وأنْ تُشَرِّفَ بنيانهُ وأنْ تَرْفَعَ مكانهُ، وأنْ تستعملنا يا مولانا بسنتهِ وأنْ تميتنا على ملتهِ،

wa 'ann tusalliya 'alaihi wa āla āālihi'adada kulli bahiimatin khalaqtaha āla ardika saghiratan aw qabiratan fi mashariqi-l'ardi wa magharibiha mimma 'ulima wa mimma la ya'lamu 'ilmahu 'illa 'anta min yaumi khalaqtad-dunya ila yaumi-lqiyamati fi kulli yaumin alfa marrah Wa 'an tusalliya 'alaihi wa āla āalihi 'adada man-lamsalli'alaihi wa 'adad man lam yusalli 'alaihi 'adada man yusalli 'alaihi ila yaumil-qiyaamati fi kulli yaumin alfa marrah

wa 'an tusalliya 'alaihi wa āla āalihi 'adadal-ahyaa'i Wal amwaati wa 'adada ma khalaqta minn hitaani-wa tairi-wa namli-wa nahli-wa hasharaat Wa 'an tusalliya 'alaihi wa āla āalihi f'illaili 'idha yaghsha wannahaari 'idha tajalla Wa 'an tusalliya 'alaihi wa āla āalihi fil-aakhirati wal uula

wa 'an tusalliya 'alaihi wa āla āalihi munzu kaana fil-mahdi sabiyyan ila 'an sora kahlam-mahdiyyan faqabaztahu ilaika 'adlam-m'ardiyyal-litab 'athahu shafi'ann hafiyya wa 'an tusalliya 'alaihi wa āla ālihi 'adada khalqika wa rida nafsika wazinata arshika wamidaada kalimaatika wa 'an tu'tiyahul-wasilata wal fadilata waddarajatar-rafi'ata wal haudal-mauruda walmaqamal-mahmuda wal 'izzal-mamduda wa-'an tu'azima burhanahu wa-'an tusharrifa bunyanahu wa-'an tarfa'a makanuhu wa 'an tasta'milana ya maulana bisunatihi wa 'an tumitana āla millatih

And bless and support him and his family by the number of large and small creatures You have created in the West and the East of Your Earth, those that are known and those of whom knowledge is Yours alone, from the time You created this world until the Day of the Rising-Up, every day a thousand times. And bless and support him and his family as many times as those who have requested blessings upon him, as many times as those who have not asked, and as many times as those who will ask until the Day of the Rising-Up, and every day a thousand times.

And bless and support him and his family by the number of every soul alive and dead, in every bird, ant, bee, insect and beast You have created. And bless and support him and his family on every darkening night and brightening day. And bless and support him and his family in the Hereafter in the First and the Last. And bless and support him and his family from when he was in the cradle until his maturity, when You took him to Yourself, justly contented, and until You finally send him as a welcome intercessor.

And bless and support him and his family in all of Your creation, to the extent of Your contentment, the weight of Your Throne will have designated, and as much as the ink for Your Words is. And grant him the Closest Access, Pre-eminence, Highest Rank, the Oft-visited Pool, the Most Praised Station, and the Greatest Honour. And ennoble his stature, enhance his proof, raise his station, and make us, dear Lord, follow his way and religion until we die.

وأَنْ تحشرنا في زمرتهِ وتحتَ لوائهِ، وأَنْ تجعلنا مِنْ رفقائهِ وأَنْ تُوردنا حوضهُ، وأَنْ تَسْقِيَنا بكأسهِ وأَنْ تَنْفَعَنا بمحبتهِ، وأَنْ تَتُوبَ علينا وأَنْ تُعافِيَنا من جميعِ البلاءِ والبلواءِ والفتنِ، ما ظهرَ منها وما بطنَ، وأَنْ ترحمنا، وأَنْ تَعْفُوَ عنا، وتَغْفِرَ لنا ولجميعِ المؤمنينَ والمؤمناتِ، والمسلمينَ والمسلماتِ، الأحياءِ منهمْ والأمواتِ، والحمدُ للهِ ربِّ العالمينَ، وهو حسبي ونعمَ الوكيلُ، ولا حولَ ولا قوةَ إلا باللهِ العليِّ العظيمِ. اللهمَّ صلِّ على سيدنا محمدٍ وعلى آلِ سيدنا محمدٍ ما سجعتِ الحمائمُ وحمتِ الحوائمُ، وسرحتِ البهائمُ ونفعتِ التمائمُ، وشُدَّتِ العمائمُ ونَمَتِ النوائمُ، اللهمَّ صلِّ على سيدنا محمدٍ وعلى آلِ سيدنا محمدٍ ما أبلجَ الإصباحُ وهَبَّتِ الرياحُ، ودَبَّتِ الأشباحُ وتعاقبَ الغدوُّ والرواحُ، وتُقُلِّدَتِ الصفاحُ واعْتُقِلَتِ الرماحُ، وصَحَّتِ الأجسادُ والأرواحُ، اللهمَّ صلِّ على سيدنا محمدٍ وعلى آلِ سيدنا محمدٍ ما دارتِ الأفلاكُ ودَجَتِ الأحلاكُ وسَبَّحَتِ الأملاكُ،

wa ānn tahshurana fi zumratihi watahta liwaā'ihii wa 'an taj'alana min-rufaqaa'ihi wa 'an turidana haudahu wa 'an tasqiyana bika'sihi wa 'an tanfa'ana bimahabbatihi wa 'an tatuuba 'alaina wa 'an tu'afiyana minn jami'il-bala'i walbalwa'i wa-lfitani ma zahara minha wa-ma batana wa-'an tarhamana wa-'an ta'fuwa 'anna Watagh-firalana wali jamii'il mu'minina wal mu'minaati wal muslimina wal muslimaatil-ahyaa'i minhum wal āmwaati wal hamdul'illahi rabbil-āalalamina Wahuwa hasbi wani'malwakilu wala haula wala quwwata 'illa b'illahil-āliyyil-'azim

Allahumma salli āla sayyidina Muhammad-in-wa āla Āli sayidina Muhammad-in ma saja'atil-hama'imu wahamati-lhawa'imu wasarahatil-baha'imu wanafa'atit-tama'imu washuddatil-'ama'imu wanamatil-nawa'imu

Allahumma salli āla sayyidina Muhammad-in-wa āla Āli sayyidina Muhammad-in-maa ablajal-isbaahu Wa habbatir-riyaahu wa dabbatil-ashbaahu wa ta 'aqabal-ghuduw-wu warrawaahu watuqullidatis-sifaahu wa'tuqilatir-rimaahu wa sahhatil-ajsadu wal-arwah

Allahumma salli āla sayyidina Muhammad-iuw-wa āla Āli sayyidina Muhammad-im-ma daaratil-aflaaku wa dajatil-ahlaaku wa sabbahtil-amlaak

And resurrect us in his company, under his banner. And put us in his assembly, water us at his Pool, and have us drink from his cup. Grant us his love, accept our repentance, help us avoid trials and tribulations, and inner and outer discord. And grant us Your mercy, pardon us and forgive us along with all the submitting men and women and believing men and women, the living and the dead. And the totality of Grace belongs to God, the Lord of all the worlds.

And He suffices me. He is the best of Protectors, and no power is there, nor strength, save with God, the Most High, the Great.

Dear God! Bless and support our noble master Muhammad and his family in the cooing of doves and circling of beasts around waterholes, the grazing of cattle, wearing of amulets, winding of turbans, and the sleeping of slumberers.

Dear God! Bless and support our noble master Muhammad and his family in the breaking dawns, the blowing winds, the creeping shade, the following mornings and evenings, the girding-on of armour, the impounding of lances, and the healing of bodies and souls.

Dear God! Bless and support our noble master Muhammad and his family in the rotation of the celestial bodies and the overshadowing of darkness, and as the angels glorify You.

اللهمَّ صلِّ على سيدِنا محمدٍ وعلى آلِ سيدنا محمدٍ كما صليتَ على سيدنا إبراهيمَ، وبارك على سيدنا محمدٍ وعلى آلِ سيدنا محمدٍ كما باركتَ على سيدنا إبراهيمَ في العالمينَ إنكَ حميدٌ مجيدٌ، اللهمَّ صلِّ على سيدنا محمدٍ وعلى آلِ سيدنا محمدٍ ما طَلَعَتِ الشمسُ وما صُلِّيَتِ الخمسُ، وما تأَلَّقَ بَرْقٌ و تَدَفَّقَ وَدْقٌ وما سَبَّحَ رَعْدٌ، اللهمَّ صلِّ على سيدنا محمدٍ وعلى آلِ سيدنا محمدٍ ملءَ السماواتِ والأرضِ وملءَ ما بينهُما وملءَ ما شِئْتَ منْ شيءٍ بعدُ، اللهمَّ كما قامَ بأعباءِ الرسالةِ، واستنقذَ الخلقَ منَ الجهالةِ، وجاهدَ أهلَ الكفرِ والضلالةِ، ودعا إلى توحيدِكَ، وقاسى الشدائدَ في إرشادِ عبيدكَ، فأعطهِ اللهمَّ سؤلهُ وبَلِّغْهُ مأمولهُ، وآتهِ الوسيلةَ والفضيلةَ والدرجةَ الرفيعةَ، وابعثهُ المقامَ المحمودَ الذي وعدتهَ، إنكَ لا تخلفُ الميعادَ، اللهمَّ واجعلنا منَ المتبعينَ لشريعتهِ، المتصفينَ بمحبتهِ، المهتدينَ بهديهِ وسيرتهِ، وتوفنا على سنتهِ ولا تحرمنا فضلَ شفاعتهِ، واحشرنا في أتباعهِ الغرِّ المحجلينَ، وأشياعهِ السابقينَ، وأصحابِ اليمينَ، يا أرحمَ الراحمينَ،

Allahumma salli āla sayyidina Muhammad-iuw-wa āla Āli sayyidina Muhammad-in kama sallaita āla sayyidina Ibraahima wa barik āla sayyidina Muhammad-in-wa āla Āli sayyidina Muhammad-in kama baarakta āla sayyidina Ibraahima fil-'alamiina innaka hamiidun-majid

Allahumma salli āla sayyidina Muhammad-iuw-wa āla Āli sayyidina Muhammad-im-ma tala-'atish-shamsu wa-ma suliyatil-khamsu wama ta-'allaqa barqun wa-tadaffaqa wadqun wa-ma sabbaha ra'du

Allahumma salli āla sayyidina Muhammad-iuw-wa āla Āli sayyidina Muhammad-im-mil'a assamawati wal 'ardi wa-mil'au ma bainahuma wa-mil'au ma shi'ta minn shai'in ba'du

Allahumma kama qama bi-'aaba'a 'irrisalati wa-stanqazal-khalqa minal-jahalati wa jahada ahlal-kufri wa-dalalati wad'aa ila tauhiidika waqaasash-shadaa 'ida fi irshaadi 'abiidika fa'aatih'illa-humma S'ulahu waballighu ma'amulahu wa 'atihil-wasilata wal-fadilata waddarajatar-rafi'ata wa-bathhul-maqamal mahmudalladhi wa 'adtahu 'innaka la tukhliful-mi'aad

Allahumma wa-j'alna minal-muttab'iina lishari'atihil-muttasifina bima-habbatihi-lmuhtadina bihadyihi wasiratihi watawafana āla sunnatihi wala tahrimna fadla shafa'atihi wahshurna fi atba'ihil-ghurril-muhajjalina wa ashya'ihis-sabiqina wa as-habil-yamini ya arhamar-rahimin

Dear God! Bless and support our noble master Muhammad and his family, just as You blessed our noble master Abraham. And sanctify our noble master Muhammad just as You sanctified our noble master Abraham in all the worlds. You are indeed the Praiseworthy, the Mighty. Dear God! Bless and support our noble master Muhammad and his family in the rising sun, performing the five daily prayers, in lightning strikes, during the falling rain, and the pealing of thunder.

Dear God! Bless and support our noble master Muhammad and his family to the fullness of Your Heavens and Earth, the fullness between them, and the fullness of whatever You may have created elsewhere. Dear God! He bore the responsibility of Your Message and delivered creation from ignorance. And he struggled against the people of disbelief and error, called to Your Unity, and endured hardships in guiding Your servants.

Dear God! Grant him his wishes, fulfil his hopes, give him the Closest Access, the Pre-eminence, the Loftiest Rank, and appoint him to the Most Praised Station You have promised him, for You never break Your promise. Dear God! Make us the followers of his law, known for our love of him, guided by his guidance and life. And allow us to die following his way, and do not deny us the favour of his intercession. And resurrect us among his followers, shining with light, and his foremost Companions, and the Companions of the Right, O the Most Merciful of the Merciful.

اللهمَّ صلِّ على ملائكتكَ والمقربينَ، وعلى أنبيائكَ والمرسلينَ، وعلى أهلِ طاعتكَ أجمعينَ، واجعلنا بالصلاةِ عليهم منَ المرحومينَ، اللهمَّ صلِّ على سيدنا محمدٍ المبعوثِ منْ تِهَامَةَ، والآمرِ بالمعروفِ والاستقامةِ، والشفيعِ لأهلِ الذنوبِ في عرصاتِ القيامةِ، اللهمَّ أَبْلغْ عنَّا نَبِيَّنا وشَفِيعَنا وحَبِيبَنا أفضلَ الصلاةِ والتسليمِ، وابعثهُ المقامَ المحمودَ الكريمَ، وآتِهِ الوسيلةَ والفضيلةَ والدرجةَ الرفيعةَ التي وعدتهُ في الموقفِ العظيمِ، وصلِّ اللهمَّ عليهِ صلاةً دائمةً متصلةً تتوالى وتدومُ، اللهمَّ صلِّ عليهِ وعلى آلِهِ ما لاحَ بارقٌ وذَرَّ شارقٌ، ووقبَ غاسقٌ وانهمرَ وادقٌ، وصلِّ عليهِ وعلى آلِهِ ملءَ اللوحِ والفضاءِ، ومثلَ نجومِ السماءِ، وعَدَدَ القطرِ والمطرِ والحصى، وصلِّ عليهِ وعلى آلِهِ صلاةً لا تُعَدُّ ولا تُحْصَى، اللهمَّ صلِّ عليهِ زنةَ عرشكَ، ومبلغَ رضاكَ، ومدادَ كلماتكَ، ومنتهى رحمتكَ،

Allahumma salli āla mala 'ikatika wal-mukarrabiina wa āla ambiyaa'ika wal mursalina wa āla Ahli taa'atika ajmaiina waj 'alna bissalaati 'alaihim minal-marhumiin

Allahumma salli āla sayidina Muhammadi-n-ilmab'uthi min tihamata wal āmiri bil ma'rufi wal istaqamati wash-shafii'i la ahlizunubi fi 'arasatil-qiyama

Allahumma ablligh ānna nabiyana washafii'ana wahabibana afdalas-salati wattaslimi wabāthhul-maqamal-mahmuudal-karima wa āatihil-fadilata wal wasilata waddarajatar-rafiiā 'tallati wa 'adtahu fil mauqifil-'azim

Wa sall'illahumma 'alaihi salaatan daa 'imatan-muttasilatan tatawaalaa wataduum Allhumma salli'alaihi wa āla ālihi ma laha bariqun-wa zarra shariqun-wa waqaba ghasiqun wa-nhamara wadiq Wasalli'alaihi wa āla ālihi mil 'allauhi wal fadaa'i wa-mithla nujuumis-sama'i wa 'adadal Alqatri wa-lmatri wal hasa wa-salli'alaihi wa āla ālihii salatan-la tu'addu wala tuhsa Allahumma sali ālaihi zinata arshika wa mablagha ridaka wamidada kalimatika wa muntaha rahmatika

Dear God! Bless Your archangels and angels, Your Prophets and Messengers, and all the people obedient to You. And may our asking for these blessings be a mercy for us.

Dear God! Bless and support our noble master Muhammad, the Envoy from Tihama, Commander and Upholder of justice, and Intercessor for the people of sin on the courtyards of the Day of the Rising-Up.

Dear God! Send to Your Prophet, Advocate and Beloved, on our behalf, the finest blessings and peace, and send him to the Most Praised and Munificent Station, and grant him the Pre-eminence, the Closest Access and the Loftiest Rank that You have promised him on the Great Day of Standing.

And bless him, dear God, with eternal, continual, continuous and everlasting blessings.

Dear God! Bless and support him and his family in the lightning which strikes, the day which dawns, the night which obscures, and the rain that falls.

And bless and support him and his family to the fullness of the Tablet and the Cosmos, in every star in the night sky, every raindrop and stone, and bless and support him and his family with blessings that are innumerable and incalculable.

Dear God! Bless and support him as much as the weight of Your Throne, to the fullness of Your Contentment, as much as the ink for Your Words is, and according to Your limitless Mercy.

اللهمَّ صلِّ عليهِ وعلى آلهِ وأزواجِهِ وذريتِهِ، وبارك عليهِ وعلى آلهِ وأزواجِهِ وذريتِهِ، كما صليتَ وباركتَ على سيدنا إبراهيمَ وعلى آلِ سيدنا إبراهيمَ إنكَ حميدٌ مجيدٌ، وجازِهِ عنا أفضلَ ما جازيتَ نبياً عنْ أمتِهِ، واجعلنا منَ المهتدينَ بمنهاجِ شريعتِهِ، واهدِنا بهديهِ، وتوفِنا على ملتِهِ، واحشرْنا يومَ الفزع الأكبرِ منَ الآمنينَ في زمرتِهِ، وأمتنا على حبهِ وحبِّ آلهِ وأصحابهِ وذريتِهِ، اللهمَّ صلِّ على سيدنا محمدٍ أفضلِ أنبيائِكَ، وأكرمِ أصفيائِكَ، وإمامِ أوليائِكَ، وخاتمِ أنبيائِكَ، وحبيبِ ربِّ العالمينَ، وشهيدِ المرسلينَ، وشفيع المذنبينَ، وسيدِ ولدِ آدمَ أجمعينَ، المرفوع الذكرِ في الملائكةِ المقربينَ، البشيرِ النذيرِ، السراج المنيرِ، الصادقِ الأمينِ، الحقِّ المبينِ، الرؤوفِ الرحيمِ، الهادي إلى الصراطِ المستقيمِ، الذي آتيتهُ سبعاً منَ المثاني والقرآنِ العظيمِ، نبيِّ الرحمةِ وهادي الأمةِ، أولُ منْ تنشقُّ عنهُ الأرضُ ويدخلُ الجنةَ، والمؤيدِ بسيدِنا جبريلَ وسيدِنا ميكائيلَ، المبشرِ بهِ في التوراةِ والإنجيلِ،

Allahummasalli'alaihi wa āla āalihi wa azwaajihi wa zurriyyatihi wa barik 'alaihi wa āla āalihi wa azwaajihi wa zurriyyatihi kama sallaita wa baarakta āla sayyidina Ibraahima wa Wa āla Āli sayyidina Ibraahima innaka hamiidun-majid

Wa jaazihi 'anna afdala ma jazai-ta nabiyan 'ann ummatihi wa-j'alna minal-muhtadina biminhaji shari'atihi wa-hdina bihadyihi watawafana āla m'illatihi wahshurna yaumal-faza'il-akbari minal-aaminiina fi zumratihii wa amitnaa āla hubbihi wa hubbi āalihii wa ashaabihi wa zurriyyatih

Allahumma salli āla sayyidina Muhamamd-in afdala anbiyaa'ika wa akrami asfiya'ika wa imami auliya'ika wa khatimi anbiya'ika

wa habibi Rabbil-'alamina washahidil-mursalina wa-shafii 'il-mudhnibina wa sayyidi uldi adama ajma'inal-marfu 'izzikri fil mala'ikatil-mukarrabinal-bashirin-naziris-sirajil- muniris-sadikil-aminil-haqqil-mubinir-ra 'ufir-rahimi

alhadi ilassiratil-mustaqim'illadhi 'ataitahu sab'an minal-mathani wal qur'anal-azima nabiyyir-rahmati wahadil-ummati auwali man tanshaqqu anhul- ardu wa yadkhulul-jannata wal mu'ayyadi bisayyidina jibrila wa sayyidina mikaa'ilal-mubashari Bihi fit-taurati wal injilil

Dear God! Bless and support him and his family, his wives and his descendants. And sanctify him and his family, his wives and his descendants, just as You sanctified our noble master Abraham and his family. You are the Praiseworthy, the Mighty.

And reward him, for us, better than You have awarded any Prophet on behalf of his nation. And place us among those guided by his law, guide us through his guidance, and have us pass away following his religion. And resurrect us among the faithful in his company on the Day of the Greatest Concern. And have us die loving him and his family, Companions, and descendants.

Dear God! Bless our noble master Muhammad, the Finest of Your Prophets, the Noblest of Your Selected Ones, Leader of Your Saints, Seal of Your Prophets, and Your Beloved. He is the Witness for the Messengers, Advocate of the sinners, and noble master of all the Children of Adam. He is the one mentioned highly among the Highest Angels, the News-Bringer, the Warner, the Shining Lamp, and the Truthful One. And he is the honest one, the compassionate and merciful one, the clear truth, and the guide to the Straight Path. And he is the one to whom You gave the Seven Duals and the Mighty Quran. He is the Prophet of Mercy and the Guide of the Nation. And he is the first upon whom the Earth breathed, and the first to enter Your Garden. He is the one supported by our noble masters Gabriel and Michael. He is the one announced in the Torah and the Gospel.

المُصطفى المُجتبى المنتخبِ أبي القاسمِ، سيدِنا محمدٍ بنِ عبدِ اللهِ بنِ عبدِ المطلبِ بنِ هاشمٍ، اللهمَّ صلِّ على ملائكتكَ المقربينَ الذين يسبحونَ الليلَ والنهارَ لا يفترونَ، ولا يعصونَ اللهَ ما أمرهمْ ويفعلونَ ما يؤمرونَ، اللهمَّ وكما اصطفيتهم سُفَرَاءَ إلى رُسُلِكَ وأُمَنَاءَ على وَحْيِكَ وَشُهَدَاءَ على خلقكَ، وخرقتَ لهمْ كُنُفَ حُجُبِكَ وأطلعتهم على مكنونِ غيبكَ، واخترتَ منهمْ خزنةً لجنتِكَ وحملةً لعرشِكَ، وجعلتهُمْ منْ أكثرِ جنودكَ، وفَضَّلْتَهُمْ على الورى، وأَسْكَنْتَهُمُ السماواتِ العُلَى، ونَزَّهْتَهُمْ عنِ المعاصي والدناءاتِ، وقَدَّسْتَهُمْ عنِ النقائصِ والآفاتِ، فصلِّ عليهمْ صلاةً دائمةً تَزيدُهُمْ بها فضلاً، وتجعلُنا بها أهلاً، اللهمَّ وصلِّ على جميعِ أنبيائكَ ورسلِكَ، الذينَ شرحتَ صدورَهُمْ وأودعتَهُمْ حكمتكَ وطوقتَهُمْ نبوتَكَ وأنزلتَ عليهمْ كُتُبَكَ، وهديتَ بهمْ خلقَكَ ودَعَوْا إلى توحيدِكَ، وشَوَّقُوا إلى وعدِكَ وخَوَّفُوا منْ وعيدِكَ، وأرشدوا إلى سبيلِكَ وقاموا بحجتِكَ ودليلِكَ، وسَلِّمِ اللهمَّ عليهمْ تسليماً،

Al-mustafal-mujtabal-muntakhabi abil-qaasimi sayyidina Muhammadib-ni Abd'illahib-ni abdil-muttalibib-ni haashim Allahumma salli āla mala'ikatika wal mukarrabinal-ladhina yusabbihunal-laila wannahara la yafturuna wala ya'sunallaha ma 'amarahum wayaf'aluna ma yu'marun

Allahumma wa kamas-tafaitahum sufaraa'a ila rusulika wa umanaa 'a āla wahyika washuhadaa 'a āla khalqika wakharaqtalahum kunufa hujubika wa atla'tahum āla maknuni Ghaibika wa-khtarta minhum khazanatan lijannatika wahamalatan li'arshika waja'altahum min akthari junudika wa fadaltahum ālal-waraa wāskantahumus-samawatil-ulaa wanazzahtahum ānil-ma'asi waddanaaāati waqaddastahum ānil-naqaa'issi wal āafati fasalli 'alaihim salaatan daa'imatan taziduhum biha fadla wataj'aluna li istighfarihim biha ahla

Allahumma wa salli āla jamii'i ambiyaa 'ika warusulikalladhiina sharahta sudurahum wa 'auda'tahum hikmataka wa-tawwaqtahum nubuwataka wa 'anzalta 'alaihim kutubaka wahadaita bihim khalqaka wa da 'au ila tauhiidika wa shauwaqu ila wa'dika wa khauwafu min-wa 'iidika wa arshadu ila sabiilika wa qaamu bihujjatika wadaliilika wasallimil-laahumma 'alaihim taslima

He is The Chosen One, the Elected One, the Selected One, and the Father of Qasim. He is our noble master Muhammad, son of Abdullah, son of Abdul Muttalib, and son of Hashim.

Dear God! Bless Your highest angels who glorify You ceaselessly, night and day, who never disobey You in what You have ordered, and carry out what they have been instructed to do.

Dear God! You have chosen Your angels to be the Envoys to Your Messengers, the Guardians of Your Revelations and the Witnesses over Your Creation. And You have allowed them to pass through the folds of Your Veils and access Your Hidden and Unseen Realms. And You have chosen some of them to be the Guardians of Your Garden and Bearers of Your Throne.

And You have made them the most numerous of Your soldiers, favoured them over mortal men, and populated the High Heavens with them. And You have freed them from disobedience and baseness, and sanctified them from misfortunes and shortcomings. Bless them eternally, and may this request be a means of increasing their favour and asking forgiveness for us.

Dear God! Bless and support all of Your Prophets and Messengers whose hearts You have opened and entrusted with Your Wisdom. You empowered them with Prophethood, to whom You revealed Your Books, and by whom Your Creation has been guided. They have called to Your Unity, looked forward to Your Promise, and feared Your Threat, those who have guided to Your Path, and upheld Your Proof and Evidence. And grant them abundant peace.

وهبْ لنا بالصلاةِ عليهِمْ أجراً عظيماً، اللهمَّ صلِّ على سيدِنا محمدٍ وعلى آلِ سيدِنا محمدٍ صلاةً دائمةً مقبولةً تُؤَدِّي بها عنَّا

حقهُ العظيمَ، اللهمَّ صلِّ على سيدِنا محمدٍ صاحبِ الحُسْنِ والجمالِ والبهجةِ والكمالِ، والبهاءِ والنورِ والوِلْدَانِ والحورِ، والغرفِ

والقصورِ واللسانِ الشَّكُورِ والقلبِ المشكورِ، والعِلْمِ المشهورِ والجيشِ المنصورِ، والبنينَ والبناتِ، والأزواجِ الطاهراتِ،

والعُلُوِّ على الدرجاتِ، والزمزمِ والمقامِ والمشعرِ الحرامِ، واجتنابِ الآثامِ وتربيةِ الأيتامِ، والحجِّ وتلاوةِ القرآنِ، وتسبيحِ الرحمنِ

وصيامِ رمضانَ، واللواءِ المعقودِ، والكرمِ والجودِ، والوفاءِ بالعهودِ، صاحبِ الرغبةِ والترغيبِ، والبَغْلَةِ والنجيبِ، والحوضِ

والقضيبِ، النبيِّ الأوابِ، الناطقِ بالصوابِ، المنعوتِ في الكتابِ، النبيِّ عبدِ اللهِ، النبيِّ كنزِ اللهِ، النبيِّ حُجَّةِ اللهِ، النبيِّ منْ

أطاعهُ فقدْ أطاعَ اللهَ، ومنْ عصاهُ فقدْ عصى اللهَ، النبيِّ العربيِّ، القرشيِّ الزمزميِّ، المكيِّ التهاميِّ،

wahab lana bissalaati 'alaihim ajran aziimaa Allahummasalli 'ala sayyidina Muhammad-iuw-wa āla Āli sayyidina Muhamamd-in salaatan daa'imatan-maqbuulatan-tu'addi biha 'anna haqqahul-'aziim

Allahumma salli āla sayyidina Muhammad-in saahibil-husni waljamĀli wal bahjati wal kamali wal bahaa 'i wannuri walwildani wal huri wal ghurafi wa-lqusuri wal-lisanish-shakuri wal qalbil-mashkuri

wal 'ilmil-mashhuri wal jaishil-mansuri wal banina wal banati wal azwajit-tahiraati wal uluwwi 'aladdarajati wazzamzami wal maqami wal mash'arielharaami wajtinabil-āathaami watarbiyatil-āitaami wal hajji watilawatil-qurāani

watasbihir-rahmani wasiyami ramadana walliwa'il-ma'qudi wal karami wal judi walwafa'i bil uhudi sahibir-raghbati wattarghibi wal baghlati wal najibi wal haudi wal qadibi Nabiyyil-auwabin-naatiqi bissowaabi

Al-man'uuti fil kitaabin-nabiyyi abd'illallahin-nabiyyi kanz'illallahin-nabiyyi hujjat'illallahinnabiyyi mann ata'ahu faqad ata'allahi wa mann asaahu faqad 'asallaha-an-nabiyyil-'arabiyyilqurashiyiz-zamzamiyyil-makiyyit-tihami

Dear God! Through this request for them, bestow on us a mighty reward. Dear God! Bless and support our noble master Muhammad and his family, blessings eternally acceptable, and discharge us of his great rights over us. Dear God! Bless our noble master Muhammad, the Possessor of beauty and handsomeness, splendour and perfection, radiance and light, youthful servants and houris, chambers and palaces. He is the Possessor of a grateful tongue and a praiseworthy heart, of renowned knowledge and victorious army, sons and daughters, pure wives of the highest ranks, the spring of Zamzam, the Maqam Ibrahim, the Holy Sanctuary, infallibility, an orphan's upbringing, the Hajj, the Qur'anic recitation, glorification of the Merciful, the Ramadan fast, the Banner, and nobility and generosity.

Dear God! Bless our noble master Muhammad, the Fulfiller of promises, the Possessor of longing for You, and the one who kindled such yearning in others. And he is the Owner of the mule (his mount), of noble birth, the Pool, the Sceptre, the Prophet of Return, the Speaker with Re.ard, the One mentioned in the Book. And he is the Prophet and Servant of God, the Prophet and Treasure of God, the Prophet and Proof of God. And he is the Prophet, obedience to whom is the same as obedience to God, and to whom disobedience is the same as disobedience to God.

Dear God! Bless our noble master Muhammad, the Arabian Prophet, the Quraishi Prophet, the Zamzami Prophet, the Meccan Prophet, and the Tihami Prophet.

صاحبِ الوجهِ الجميلِ، والطرفِ الكحيلِ، والخدِّ الأسيلِ، والكوثرِ والسلسبيلِ، قاهرِ المضادينَ مبيدِ الكافرينَ، وقاتلِ المشركينَ، قائدِ الغرِّ المحجلينَ إلى جناتِ النعيم وجوارِ الكريم، صاحبِ سيدنا جبريلَ عليهِ السلامُ، ورسولِ ربِّ العالمينَ، وشفيع المذنبين، وغايةِ الغمامِ، ومصباحِ الظلامِ، وقمرِ التمام، صلى اللهُ عليهِ وعلى آلهِ المصطفينَ مِنْ أطهرِ جِبلّة ، صلاةً دائمةً على الأبدِ غيرَ مُضْمَحِلّةَ، صلى اللهُ عليهِ وعلى آلهِ صلاةً يتجددُ بها حبُورُهُ، ويَشْرُفُ بها في الميعادِ بعثُهُ ونُشُورُهُ، فصلى اللهُ عليهِ وعلى آلهِ الأنجُمِ الطوالِعِ، صلاةً تجودُ عليهِم أَجْوَدَ الغُيُوثِ الهَوَامِعِ، أَرْسَلَهُ مِنْ أَرْجَحِ العرب ميزاناً وأوضَحِها بياناً، وأفصَحِها لساناً وأشمَخِها إيماناً وأعلاها مقاماً وأحلاها كلاماً، وأوفاها ذِمَامَاً وأصْفَاها رَغَامَاً، فَأَوْضَحَ الطريقةَ، ونصحَ الخليقةَ، وشَهَرَ الإسلامَ وكَسَّرَ الأصنامَ، وأَظْهَرَ الأحكامَ وحَظَرَ الحرامَ وعمَّ بالإنعامِ، صلى اللهُ عليهِ وعلى آلهِ في كلِّ مَحْفَلٍ ومَقَامٍ، أفضلَ الصلاةِ والسلامِ،

saahibil-wajhil-jamiili wa-ttarfil-kahili wal-khadil-‘assili wal-kauthari wa-ssal-sabili qahiril-muda-adina mubidil-kafirina wa qatilil-mushrikina qa‘idil-ghurril-muhajjalina ila jannatin-na’imi wajawaril-karimi saahibi sayyidina jibriila ‘Alaihis-salaamu warasuuli rabbil-’alamina washafii‘il-muznibiina waghaayatil-ghamaam Wa misbaahiz-zhalaami waqamarit-tamaami sallallahu ’alaihi wa āla āalihil-mustafaina minn athari jib’illatin salaatan daa ‘imatan ‘alal-abadi ghaira mudhmah’illatin

sallallahu ‘alaihi wa āla āalihi salatan-yatajaddadu biha hubuuruhu wayusharrafu biha fil mi ‘aadi ba’thuhu wanushuuruhu fasallallahu ‘alaihi wa āla āalihil-anjumit-tawali ‘i salaatan tajuudu ‘alaihim ajwadal-ghuyuuthil-hawaami ‘i

arsalahu minn arjahil-arabi mi’idhanan-wa audhahiha Bayanaw-wa afsahiha lisanan wa ashmakhiha ‘imanan wa ‘aalaha maqaman wa ahlaha kalaman wa aufaha zimaman wa asfaha raghaman Fa ‘audahat-tariqata wanasahal-khaliqata wa shaharal-islama wa kassaral-‘asnama wa ‘azharal-‘ahkama wahazaral-harama wa ‘amma bil-in‘ami sallallahu ‘alaihi wa āla āalihi fi kulli mahfilin-wa maqaamin afdhalas-salaati wassalaami

He is the Possessor of the most handsome face, the naturally mascaraed eyelashes, the noble cheeks, and the springs of Kawthar and Salsabeel. He is the Conqueror of the enemies, the Destroyer of the disbelievers, the Fighter against the associators, the Guide to the Divine Garden near the Munificent, for those with shining faces and limbs. He is the Companion of our noble master Gabriel, peace be upon him, the Messenger of the Lord of all the Worlds. And he is the Advocate for sinners even though their sins reach the limits of the clouds, the Lamp in the Darkness, and the Full Moon, may Your blessings be upon him. The blessings of God be on him and his most purely chosen family, blessings eternal and everlasting, never diminishing.

Dear God! Bless and support our noble master Muhammad through which his happiness is renewed, and his resurrection is honoured on the Promised Day. Bless and support him and his family, the Rising Stars, with blessings more generous than abundant rainfall. Send Your blessings to the One who, of all Arabs, is more just, more eloquent, and greater in faith. And he is higher in station, more articulate in speech, more careful of the rights of others and purer in his aversion towards his enemies.

He enlightened the Path, advised creation, made Islam known, smashed the idols, made justice appear, and forbade the prohibited, thus spreading favours to the whole world. May God bestow His blessings upon him and his family at every gathering and every spot. Dear God! Bestow the best of Your blessings and abundant peace upon him and his family, over and over again.

صلى اللهُ عليهِ وعلى آلِهِ عَوْداً وبَدْءاً صلاةً تكونُ ذَخِيرَةً وَوِرْداً، صلى اللهُ عليهِ وعلى آلِهِ صلاةً تامةً زاكيةً، وصلى اللهُ عليهِ وعلى آلِهِ صلاةً يتبعها رَوْحٌ ورَيْحَانٌ، ويَعْقُبُها مَغْفِرَةٌ ورِضْوَانٌ، وصلى اللهُ على أفضلِ منْ طابَ منهُ النِّجَارُ، وسَمَا بهِ الفَخَارُ، واستنارَتْ بنورِ جبينهِ الأقمارُ، وتضاءلَتْ عندَ جودِ يمينهِ الغمائمُ والبحارُ، سيدِنا ونبيِّنا محمدٍ الذي بباهرِ آياتهِ أضاءتْ الأنجادُ والأغوارُ، وبمعجزاتِ آياتهِ نطقَ الكتابُ وتواترتِ الأخبارُ، صلى اللهُ عليهِ وعلى آلِهِ وأصحابهِ الذينَ هاجروا لنصرتهِ، ونصروهُ في هجرتهِ، فنعمَ المهاجرونَ ونعمَ الأنصارُ، صلاةً ناميةً دائمةً ما سجعتْ في أيْكِها الأطيارُ، وهمعتْ بوبلِها الدِّيمَةُ المِدْرَارُ، ضاعفَ اللهُ عليهِ دائمَ صلواتِهِ، اللهمَّ صلِّ على سيدنا محمدٍ وعلى آلِهِ الطيبينَ الكرامِ، صلاةً موصولةً دائمةَ الاتصالِ بدوامِ ذي الجلالِ والإكرامِ، اللهمَّ صلِّ على سيدنا محمدٍ الذي هو قطبُ الجلالةِ، وشمسُ النبوةِ والرسالةِ، والهادِي منَ الضلالةِ، والمنقذُ منَ الجهالةِ، ﷺ صلاةً دائمةَ الاتصالِ والتوالي، متعاقبةً بتعاقبُ الأيامِ والليالي.

sallallahu 'alaihi wa āla āalihi 'audan-wa bad'a Salaatan taquunu zakhiiratan-wa wirdan sallallahu 'alaihi wa āla āalihi salaatan taa 'ammatan zaakiyataw-wa sallallahu 'alaihi wa āla āalihi salatan-yatba 'uha Ruuhun-wa rihaanuw-wa ya'qubuha maghfiratuw-wa ridhwaan Wa sallallahu āla afdala mann taba minhun-nijaaru wasama bihil-fakhaaru wastanaarat binuuri jabiinihil-aqmaar Watadhaa'alat 'inda juudi yamiinihil-ghamaa 'imu wal biharu sayyidina wanabiyyinaa Muhammadi-n'illazi bibaahirii aayaatihii adhaa'atil-anjaadu wal aghwaaru wabimu'j'idhati aayytihii nataqal-kitaabu watawaa taratil-akhbaaru

sallallahu 'alaihi wa āla āalihi wa ashaabihil-ladhina haajaru linusratihii wanasaruuhu fi hijratihii fani'mal-muhaajiruna wa ni'mal-ansaru salatan namiyatan da'iamatan ma saja'at fi aikihal 'atyaru wa hama'at biwablihad-dimatul-midraru da'afallaahu 'alahi da'ima salawatihi

Allahumma salli āla sayyidina Muhammad-iuw-wa āla āalihit-taiyibiinal-kiraami salaatam-mausuulatan daa 'imatal-ittisaali bidawaami ziljil Āli wal ikraam Allahumma salli āla sayyidina Muhammadi-n'illazi huwa qutbul-jalaalati wash-shamsun-nubuwwati warrisaalati walhaadi minadh-dhalaalati walmunqizu minal-jahaalati sallallahu 'Alaihi wasallama salaatan daa'imatal-ittisaali wattawĀli muta'aaqibatan bita'aqubil-ayyaami wallayaali.

Blessings are a source of treasure. And may God bless him and his family, complete and pure blessings ensured by fragrances and scents, succeeded by forgiveness and satisfaction. And the blessings of God be upon the One through whom the lineage of humanity was most permeated with goodness. And through whom God's glory is exalted, and through the light of whose cheeks the moon is illuminated. And the generosity of his right hand illuminates the clouds and seas. Our noble master and Prophet Muhammad, by the splendour of his signs, illustrates the highlands and the lowlands. By the miracles of his sublime character, the Book was enunciated, and the Good News was transmitted.

The blessings of God be upon him and his family, and his Companions who emigrated to help him and they helped him to emigrate. And blessed be the Emigrants and Helpers, blessings that grow and are eternal for as long as birds sing in the trees, and rain streams down in abundance. And multiply the eternal blessings upon him. Dear God! Bless and support our noble master Muhammad and his good and honourable family. Bless him with blessings that are perpetual and eternally bound up with the Owner of Majesty and Nobility. Dear God! Bless and support our noble master Muhammad, the Pole of Magnificence, the Sun of the Message and Prophethood, the Guide away from error, and the Critic of ignorance. The blessings and abundant peace of God be upon him, eternal blessings successively repeating in accordance with the alternation of days and nights.

الحزبُ الثامنُ وردِ يومِ الاثنين

بسمِ اللهِ الرحمنِ الرحيمِ

اللهمَّ صلِّ على سيدنا محمدٍ النبيِّ الزاهدِ، رسولِ المَلِكِ الصمدِ الواحدِ، صلى الله عليه وسلم صلاةً دائمةً إلى مُنتهى الأبدِ بلا انقطاع ولا نفادٍ، صلاةً تنجينا بها منْ حرِّ جهنمَ وبئسَ المهادِ، اللهمَّ صلِّ على سيدنا محمدٍ النبيِّ الأميِّ وعلى آلهِ وسَلِّمْ، صلاةً لا يُحْصَى لَها عَدَدٌ، ولا يُعَدُّ لها مددٌ، اللهمَّ صلِّ على سيدنا محمدٍ صلاةً تكرمُ بها مثواهُ، وتبلغُ بها يومَ القيامةِ منَ الشفاعةِ رضاهُ، اللهمَّ صلِّ على سيدنا محمدٍ النبيِّ الأصيلِ السيدِ النبيلِ، الذي جاءَ بالوحيِ والتنزيلِ وأوضحَ بيانَ التأويلِ، وجاءهُ الأمينُ سيدنا جبريلُ عليهِ السلامُ بالكرامةِ والتفضيلِ، وأسرى بهِ المَلِكُ الجليلُ في الليلِ البهيمِ الطويلِ، فكشفَ لهُ عنْ أعلى الملكوتِ وأراهُ سناءَ الجبروتِ، ونظرَ إلى قدرةِ الحيِّ الدائمِ الباقي الذي لا يموتُ،

Allahumma salli āla sayyidina Muhammadi-nin-nabiyyiz-zaahidi rasuulil-malkis-saamadil-waahidi sallallahu 'alaihi wassallama salaatan daa 'imatan ila muntahal-abadi bilan-qita'in wala nafadin salatan tunjina biha min harri jahannama wa-bai'sal-mihad

Allahumma salli āla sayyidina Muhammidi-nin-nabiyyil-ummiyi wa āla ālihi wasallim salatan-la yuhsaa lahaa 'adadun-walaa yu'addu lahaa madad Alalahumma salli āla sayyidina Muhammadin salaatan Tukrimu biha mathwaahu watuballighu biha yaumal-qiyaamati minash-shafaa-'ati ridah

Allahumma salli āla sayyidina Muhammadi-nin-nabiyil-aseelis-sayyidin-nabil'illazi jaa'a bil-wahyi watanziili wa-audhaha bayaanat-taaviili wa jaa'ahul-amiinu saiyidunaa Jibriilu alaihis-salaamu bilkaramati wat-tafdiil wa asra bihil-malikul-jalilu fillailil-bahimit-tawili fakashafa lahu 'an 'alal-malakuti wa arahu sana'al jabaruti wanazara 'ila qudratil-hayyid-da'imil-baq'illazi la yamuut

Monday - The Eighth Part

BISMILLA HIRRAHMAAN NIRRAHIM

Dear God! Bless and support our noble master Muhammad, the spiritual Prophet, the Messenger of the Only Eternal King. And God's blessings and peace be upon him, eternal blessings that last for all eternity, without break or depletion, blessings that save us from the heat of the Hell Fire, an evil resting place.

Dear God! Bless, support and grant peace to our noble master Muhammad - the Prophet sent to all nations, and his Family, blessings that are uncountable and whose supply is never impeded.

Dear God! Bless and support our noble master Muhammad, blessings which ennoble his abode and procure Your contentment from his intercession on the Day of the Rising-Up.

Dear God! Bless and support our noble master Muhammad, the Prophet of noble origin, the high-bred noble master who came with inspiration and revelation and clarified the meaning of interpretation. And to whom came the Honest One, our noble master Archangel Gabriel, peace be upon him, with honour and dignity. And he journeyed with him to the King, the Glorious One, on the Night Journey, and revealed to him the Heights of the True Kingdom of Heaven. And he was shown the supremacy of the Omnipotence of the Heavens. And he saw the Power of the Ever-Living, the Eternal, the Ever-Abiding, the One Who never dies.

صلى الله عليه وسلم صلاةً مقرونةً بالجمالِ، والحُسْنِ والكمالِ والخيرِ والإفضالِ، اللهمَّ صلِّ على سيدنا محمدٍ وعلى آلِ سيدنا محمدٍ عَدَدَ الأقطارِ، وصلِّ على سيدنا محمدٍ وعلى آلِ سيدنا محمدٍ عَدَدَ ورقِ الأشجارِ، وصلِّ على سيدنا محمدٍ وعلى آلِ سيدنا محمدٍ عَدَدَ زبدِ البحارِ، وصلِّ على سيدنا محمدٍ وعلى آلِ سيدنا محمدٍ عَدَدَ الأنهارِ، وصلِّ على سيدنا محمدٍ وعلى آلِ سيدنا محمدٍ عَدَدَ رملِ الصحاري والقفارِ، وصلِّ على سيدنا محمدٍ وعلى آلِ سيدنا محمدٍ عَدَدَ ثقلِ الجبالِ والأحجارِ، وصلِّ على سيدنا محمدٍ وعلى آلِ سيدنا محمدٍ عَدَدَ أهلِ الجنةِ وأهلِ النارِ، وصلِّ على سيدنا محمدٍ وعلى آلِ سيدنا محمدٍ عَدَدَ الأبرارِ والفجارِ، وصلِّ على سيدنا محمدٍ وعلى آلِ سيدنا محمدٍ عَدَدَ ما يَختلفُ بهِ الليلُ والنهارُ، واجعلِ اللهمَّ صلاتنا عليهِ حجاباً منْ عذابِ النارِ، وسبباً لإباحةِ دارِ القرارِ، إنكَ أنتَ العزيزُ الغفارُ،

Sallallahu 'alaihi wasallama salaatam-maqruunatam-biljamĀli wal-husni wal-kamali wal-khairi wal-ifdhaal Alalhumma salli āla sayyidina Muhammad-in wa āla Āli sayyidina Muhammad-in 'adadal-aqtaar

wa salli āla sayyidina Muhammad-iuw-wa'ala sayyidina Muhammad-in 'adada waraqil-ashjaar Wa salli āla sayyidina Muhammad-iuw-wa āla Āli sayyidina Muhammad-in 'adada zabadil-bihar Wa salli āla Muhammad-iuw 'adadal-anhaar wasalli'aala sayyidina Muhammad-iuw-wa āla sayyidina Muhammad-in 'adada ramlis-sahaaraa Wal qifaar Wa salli āla sayyidina Muhammad-iuw-wa āla Āli sayyidina Muhammad-in 'adada thiqlil-jibĀli wa ahjaar

wa salli āla sayyidina Muhammad-in-wa āla Āli sayyidina Muhammad-in 'adada ahlil-jannati wa ahlinnar Wa salli āla sayyidina Muhammad-iuw-wa āla Āli sayyidina Muhammad-in 'adadal-abraari wal fujjaar wa salli āla sayyidina Muhammad-in-wa āla Āli sayyidina Muhammad-in 'adada maa yakhtalifu bihil-lailu wannahar Waj'al'illa-humma salatanaa 'alahi hijaban min 'azabinnari wa sababan-li'ibahati daril qarari innaka 'anta al'azizu-lghaffar

God's blessings and peace be upon him, blessings permeated with beauty, charm and perfection, goodness and favour. Dear God! Bless and support our noble master Muhammad and his family as many times as there are drops of rain. And bless and support our noble master Muhammad and his family as many times as there are leaves on all the trees.

And bless and support our noble master Muhammad and his family in as much profusion as there is foam upon the oceans. And bless and support our noble master Muhammad and his family by the number of rivers there are. And bless our noble master Muhammad and his family as many times as there are grains of sand in the deserts and the wilderness.

And bless and support our noble master Muhammad and his family as much as the weight of all mountains and rocks. And bless and support our noble master Muhammad and his family as many times as there are dwellers in The Garden and dwellers in The Hellfire. And bless our noble master Muhammad and his family by the number of righteous ones and corrupt ones.

And bless and support our noble master Muhammad and his family by the number of times the night has alternated with the day. And make, dear God, our asking for blessings upon him a shield that protects us from the torment of The Hellfire and a means of gaining permission to enter the Abode of Permanence. You are the Mighty, the Forgiving.

وصلى الله على سيدنا محمدٍ وعلى آلهِ- الطيبينَ وذريتهِ المباركينَ، وصحابتهِ الأكرمينَ، وأزواجهِ أمهاتِ المؤمنينَ، صلاةً موصولةً تتردّدُ إلى يومِ الدينِ، (اللهمَّ صلِّ عَلى سيدِ الأبرارِ، وزَيْنِ المرسلينَ الأخيارِ، وأكرمَ مِنْ أظلمَ عليهِ الليلُ وأشرقَ عليهِ النهارُ) (ثلاثاً)، اللهمَّ يا ذا المنِّ الذي لا يكافى امتنانه، والطولِ الذي لا يُجازى إنعامُهُ وإحسانُهُ، نسألُكَ بكَ ولا نسألُكَ بأحدٍ غيرِكَ، أنْ تطلقَ ألسنتنا عندَ السؤالِ، وتوفقنا لصالح الأعمالِ، وتجعلنا منَ الآمنينَ يومَ الرَّجفِ والزلزالِ، يا ذا العزة والجلالِ، أسألُكَ يا نورَ النورِ، قبلَ الأزمنةِ والدهورِ، أنتَ الباقي بلا زوالٍ، الغنيُّ بلا مثالٍ، القدوسُ الطاهرُ، العليُّ القاهرُ، الذي لا يحيطُ بهِ مكانٌ، ولا يشتملُ عليهِ زمانٌ، أسألُكَ بأسمائكَ الحسنى كلها، وبأعظمِ أسمائكَ إليكَ وأشرفِها عندكَ منزلةً وأجزلِها عندكَ ثواباً وأسرَعِها مِنكَ إجابةً، وباسمِكَ المخزونِ المكنونِ، الجليلِ الأجلِّ، الكبيرِ الأكبرِ، العظيمِ الأعظمِ، الذي تحبُّهُ وترضى عمن دعاكَ بهِ وتستجيبُ لهُ دعاءهُ،

Wa sallallahu āla sayidina Muhammad-iuw-wa āla āalihit-taiyibiina wa zurriyatihil-mubaarakiina wasahabatihil-akramiina wa azwaajihii ummahaatil-mu'miniina salatan-mausuulatan tata –rad-dadu ila yaumiddiin Alalhumma salli āla sayyidil abraari wa zainil mursalinal akhyaari wal akrami man azlama 'alahil lailu wa ashraqa 'alaihin nihaar (Thalaatha)

Allahumma ya dhal-manne alladhi la yukafam-tinanuhu wattaul-lalladhi la yujaza in'amuhu wa 'ihsanuhu nas'aluka bika wala nas'aluka bi'ahadin ghairika 'an tutliqa Alsinatana 'I-nassu'Āli watuwaffiqana lisalihil-'aamAli wataj'alana minal-aaminina yaumar-rajfi wazzalazili ya zal-'izzati waljalal As'aluka ya nuuran-nuuri qablal-azminati wadduhuur Antal-baaqi bilazawĀli nil-ghaniyyu bilamithaalinil-qudduusut-taahirul-'aliyyul-qaahirul-lazi la yuhiitu bihi makaanuw-wala yashtamilu 'alaihizamaan As'aluka bi-'asmā'ikal-husna kulliha wa-bi'azami asma'ika ilayka wa-ashrafiha 'indaka manzilatan wa-'ajzaliha 'indaka thawaban wa-asra'iha minka ijabatan wa-bismikal-makhzunil-maknuni Al-jalilil-ajallil-kabiril-akbaril-azimil-'aazam'illazi tuhibbuhu watarda 'amman daāka bihi watastajibu lahuu dua'ah

And may the blessings and peace of God be upon our noble master Muhammad, his virtuous and blessed descendants, his honoured Companions and his pure wives - the Mothers of the Believers - continuous blessings until the Day of Judgement. Dear God! Bless and support the noble master of the righteous, the Ornament of the Messengers, the Best and Noblest ever to have been covered in the darkness of night or bathed in the light of day. (three times)

Dear God! O Noble Master of Favour, Whose Strength and Might are unequalled. Whose Favour and Virtue are beyond compare, we ask You and no one else but You to loosen our tongues in beseeching You, grant us success in doing good works, and make us among the safe ones on the Day of Convulsions and Earthquakes, O Maker of Might and Glory. I ask You, dear Light of the Light, which was before Time and Eternity. You are the Abiding One, with no end, the Rich with no equal, the Holy, the Pure, the Most High, the Subduing, the One Who is neither contained by time nor encompassed by space.

I ask You by all of Your most beautiful names and greatest names, and by the rank most noble to You, and by the reward most plentiful with You, and by your promptest response. And in Your Hidden and Protected Name, the Most Magnificent of the Magnificent, the Greatest of the Great, the Most Exalted of the Exalted, the One Who responds to and makes contented him who calls upon You, and whose prayer is accepted.

أَسْأَلُكَ اللهمَّ بلا إلهَ إلا أَنتَ الحنانُ المنانُ، بديعُ السماواتِ والأرضِ، ذو الجلالِ والإكرام، عالِمُ الغيب والشهادةِ، الكبيرُ المتعالُ، وأسألكَ باسمكَ العظيمِ الأعظم، الذي إذا دعيتَ بهِ أجبتَ، وإذا سُئلتَ بهِ أعطيتَ، وأسألكَ باسمكَ الذي يذلُّ لعظمتهِ العظماءُ والملوكُ والسباعُ والهوامُّ، وكلُّ شيءٍ خلقتهُ يا اللهُ، يا ربِّ استجبْ دعوتي، يا مَنْ لهُ العزةُ والجبروتُ، يا ذا المُلْكِ والملكوتِ، يا مَنْ هو حيٌّ لا يموتُ، سبحانكَ ربي ما أعظمَ شأنَكَ، وأرفعَ مكانَكَ، أنتَ ربي، يا مُتَقَدِّساً في جبروتِهِ، إليكَ أرغبُ، وإياكَ أرهبُ، يا عظيمُ يا كبيرُ، يا جبارُ يا قادرُ يا قويُّ، تباركتَ يا عظيمُ، تعاليتَ يا عليمُ، سبحانكَ يا عظيمُ، سبحانكَ يا جليلُ، أسألكَ باسمِكَ العظيم التام الكبيرِ، أنْ لا تُسَلِّطَ علينا جباراً عنيداً، ولا شيطاناً مريداً، ولا إنساناً حسوداً، ولا ضعيفاً منْ خلقِكَ ولا شديداً، ولا بارّاً ولا فاجراً ولا عبيداً ولا عنيداً، اللهمَّ إني أسألُكَ فإني أشهدُ أنكَ أنتَ اللهُ الذي لا إلهَ إلا أنتَ الواحدُ الأحدُ الصمدُ، الذي لم يلدْ ولم يولدْ، ولم يكنْ لهُ كفواً أحدٌ،

As'aluka allahumma bila 'ilaha 'illa antal-hannanul-munnanu badi'ussamawati wal 'ardi zuljlali wal 'ikrami 'alimul-ghaibi wash-shahadatil-kabiirul-muta'al wa as'aluka bi ismika-l'aazim'illadhi 'idha du'ita bihi ajabta wa 'idha su'ilta bihi a'ataita

wa as'aluka bi-ismikalladhi yazillu li'azamatihil-'uzama'u wal muluku wassiba'u wal hawa-ammu wakullu shai'in khalaqtahu Ya Allahu ya rabbis-tajib da'wati ya man-lahul-'izzatu waljabarutu ya zalmulki wal malakuti ya man huwa hayyul-la yamutu

subhanaka rabbi ma 'aazama shanaka wa arfa'a makanaka anta rabbi ya mutaqaddisan fi jabaruutihi ilaika ārghabu wa iyyaka ārhabu ya 'azzimu ya kabiru ya jabbaru ya qadiru ya qawwiyun tabarakta ya 'azimu ta'a laita ya 'alimu subhanaka ya 'azimu subhanaka ya jalilu as'aluka bi-ismikal-'azimit-ta'ammil-kabiri anl-la tusallita 'alaina jabbaran ' anidan wala shaitanan maridan wala insanan hasudan wala da'ifan min-khalqika wala shadeedan wala barran wala fajiran wala 'abidan wala 'anida Allahumma inni as'aluka fa inni ashhadu annaka antalla-hullazi la ilaaha 'illa antal-waahidul-ahaduss- samadullazi lamyalid walam yulad walam yakullahu kufwan ahad

I ask You, dear God! There is no god but You, the Compassionate, the Benefactor, the Originator of the Heavens and the Earth, Noble Master of Glory and Honour, Knower of the Unwitnessed and the Seen, the Greatest, the Exalted.

I ask You by Your Greatest Name in which, when we pray, our prayer is answered, and when we make a request, our request is granted. And I ask You by the Name which humbles, with its Might, the kings, the mighty ones, the lions, the reptiles and everything You have created. Dear God! Dear Lord, accept my prayer, O You to Whom belongs Majesty and Omnipotence. O the Noble Master of Sovereignty and the True Kingdom, You are the Ever-Living, Who never dies. Exalted are You, dear Lord. Nothing is more excellent than Your Status, and there is nothing higher than You. You are my Lord.

O the Holy One! In Your Omnipotence, I beseech You, and I fear You. O the Greatest One! O the Majestic! O the Most Powerful! O the Almighty! O the Strongest! You have blessed Yourself. You have exalted Yourself. O the All-Knowing! Exalted are You. O the Splendid One! I ask You by Your Greatest, Perfect and Majestic names, not to give dominion over me to the high-handed, the stubborn, the rebellious Satan, the envious one, the weak among Your creation, the oppressive one, the hateful one, the corrupt one, the enslaved one, or the wilful one.

Dear God! I bear witness that You are God, and there is no deity but You, the One, the Only, the Eternal, Who neither begets nor was begotten. And there is nothing like unto You.

يا هو يا مَنْ لا هو إلا هو، يا مَنْ لا إلهَ إلا هو، يا أزليُّ يا أبديُّ، يا دهريُّ يا ديمومِيُّ، يا مَنْ هو الحيُّ الذي لا يموتُ، يا إلهَنا وإلهَ
كلِّ شيءٍ إلهاً واحداً، لا إلهَ إلا أنتَ، اللهمَّ فاطرَ السماواتِ والأرضَ، عالمَ الغيبِ والشهادةِ، الرحمنَ الرحيمَ، الحيَّ القيومَ الديانَ،
الحنانَ المنانَ، الباعثَ الوارثَ، ذا الجلالِ والإكرام، قلوبُ الخلائقِ بيدكَ، نواصيهِمْ إليكَ، فأنتَ تزرعُ الخيرَ في قلوبهِمْ، وتمحو الشرَّ
إذا شئتَ مِنْهُمْ، فأسألُكَ اللهمَّ أنْ تمحوَ مِنْ قلبي كلَّ شيءٍ تكرَهُهُ، وأنْ تحشوَ قلبي مِنْ خشيتِكَ، ومعرفتِكَ ورهبتِكَ، والرغبةِ فيما
عندكَ، والأمنِ والعافيةِ، واعطفْ علينا بالرحمةِ والبركةِ منكَ، وألهمنا الصوابَ والحكمةَ، فنسألُكَ اللهمَّ علمَ الخائفينَ، وإنابةَ
المخبتينَ، وإخلاصَ الموقنينَ، وشكرَ الصابرينَ، وتوبةَ الصديقينَ، ونسألُكَ اللهمَّ بنورِ وجهكَ الذي ملأَ أركانَ عرشِكَ، أنْ تزرعَ في
قلبي معرفتَكَ حتى أعرفَكَ حقَّ معرفتِكَ، كما ينبغي أنْ تُعْرَفَ بهِ، وصلى اللهُ على سيدنا محمدٍ خاتمِ النبيينَ، وإمامِ المرسلينَ، وعلى
آلهِ وصحبهِ وسلم تسليماً، والحمدُ للهِ ربِّ العالمينَ وهو حسبنا ونعم الوكيل.

وَلَا حَوْلَ وَلَا قُوَّةَ إِلَّا بِاللهِ الْعَلِيِّ الْعَظِيمِ اللَّهُمَّ اغْفِرْ لِمُؤَلِّفِهِ . وَارْحَمْهُ وَاجْعَلْهُ مِنَ الْمَحْشُورِينَ فِي زُمْرَةِ النَّبِيِّينَ وَالصديقين يَوْمَ
الْقِيَامَةِ بِفَضْلِكَ يَا رَحْمَانُ.

yaa houwa ya-man la houwa 'illa houwa ya-man la 'ilaha 'illa houwa ya azaliyu ya abadiyu ya dahriyu
ya daimumiyu ya man huwal-hayyullazi la yamuutu ya ilahana wa ilaha kulli sha'in ilaahan-wahidal-la
ilaha 'illa anta Allahumma Faateras-samaawaati wal 'ardi 'aalimal-ghaibi wash-shahadatir-rahmaanir-
rahiimal-haiyal-qayuumad -daiyaanal-hannaanal mannaanal baa 'I-thal-waaritha zaljal Āli wal 'ikram
Qulubul-khala'iki biyadika nawasihim ilaika fa anta tazra'ul-khaira fi qulubihim watamhush-sharra 'idha
shi'ta minhum fansālukallahumma ān tamhu minn qalbi qulla shain takrahuhuu wa 'an tahshuwa qalbi
min khashyatika wa ma'rifatika warahbatika warraghbata fima 'indaka wal 'amna wal ' afiyata wa-'tif
'alaina bir-rahmati wal barakati minka wa alhimna-assawaba wal hikmah

fansālukallahumma 'ilmal-khaa 'ifiina wa inaabatal-mukhbitina wa ikhlasal-muqinina wa shukras-
sabirina wataubatas-siddiqina Wanasālukallahumma binuuri wajhikalladhi malaā arkana ārshika an
tazra'a fi qalbi māarifatika hatta āarifaka haqqa māarifatika kama yambaghi ān tu'rafa bihi wasallallahu
āla saiyidina wa maulaana Muhammad-in khatimin-nabiyyināā wa imamil-mursalina wa āla Āalihii wa
sahbihi wasallama tasliman-walhamdu l'illahi rabbil-'aalamiin wa huwa hasbuna wa ni'mal-wakilu

O the One, other than Whom there is no god but He. O He! O the One! There is no god but You. O
the Infinite One! O the Eternal! O my Destiny! O the Everlasting One! O the One Who is the Ever-Living
Who does not die. O our God and God of everything! God Alone! There is no god but You. Dear God!
You are the Creator of the Heavens and the Earth, the All-Knowing One of the Unwitnessed and the
Seen. You are the Compassionate, the Merciful, the Ever-Living, the Ever-Rising, the Judge, the
Benefactor. The Munificent, the Reviver, the Inheritor, the Noble Master of Honour and Glory. The
hearts of all creatures are in Your hands, and we entrust them to You. And You cause goodness to grow
in our hearts, and You erase the evil from them as You like.

So I ask You, dear God, to fill our hearts with reverence of You and erase everything that You hate
from our hearts. And fill our hearts with knowledge of You, awe of You, longing for what is with You,
and security and good health. And have mercy on us, with Your blessings and kindness. And inspire in
us that which is proper and wise. And I ask You, dear God, for the knowledge of those who revere You,
the repentance of the humble, the sincerity of the certain, the gratitude of the patient, and the repentance
of the truthful ones. And I ask You, dear God, by the Light of Your Face that fills every corner of Your
Throne, that You cause knowledge of You to grow in our hearts until we know You and Your True
Knowledge, in a way that You should be known. And God's blessings and abundant peace be upon our
noble master Muhammad, Seal of the Prophets and Leader of the Messengers, his family and
Companions. And the totality of Grace belongs to God, the Lord of all the Worlds. In Him we place all
our trust.

There is no power and no strength except through Allah, the Most High, the Most Great. O Allah,
forgive its author, have mercy on him, and gather him among the company of the Prophets and the
Truthful Ones on the Day of Judgment – by Your Grace, O the Most Merciful.

دعاء يقرأ عقيب دلائل الخيرات

اللَّهُمَّ اشْرَحْ بِالصَّلاةِ عَلَيْهِ صُدُورَنَا، وَيَسِّرْ بِهَا أُمُورَنَا، وَفَرِّجْ بِهَا هُمُومَنَا، وَاكْشِفْ بِهَا غُمُومَنَا، وَاغْفِرْ بِهَا ذُنُوبَنَا، وَاقْضِ بِهَا دُيُونَنَا، وَأَصْلِحْ بِهَا أَحْوَالَنَا، وَبَلِّغْ بِهَا آمَالَنَا، وَتَقَبَّلْ بِهَا تَوْبَتَنَا، وَاغْسِلْ بِهَا حَوْبَتَنَا، وَانْصُرْ بِهَا حُجَّتَنَا، وَطَهِّرْ بِهَا أَلْسِنَتَنَا، وَآنِسْ بِهَا وَحْشَتَنَا، وَارْحَمْ بِهَا غُرْبَتَنَا، وَاجْعَلْهَا نُوراً بَيْنَ أَيْدِينَا، وَمِنْ خَلْفِنَا، وَعَنْ أَيْمَانِنَا، وَعَنْ شَمَائِلِنَا، وَمِنْ فَوْقِنَا، وَمِنْ تَحْتِنَا، وَفِي حَيَاتِنَا، وَمَوْتِنَا، وَفِي قُبُورِنَا، وَحَشْرِنَا، وَنَشْرِنَا، وَظِلّاً فِي يَوم الْقِيَامَةِ عَلَى رُؤُوسِنَا، وَثَقِّلْ بِهَا مَوَازِينَ حَسَنَاتِنَا، وَأَدِمْ بَرَكَاتِهَا عَلَيْنَا حَتَّى نَلْقَى نَبِيَّنَا وَسَيِّدَنَا مُحَمَّدًا صَلَّى الله عَلَيْهِ وَسَلَّمَ، وَنَحْنُ آمِنُونَ مُطْمَئِنُّونَ فَرِحُونَ مُسْتَبْشِرُونَ، وَلَا تُفَرِّقْ بَيْنَنَا وَبَيْنَهُ حَتَّى تُدْخِلَنَا مُدْخَلَهُ، وَتُؤْوِينَا إِلَى جِوَارِهِ الْكَرِيمِ مَعَ الَّذِينَ أَنْعَمْتَ عَلَيْهِمْ مِنَ النَّبِيِّينَ وَالصِّدِّيقِينَ وَالشُّهَدَاءِ وَالصَّالِحِينَ، وَحَسُنَ أُولَآئِكَ رَفِيقاً.

Allāhumma-shraḥ biṣṣalāti ʿalayhi sudūrana, wa yassir bihā umūranā, wa farrij bihā humūmanā, wakshif bihā ghumūmanā, waghfir bihā dhunūbanā, waqdi bihā duyūnanā, wa aṣliḥ bihā aḥwālanā, wa balligh bihā āmālanā, wa taqabbal bihā tawbatanā, waghsil bihā ḥawbatanā, wanṣur bihā ḥujjatanā, wa ṭahhir bihā al sinatanā, wa ānis bihā waḥshatanā, warḥam bihā ghurbatanā, wajʿalhā nūran bayna aydīnā wa min khalfinā wa ʿan aymānina wa ʿan shamāʾilinā, wa min fawqinā wa min taḥtinā, wa fī ḥayātina wa mawtinā, wa fī qubūrinā wa ḥashrinā wa nashrinā, wa ẓillan fī yawmal qiyāmati ʿalā ruʾūsina, wa thaqqil bihā ya rabbi mawāzīna ḥasanātinā, wa adim barakātihā ʿalaynā ḥattā nalqa nabiyyinā wa sayyidinā Muḥammadan ṣallAllahu ʿalayhi wa ṣallama, wa naḥnu āminūna muṭmaʾinnūna fariḥūna mustabshirūna, wa lā tufarriq baynanā wa-baynahu ḥatā tudkhilanā mudkhalahu, wa taʿwiyanā ila jiwarihil karīmi maʿalladhīna ʿanʿamta ʿalayhim min annabiyīna waṣ-ṣiddīqīna wash-shuhadāʾi waṣ ṣāliḥīna, wa-ḥasuna ūlāʾika rafīqa.

Dua of Completion (Final Dua)

Dear God! Through our asking for blessings upon Your Prophet (ﷺ), expand our hearts and ease our affairs, dispel our anxieties and remove our sorrows. And thereby forgive our sins, relieve our debts, and improve our state. And fulfill our hopes, accept our repentance, and cleanse our misdeeds. And thereby champion our aspirations. Make our tongues pure, and let us not be lonely. And ease our separation. Make our prayers for him a light in front of us and behind us. And to our right and our left. And above us and beneath us. And in our lives and our deaths. And in our gatherings and our graves and our resurrection. And provide shade for us on the Day of the Rising-Up. And weigh down our scales thereby with good deeds. And repeat these blessings on us until we meet with our Prophet and noble master Muhammad, may Your peace and blessings be upon him and his family. We believe, we are certain, we are overjoyed, and the receivers of good news. Do not separate us from him and admit us through his entrance hall. Accommodate us in his noble neighbourhood with those You have favoured amongst the Prophets, the truthful ones, martyrs and righteous ones; they are the best of company.

اللَّهُمَّ إِنَّا آمَنَّا بِهِ صَلَّى اللهُ عَلَيْهِ وَسَلَّمَ وَلَمْ نَرَهُ، فَمَتِّعْنَا اللَّهُمَّ فِي الدَّارَيْنِ بِرُؤْيَتِهِ، وَثَبِّتْ قُلُوبَنَا عَلَى مَحَبَّتِهِ، وَاسْتَعْمِلْنَا عَلَى سُنَّتِهِ، وَتَوَفَّنَا عَلَى مِلَّتِهِ وَاحْشُرْنَا فِي زُمْرَتِهِ النَّاجِيَةِ وَحِزْبِهِ الْمُفْلِحِينَ، وَانْفَعْنَا بِمَا انْطَوَتْ عَلَيْهِ قُلُوبُنَا مِنْ مَحَبَّتِهِ صَلَّى اللهُ عَلَيْهِ وَسَلَّمَ يَوْمَ لَا جَدَّ وَلَا مَالَ وَلَا بَنِينَ، وَأَوْرِدْنَا حَوْضَهُ الْأَصْفَى، وَاسْقِنَا بِكَأْسِهِ الْأَوْفَى، وَيَسِّرْ عَلَيْنَا زِيَارَةَ حَرَمِكَ وَحَرَمِهِ مِنْ قَبْلِ أَنْ تُمِيتَنَا، وَأَدِمْ عَلَيْنَا الْإِقَامَةَ بِحَرَمِكَ وَحَرَمِهِ صَلَّى اللهُ عَلَيْهِ وَسَلَّمَ إِلَى أَنْ نُتَوَفَّى.

اللَّهُمَّ إِنَّا نَسْتَشْفِعُ بِهِ إِلَيْكَ إِذْ هُوَ أَوْجَهُ الشُّفَعَاءِ إِلَيْكَ، وَنُقْسِمُ بِهِ عَلَيْكَ إِذْ هُوَ أَعْظَمُ مَنْ أُقْسِمَ بِحَقِّهِ عَلَيْكَ، وَنَتَوَسَّلُ بِهِ إِلَيْكَ إِذْ هُوَ أَقْرَبُ الْوَسَائِلِ إِلَيْكَ، نَشْكُو إِلَيْكَ يَا رَبِّ قَسْوَةَ قُلُوبِنَا، وَكَثْرَةَ ذُنُوبِنَا، وَطُولَ آمَالِنَا، وَتَكَاسُلَنَا عَنِ الطَّاعَاتِ، وَهُجُومَنَا عَلَى الْمُخَالَفَاتِ، فَنِعْمَ الْمُشْتَكَى إِلَيْهِ أَنْتَ يَا رَبِّ، بِكَ نَسْتَنْصِرُ عَلَى أَعْدَائِنَا وَأَنْفُسِنَا فَانْصُرْنَا، وَعَلَى فَضْلِكَ نَتَوَكَّلُ فِي صَلَاحِنَا، فَلَا تَكِلْنَا إِلَى غَيْرِكَ يَا رَبَّنَا، وَإِلَى جَنَابِ رَسُولِكَ صَلَّى اللهُ عَلَيْهِ وَسَلَّمَ نَنْتَسِبُ فَلَا تُبَعِّدْنَا، وَبِبَابِكَ نَقِفُ فَلَا تَطْرُدْنَا، وَإِيَّاكَ نَسْأَلُ فَلَا تُخَيِّبْنَا.

Allahumma innā āmannā bihi ṣallAllahu ʿalayhi wa ṣallama wa lam narahu, famattiʿnAllahuma fiddāraini biruʾyatihi, wa thabbit qulūbana ʿalā maḥabbatihi, wastaʿmilna ʿalā sunnatihi, wa tawaffanā ʿalā millatihi, waḥshurna fī zumratihin nājiyati wa ḥizbihil mufliḥīna, wanfaʿna biman ṭawat ʿalayhi qulūbuna min maḥabbatihi ṣallAllahu ʿalayhi wa ṣallama yawma lā jadda wa lā māla wa lā banīn, wa awridnā ḥawḍahul aṣfa, wasqinā bikaʾ sihil ʿawfa, wa yassir ʿalaynā ziyarata ḥaramika wa ḥaramihi min qabli ʿan tumītana, wa adim ʿaynal iqāmata biḥaramika wa ḥaramihi ṣallallahu ʿalayhi waṣallama ilā an natawaffa.

Allahumma innā nastashfiʿu bihi ilayka iza huwa awjahu-shufaʿāi ilayka, wa-nuqsimu bihi ʿalayka iza huwa aʿẓamu man ʿaqsama bi-ḥaqihi ʿalayka, wa natawasalu bihi ilayka iza huwa aqrabul wasāʾili ilayka, nashkū ilayka yā rabbi qaswata qulūbina, wa kathrata dhunūbinā, wa ṭūla āmālinā, wa fasada ʿāmālina, wa takasulanā ʿaniṭṭaʿāti, wa hujūmanā ʿalal mukhālafāti, faniʿmal mushtaka ilayhi anta yā rabbi bika nastanṣiru ʿalā aʿdāʾina wa anfusinā fanṣurnā, wa-ʿalā faḍlika natawakalu fī ṣalāḥinā, falā takilnā ilā ghayrika yā rabana, wa ilā janābi rasūlika ṣallallahu ʿalayhi wa ṣallama nantasibu falā tubaʿidnā, wa bibābika naqifu falā taṭrudnā, wa iyyāka nasʾalu falā tukhayibunā.

Dear God! We have believed in him, peace and blessings be upon him, without seeing him, so make us enjoy, dear God, a vision of him in both realms, and keep our hearts forever in love with him and establish us on his path. And cause us to complete our lives while adhering to his religion. And raise us in his secure company and party of success. And avail us of love for him, peace and blessings be upon him, which is sealed in our hearts on the Day when there will be no ancestors, wealth, and sons (to speak for us). And have us drink at his pure wellspring and from his full chalice. And ease for us a visit to Your sanctuary (in Mecca) and his holy place (Medina) before You cause us to die. And make our stay at Your sanctuary and his station last until we pass away.

Dear God! We seek his intercession with You, for he is the most lauded by You. And we urge You, through him, for he is the best to entreat You (on our behalf). We seek a way to You through him, for his is the nearest access to You. We lament to You, O Lord, about the hardness of our hearts, the abundance of our sins, the extent of our hopes, and the imperfection of our actions. And our reluctance to do good deeds and our haste to commit bad deeds. Bestow upon the ones who seek Your help, O Lord, triumph over our enemies. Support our souls and, through Your Grace, make us rely solely upon our good deeds and no other considerations. O our Lord, we associate ourselves with the honour of Your Messenger, peace and blessings be upon him, so do not keep us away. We stop at Your door, so do not turn us away. We implore You alone, so do not thwart us.

اللَّهُمَّ ارْحَمْ تَضَرُّعَنَا، وَآمِنْ خَوْفَنَا، وَتَقَبَّلْ أَعْمَالَنَا، وَأَصْلِحْ أَحْوَالَنَا، وَاجْعَلْ بِطَاعَتِكَ اشْتِغَالَنَا، وَإِلَى الْخَيْرِ مَآلَنَا، وَحَقِّقْ بِالزِّيَادَةِ آمَالَنَا، وَاخْتِمْ بِالسَّعَادَةِ آجَالَنَا. هَذَا ذُلُّنَا ظَاهِرٌ بَيْنَ يَدَيْكَ، وَحَالُنَا لَا يَخْفَى عَلَيْكَ، أَمَرْتَنَا فَتَرَكْنَا، وَنَهَيْتَنَا فَارْتَكَبْنَا، وَلَا يَسَعُنَا إِلَّا عَفْوُكَ فَاعْفُ عَنَّا يَا خَيْرَ مَأْمُولٍ، وَأَكْرَمَ مَسْئُولٍ، إِنَّكَ عَفُوٌّ غَفُورٌ رَءُوفٌ رَحِيمٌ يَا أَرْحَمَ الرَّاحِمِينَ. وَصَلَّى اللهُ عَلَى سَيِّدِنَا مُحَمَّدٍ وَعَلَى آلِهِ وَصَحْبِهِ وَسَلَّمَ تَسْلِيماً، وَالْحَمْدُ للهِ رَبِّ الْعَالَمِينَ.

Allahummarḥam taḍarruʿanā, wa āmin khawfanā, wa taqabbal ʿamālanā, wa aṣliḥ aḥwālanā, wajʿal biṭāʿatikash tighālanā, wa ilāl khayri mālanā, wa ḥaqqiq bizziyādati āmālanā, wakhtim bissaʿādati ājālanā, hadhā dhullunā ẓāhirun bayna yadayka, wa ḥālunā la yakhfa ʿalayka, amartanā fataraknā, wa nahaytanā fartakabnā, wa lā yasʿunā illā ʿafwuka, faʿfu ʿannā yā khayra maʾmūlin, wa akrami masʾūlin, innaka ʿafuwwun ghafūrun raʾūfun raḥīmun, yā arḥamar raḥimīna, wa ṣallAllahu ʿalā sayyidinā Muḥammadin wa ʿalā ālihi wa ṣaḥbihi wa ṣallama taslīman, walḥamduliLlahi rabbil ʿālamīn.

Dear God! Have mercy upon our beseeching, and allay our fears. Accept our actions and make us righteous. Make obedience to You our main occupation. And cause us to spend our wealth only for good. And fulfill our hopes and more. And seal our final destination with bliss. Thus is our lowly state made clear to You and is not hidden from You. You have commanded us, and we have been remiss. You have forbidden us, and we have disobeyed. Nothing is more expansive than Your clemency. So pardon us, O Best Gratifier of Hopes. And Most Generous Redeemer of Petitions. You are the Merciful, the Forgiver, the Pardoner, O Most Merciful of the Merciful. And God's blessings and abundant peace be upon our noble master Muhammad and his family and Companions, and all praise is due to God, the Lord of all the Worlds.

بعض معجزات النبي ﷺ

Some of the Reported Miracles of the Prophet ﷺ

بعض من معجزات النبي صلى الله عليه وسلم

معجزات الحبيب محمد صلى الله عليه وسلم كثيرة نذكر بعضها كما وردت في الكتاب والسنة. أرسل الله تعالى رسوله الكريم محمد -صلى الله عليه وسلم- رحمة للعالمين، وختم به الرسالات السماوية، وقد أيده بالعديد من المعجزات المتنوعة إلى جانب معجزته الخالدة القرآن الكريم، ومن هذه المعجزات: الإسراء والمعراج انشقاق القمر، دعاؤه المستجاب، تكثير الطعام والماء، تسبيح الحصى في يديه، نبع الماء من بين أصابعه الشريفة، شفاء المرضى بريقه – صلى الله عليه وسلم – كما جرى لعلي بن أبي طالب، الإخبار عن أمور ستقع بالمستقبل، وصف غزوة مؤتة وهو في المدينة.

God Almighty sent His Noble Messenger Muhammad (ﷺ) as a mercy to all the worlds, and he (ﷺ)sealed the heavenly messages. He (ﷺ) communicated with animals and inanimate objects, healed the sick, told about things that would happen in the future, and described the battle of Mu'tah while he (ﷺ) was in Medina. And Angel Gabriel opened his (ﷺ) chest to purify it from evil.

1)أعظم معجزاته صلى الله عليه وسلم (القرآن الكريم).

Some of the reported miracles of the Prophet (ﷺ):

1. The Holy Qur'an

قال تعالى: ﴿ قُلْ لَئِنِ اجْتَمَعَتِ الْإِنْسُ وَالْجِنُّ عَلَى أَنْ يَأْتُوا بِمِثْلِ هَذَا الْقُرْآنِ لَا يَأْتُونَ بِمِثْلِهِ وَلَوْ كَانَ بَعْضُهُمْ لِبَعْضٍ ظَهِيرًا ﴾ [الإسراء: 88] .

Say: "If all mankind and all jinn were to come together to bring the like of this Qur'ān, they could not produce its like, even if they were to exert all their strength in aiding one another!" [Q 17:88]

قال الله -تعالى-: (ذَلِكَ الْكِتَابُ لَا رَيْبَ ۛ فِيهِ ۛ هُدًى لِّلْمُتَّقِينَ) [البقرة: 2].

This is the Book in which there is no doubt, a guide for all who are conscious of God. [Q 2:2]

وقال سبحانه-: (وَإِنَّهُ لَتَنزِيلُ رَبِّ الْعَالَمِينَ). [الشعراء: 192]

Now, behold, this [divine writ] has indeed been bestowed from on high by the Sustainer of all the worlds: [Q 26:192]

وقد ثبت عن أبي هريرة -رضي الله عنه- عن رسول الله – ﷺ – قال: (ما مِنَ الْأَنْبِيَاءِ نَبِيٌّ إِلَّا أُعْطِيَ مِنَ الْآيَاتِ ما مِثْلُهُ أُومِنَ، أَوْ آمَنَ، عليه الْبَشَرُ، وإِنَّما كانَ الذي أُوتِيتُ وَحْيًا أَوْحَاهُ اللَّهُ إِلَيَّ، فأَرْجُو أَنِّي أَكْثَرُهُمْ تَابِعًا يَومَ الْقِيَامَةِ).

Abu Huraira (may God be content with him) reported that the Prophet (ﷺ) said, "There has been no prophet among all the prophets, but he was given miracles because of which people had security or had belief. But I have been given the Divine revelation which God has revealed to me. So, I hope my followers will be more than any other prophet on the Day of the Rising Up." [1]

٢) الإسراء والمعراج

2. Israaʾ wal Miraj (The Night Journey)

قال الله تعالى—: (سُبْحانَ الَّذي أَسْرى بِعَبْدِهِ لَيْلاً مِنَ المَسْجِدِ الحَرامِ إِلَى المَسْجِدِ الأَقْصَى الَّذي بارَكْنا حَوْلَهُ لِنُرِيَهُ مِنْ آياتِنا إِنَّهُ هُوَ السَّميعُ البَصيرُ). [الإسراء: ١].

Glory be to Him Who transported His Servant by night from the Sacred Mosque (in Mecca) to the Farthest Mosque (in Jerusalem) whose surroundings We have blessed, that We might show him some of Our signs. Truly He is the All-Hearing, the All-Seeing. [Q 17:1]

وقال تعالى—: (أَفَتُمارُونَهُ عَلَى ما يَرَى* وَلَقَدْ رَآهُ نَزْلَةً أُخْرَى* عِندَ سِدْرَةِ المُنْتَهَى* عِندَها جَنَّةُ المَأْوَى* إِذْ يَغْشَى السِّدْرَةَ ما يَغْشَى* ما زاغَ البَصَرُ وَما طَغَى* لَقَدْ رَأَى مِنْ آياتِ رَبِّهِ الكُبْرَى). [النجم: ١٢–١٨].

*… will you then dispute with him about what he saw? * And, indeed, he saw it descend a second time * by the lote tree of the farthest limit, * near to the Garden of Refuge, * with the lote tree veiled in a veil of nameless splendour. * [And withal,] the gaze did not waver, nor did it stray: * indeed did he saw some the most profound of his Sustainer's signs.* [Q 53:12-18]

٣) انشقاق القمر

3. The Moon being split in half

عن أنس بن مالك أنَّ أَهْلَ مَكَّةَ سَأَلوا رَسولَ اللهِ ﷺ أَنْ يُرِيَهُمْ آيَةً، فَأَراهُمُ القَمَرَ شِقَّتَيْنِ، حَتَّى رَأَوْا حِراءً بَيْنَهُما.

Anas bin Malik (may God be content with him) narrated that the people of Mecca asked God's Messenger (ﷺ) to show them a miracle. He (ﷺ) showed them the moon in two halves, and they saw Mount Hiraʾ between the two halves. [2]

٤) دعاؤه المستجاب:

4. His (ﷺ) supplications being answered

جـ- دعاؤه – صلى الله عليه وسلم – لأنس بن مالك بكثرة المال والولد وهو مشهور. ويروى عن أنس – رضي الله عنه – في حديثه: " جاءَتْ بي أُمِّي أُمُّ أَنَسٍ إلى رَسولِ اللهِ ﷺ، وَقَدْ أَزَّرَتْني بِنِصْفِ خِمارِها، وَرَدَّتْني بِنِصْفِهِ، فَقالَتْ: يا رَسولَ اللهِ، هذا أُنَيْسٌ ابْني، أَتَيْتُكَ بِهِ يَخْدُمُكَ فادْعُ اللَّهَ له، فَقالَ: اللَّهُمَّ أَكْثِرْ مالَهُ وَوَلَدَهُ. قالَ أَنَسٌ: فَوَاللهِ إنَّ مالي لَكَثيرٌ، وإنَّ وَلَدي وَوَلَدَ وَلَدي لَيَتَعادُّونَ عَلَى نَحْوِ المِئَةِ، اليَومَ.

---

(1) The speaker: Al-Bukhari – Source: Sahih Al-Bukhari – page or number: 7274. Conclusion of the speaker: sound.
(2) The speaker: Al-Bukhari – Source: Sahih Al-Bukhari – page or number: 3868. Conclusion of the speaker: sound.

Anas (may God be content with him) narrated, "My mother, Umm Anas, came to God's Messenger (ﷺ). She made my lower garment out of the half of her headdress, and she used the other half to cover my upper body and said, "God's Messenger, here is my son Anas. I have brought him to you so that he can serve you. Invoke the blessings of God upon him." The Holy Prophet (ﷺ) said, "O God, increase his wealth and progeny." Anas said, "By God, my fortune is now immense, and my children and grandchildren are more than one hundred.[1]

5)تكثير الطعام والماء:

أ– ومن ذلك قصة أبي هريرة حيث روى عشرات الرجال من قدح لبن ناولهم إياه نبينا محمد – صلى الله عليه وسلم –.
(والقصة في صحيح البخاري).

ب – قصة جابر بن عبد الله في غزوة الخندق وإطعامه للمئات من الصحابة من قدر واحد.
(والقصة في صحيح البخاري وفي مسلم وفي مسند الإمام أحمد)

5. Food and water being increased

A. The narration of Abu Hurairah, where dozens of men narrated about a glass of milk that Prophet Muhammad (ﷺ) gave them. (This story is in Sahih Al-Bukhari.)

B. The narration of Jabir bin Abdullah at the Battle of the Trench when the Prophet (ﷺ) fed hundreds of companions from one pot. (This story is in Sahih al-Bukhari, in Muslim, and the Musnad of Imam Ahmad.)

6)تسبيح الحصى في يديه - ﷺ

6. Pebbles in his (ﷺ) hand glorifying God

عن أبي ذرٍ رضي الله عنه قال: إني لشاهدٌ عند النبي صلى الله عليه وسلم وفي يدهِ حَصَى فسبّحنَ، ثم دفعهنّ إلى أبي بكرٍ فسبّحنَ في يدهِ، ثم دفعهنّ إلى عمرُ فسبّحنَ في يدهِ، ثم دفعهنّ إلى عثمانَ فسبّحنَ في يدهِ، ثم دفعهنّ إلينَا فلم يُسبّحنَ في يدِ أحدٍ منا.

Abu Dharr (may God be content with him) narrated, "I witnessed the Prophet (ﷺ) holding pebbles in his hand, and they glorified God.[2]

---

(1) The speaker: Muslim – Source: Sahih Muslim – page or number: 2481. Conclusion of the speaker: sound.
(2) The speaker: Ibn Hajar Al-Asqalani – Source: muafaqat alkhabar alkhabar – page or number: 1/215
Conclusion of the speaker: [His men] are all trustworthy

7. Water flowing from his (ﷺ) fingers

وعن عبد الله بن مسعود رضي الله عنه قال كُنَّا نَعُدُّ الآيَاتِ بَرَكَةً، وأَنتُمْ تَعُدُّونَهَا تَخْوِيفًا؛ كُنَّا مع رَسُولِ اللَّهِ صَلَّى الله عليه وسلَّمَ في سَفَرٍ، فَقَلَّ المَاءُ، فقَالَ: اطْلُبُوا فَضْلَةً من مَاءٍ، فجَاؤُوا بإنَاءٍ فيه مَاءٌ قَلِيلٌ، فأَدْخَلَ يَدَهُ في الإنَاءِ، ثُمَّ قَالَ: حَيَّ على الطَّهُورِ المُبَارَكِ، والبَرَكَةُ مِنَ اللَّهِ. فَلَقَدْ رَأَيْتُ المَاءَ يَنْبُعُ مِن بَيْنِ أصَابِعِ رَسُولِ اللَّهِ صَلَّى اللهُ عليه وسلَّمَ، ولَقَدْ كُنَّا نَسْمَعُ تَسْبِيحَ الطَّعَامِ وهو يُؤْكَلُ.

`Abdullah (may God be content with him) narrated that he used to consider miracles as God's Blessings, but the people considered them to be a warning. He said, "Once we were with God's Messenger (ﷺ) on a journey, and we ran short of water. He (ﷺ) said, 'Bring the water remaining with you.' The people brought a bowl containing a little water, and he placed his right hand in the bowl and said, 'Come to the blessed water, and the Blessing is from God.' I saw the water flowing from among the fingers of God's Messenger (ﷺ) and, no doubt, we heard the meal glorifying God when it was being eaten (by him)." [1]

وعن جابر بن سمرة رضي الله عنه قال قال رسول الله ﷺ إنِّي لأَعْرِفُ حَجَرًا بمَكَّةَ كانَ يُسَلِّمُ عَلَيَّ قَبْلَ أَنْ أُبْعَثَ إنِّي لأَعْرِفُهُ الآنَ.

8. Inanimate objects speaking to him (ﷺ)

Jabir bin Samura (may God be pleased with him) narrated that he heard God's Messenger (ﷺ) say, "I recognize the stone in Mecca which used to greet me with salutations before my advent as a Prophet, and I recognize it even now." [2]

عن علي بن أبي طالب رضي الله عنه قال كنتُ مع النَّبِيِّ ﷺ بمَكَّةَ، فخَرَجنا في بَعضِ نواحِيها فما استقبلَه جبلٌ ولا شجرٌ إلَّا وهوَ يقولُ: السَّلامُ عليكَ يا رسولَ اللَّهِ.

Imam 'Ali bin Abi Talib (may God bless him) narrated, "I was with the Prophet (ﷺ) in Mecca. We left to one of its districts, no mountain or tree was in front of him (ﷺ) saying: 'Peace be upon you, O Messenger of God.'" [3]

---

(1) The speaker: Al-Bukhari – Source: Sahih Al-Bukhari – page or number: 3579. Conclusion of the speaker: sound.
(2) The speaker: Muslim – Source: Sahih Muslim – page or number: 2277. Conclusion of the speaker: sound.
(3) the speaker: Al-Albani – Source: Da'ifa Tirmidhi – page or number: 3626. Conclusion of the speaker: is weak.

وعن أبو حميد الساعدي رضي الله عنه أَقْبَلْنا مع النبيِّ ﷺ مِن غَزْوَةِ تَبُوكَ، حتَّى إذا أَشْرَفْنا عَلَى المَدِينَةِ قالَ: هذِه طابَةُ، وهذا أُحُدٌ، جَبَلٌ يُحِبُّنا ونُحِبُّهُ.

Abu Humaid (may God be pleased with him) narrated, "We returned in the company of the Prophet (ﷺ) from the Holy Battle of Tabuk. And when we came upon Medina, the Prophet (ﷺ) said, "This is Teeba, and this is Uhud, a mountain that loves us, and we love it." [1]

9)شفاء المرضى بريقه - صلى اللّه عليه وسلم - كما جرى لعلي بن أبي طالب كما في صحيح البخاري.

9. The sick being healed

وعن سهل بن سعد الساعدي أنَّ رَسولَ اللَّهِ ﷺ قالَ يَومَ خَيْبَرَ: لَأُعْطِيَنَّ هذِه الرَّايَةَ غَدًا رَجُلاً يَفْتَحُ اللَّهُ عَلَى يَدَيْهِ، يُحِبُّ اللَّهَ ورَسولَه، ويُحِبُّهُ اللَّهُ ورَسولُهُ، قالَ: فَبَاتَ النَّاسُ يَدُوكُونَ لَيْلَتَهُمْ: أَيُّهُمْ يُعْطَاهَا؟ فَلَمَّا أَصْبَحَ النَّاسُ غَدَوْا عَلَى رَسولِ اللَّهِ صلَّى اللهُ عليه وسلَّمَ كُلُّهُمْ يَرْجُو أَنْ يُعْطَاهَا، فَقالَ: أَيْنَ عَلِيُّ بنُ أَبِي طَالِبٍ؟ فقِيلَ: هو -يا رَسولَ اللَّهِ- يَشْتَكِي عَيْنَيْهِ، قالَ: فأَرْسِلُوا إلَيْهِ. فأُتِيَ به فَبَصَقَ رَسولُ اللَّهِ صلَّى اللهُ عليه وسلَّمَ في عَيْنَيْهِ ودَعَا له، فَبَرَأَ حتَّى كَأَنْ لَمْ يَكُنْ به وجَعٌ، فأَعْطَاهُ الرَّايَةَ، إلخ الحديث.

Sahl (may God be pleased with him) narrated that during the Battle of Khaibar, the Prophet (ﷺ) said, "Tomorrow I will give the banner to someone who will be given victory (by God) and who loves God and His Apostle and is loved by God and His Apostle." So the people wondered all night as to who would receive the banner. In the morning, they all hoped that he (ﷺ) would be that person. God's Messenger (ﷺ) said, "Where is `Ali?" He was told that `Ali was suffering from eye trouble, so he (ﷺ) applied saliva to Ali's eyes and invoked God to cure him. Ali was at once cured as if he had no ailment. The Prophet (ﷺ) gave him the banner. Ali said, "Should I fight them until they become Muslims?" The Prophet (ﷺ) said, "Go to them calmly and patiently until you enter their land. Then, invite them to Islam, and tell them of what is enjoined upon them, for, by God, if God gives guidance to someone through you, it is better for you than possessing red camels." [2]

---

(1) The speaker: Al-Bukhari – Source: Sahih Al-Bukhari – page or number: 4422. Conclusion of the speaker: sound.
(2) The speaker: Al-Bukhari – Source: Sahih Al-Bukhari – page or number: 4210. Conclusion of the speaker: sound.

10. Telling about things that will happen in the future

وقد أخبر النبي –صلى الله عليه وسلم– بأمور غيبية كثيرة كُلّ خبر منها معجزة في ذاته، منها ما حدث في حياته ومنها ما حدث بعدها ومنها ما لم يحدث بعد، يقول حذيفة بن اليمان– رضي الله عنه–: (لَقَدْ خَطَبَنَا النَّبيُّ صَلَّى اللهُ عليه وسلَّمَ خُطْبَةً، ما تَرَكَ فِيهَا شيئًا إلى قِيَامِ السَّاعَةِ إلَّا ذَكَرَهُ، عَلِمَهُ مَن عَلِمَهُ وجَهِلَهُ مَن جَهِلَهُ، إنْ كُنْتُ لَأَرَى الشَّيْءَ قَدْ نَسِيتُ، فأعْرِفُ ما يَعْرِفُ الرَّجُلُ إذَا غَابَ عنْه فَرَآهُ فَعَرَفَهُ).

Hudhaifa (may God be pleased with him) narrated, "The Prophet (ﷺ) once delivered a speech in front of us wherein he (ﷺ) left out nothing but mentioned everything that would happen until the Final Hour. Some of us stored this in our memories, and some forgot it. After that speech, I began to see events taking place (which had been referred to in the speech), but I had forgotten them (before their occurrence). Then I would recognize such events as a man recognizes another man who has been absent and then sees and recognizes him."[1]

11. Describing the Battle of Mutah while he (ﷺ) was in Medina

من معجزات النبي –صلى الله عليه وسلم– معرفته لأحداث ووقائع غزوة مؤتة، وهي من المعارك التي لم يشارك النبي –صلى الله عليه وسلم– بها، وحدثت على أطراف بلاد الشام في السنة الثامنة للهجرة، فقد رأى النبي –صلى الله عليه وسلم– أحداثها وهو جالس في المدينة، حيث روي عن النبي –صلى الله عليه وسلم– أنّه جلس على المنبر في المسجد والناس من حوله فأخذ يُحدّثهم عن أحداثها بالتّفصيل حتى أنّه أخبرهم باستشهاد القادة الثلاث، فلمّا عاد الجيش وجد الناس وقائعها مطابقةً لما أخبر عنه النبي –صلى الله عليه وسلم–.

Among the miracles of the Prophet (ﷺ) was his knowledge of the events and incidents of the Battle of Mutah. This was one of the battles in which the Prophet (ﷺ) did not participate. It took place on the outskirts of the Levant in the eighth year of migration. The Prophet (ﷺ) saw its events while he was sitting in Medina. The Prophet (ﷺ) sat on the pulpit in the mosque with the people around him and told them about its events in detail until he (ﷺ) told them of the martyrdom of the three leaders. Peace be upon him.

---

(1) The speaker: Al-Bukhari – Source: Sahih Al-Bukhari – page or number: 6604. Conclusion of the speaker: sound.

قال أنس بن مالك -رضي الله عنه-: (أنَّ النبيَّ ﷺ، أنَّ النبيَّ صَلَّى اللهُ عليه وسلَّمَ نَعَى زَيْدًا، وجَعْفَرًا، وابْنَ رَوَاحَةَ لِلنَّاسِ قَبْلَ أنْ يَأْتِيَهُمْ خَبَرُهُمْ، فقالَ: أخَذَ الرَّايَةَ زَيْدٌ فأُصِيبَ، ثُمَّ أخَذَ جَعْفَرٌ فأُصِيبَ، ثُمَّ أخَذَ ابنُ رَوَاحَةَ فأُصِيبَ وعَيْنَاهُ تَذْرِفَانِ: حتَّى أخَذَ الرَّايَةَ سَيْفٌ مِن سُيُوفِ اللَّهِ، حتَّى فَتَحَ اللَّهُ عليهم)

Anas (may God be content with him) narrated that the Prophet (ﷺ) had informed the people about the deaths of Zaid, Ja`far and Ibn Rawaha before the news of their deaths had reached them. With his eyes overflowing with tears, he said, "Zaid took the banner and was martyred; then Ja`far took the banner and was martyred, and then Ibn Rawaha took the banner and was also martyred. Finally, the banner was taken by one of God's Swords (Khalid bin Al-Walid), and God gave them (the Muslims) victory." [1]

---

(1) The speaker: Al-Bukhari – Source: Sahih Al-Bukhari – page or number: 4262. Conclusion of the speaker: sound.

Bibliography

1- https://salawat.net/dalayel2

2- https://dalailalkhayrat.com/

3- https://salawathub.com/

4- https://www.deenislam.co.uk/dalail

1- Fereig, Sami M., Remembrance of God in Islam. Published by Fercan Corporation, Waterloo, Ontario, 2021.

2- Fereig, Sami M., The Path to Contentment in Islam. Published by Fercan Corporation, Waterloo, Ontario, 2021.

3- Lings, Martin. Muhammad. Cambridge: Islamic Texts Society, 1991.

4- Nasr, Seyyed Hossein. Muhammad: Man of God. Chicago: Kazi Publications, 1995.

5- Ogunnaike, Oludamini. Poetry in Praise of Prophetic Perfection: A Study of West African Arabic Madīḥ Poetry and Its Precedents. Cambridge: Islamic Texts Society, 2020.

6- Schimmel, Annemarie. And Muhammad is His Messenger: The Veneration of the Prophet in Islamic Piety. Chapel Hill: University of North Carolina Press, 1985.

١- التفسير الميسر – المؤلف نخبة من أساتذة التفسير – مجمع الملك فهد لطباعة المصحف الشريف – الطبعة الثانية – 1430 هـ – 2009م.

٢- الدلالات الواضحات على دلائل الخيرات وشوارق الأنوار في ذكر الصلاة والسلام على النبي المختار ﷺ للإمام أبي عبد الله محمد بن سليمان الجزولي. المؤلف: يوسف بن إسماعيل النبهاني. الناشر: دار المقطم للنشر والتوزيع – مصر – 2009.

٣- الرحيق المختوم. المؤلف: صفي الرحمن المباركفوري – الناشر: وزارة الأوقاف القطرية – قطر – 1428هـ–2007م.

٤- الروضات العرشية في الكلام على الصلوات المشيشية. المؤلف: عبد السلام بن مشيش. تحقيق أحمد فريد المزيدي. الناشر: دار الأفاق العربية – مصر – الطبعة الأولى – 2010.

٥- السيرة النبوية. المؤلف: أبو الفداء إسماعيل بن عمر بن كثير القرشي الدمشقي – المحقق: مصطفى عبد الواحد – الناشر: دار المعرفة للطباعة والنشر – بيروت – 1396هـ – 1976م.

٦- السيرة النبوية. المؤلف: عبد الملك بن هشام بن أيوب الحميري المعافري – علق عليها وأخرج أحاديثها، وصنع فهارسها: عمر عبد السلام تدمري – الناشر: دار الكتاب العربي – بيروت – الطبعة الثالثة –1410هـ –1990م.

٧- القول الأسمى في بيان صفات وأسماء الله الحسنى. المؤلف: الشيخ محمد بن صالح العثيمين – جمعه وأعده: عرفان بن سليم العشا حسونة الدمشقي – الناشر: دار الفكر – بيروت 1426 هـ –2005م.

٨- أسماء الله الحسنى الثابتة في الكتاب والسنة. المؤلف: محمود عبد الرازق الرضواني – الناشر: مكتبة سلسبيل – القاهرة – الطبعة الأولى – 1426هـ.

9- دلائل الخيرات وشوارق الأنوار في ذكر الصلاة على النبي المختار صلى الله عليه وسلم. المؤلف: أبى عبد الله محمد بن سليمان الجزولي. الناشر: المكتبة العصرية للطباعة والنشر – مصر – 2008.

10- سنن الترمذي. تعليق الشيوخ: أحمد محمد شاكر وعبد العزيز بن عبد الله بن باز ومحمد ناصر الدين الالباني ومحمد بن صالح العثيمين ومحمد حامد الفقي وعبد الله بن عبد الرحمن البسام وصالح بن فوزان الفوزان وعبد المحسن بن حمد العباد وعبد العزيز الراجحي – الناشر: شركة الفلاح للنشر والتوزيع – مصر – الطبعة الأولى – 1439هـ – 2018م.

11- سنن النسائي. تعليق الشيوخ: أحمد محمد شاكر وعبد العزيز بن عبد الله بن باز ومحمد ناصر الدين الالباني ومحمد بن صالح العثيمين ومحمد حامد الفقي وعبد الله بن عبد الرحمن البسام وصالح بن فوزان الفوزان وعبد المحسن بن حمد العباد وعبد العزيز الراجحي – الناشر: شركة الفلاح للنشر والتوزيع – مصر – الطبعة الأولى – 1439هـ – 2018م.

12- سنن أبي داود. تعليق الشيوخ: أحمد محمد شاكر وعبد العزيز بن عبد الله بن باز ومحمد ناصر الدين الالباني ومحمد بن صالح العثيمين ومحمد حامد الفقي وعبد الله بن عبد الرحمن البسام وصالح بن فوزان الفوزان وعبد المحسن بن حمد العباد وعبد العزيز الراجحي – الناشر: شركة الفلاح للنشر والتوزيع – مصر – الطبعة الأولى – 1439هـ –2018م.

13- شموس الأنوار ومعادن الأسرار على صلاة القطب الأكبر مولانا عبد السلام بن مشيش (سلسلة الأنوار الإلهية). المؤلف: العارف بالله سيدي محمد المرون. الناشر: دار الكتب العلمية – بيروت – 2008.

14- صحيح الإمام البخاري. المحقق: محمد فؤاد عبد الباقي – الناشر: مكتبة الامام مسلم للنشر والتوزيع – مصر الطبعة الأولى – 1436هـ – 2015م.

15- صحيح الإمام مسلم شرح النووي. المحقق: محمد فؤاد عبد الباقي– الناشر: مكتبة أبي سهيل – تنزانيا – منارة الإسلام للنشر والتوزيع – مصر – الطبعة الأولى –1441هـ–2020م.

16- فاذكروني أذكركم. المؤلف: عبد الحليم محمود – الناشر: دار المعارف – القاهرة – 1981.

17- لسان العرب – ابن منظور الأنصاري–دار صادر – بيروت – الطبعة الثالثة –1414 هـ–1994م.

18- مسند الإمام أحمد بن حنبل. المحقق: أحمد محمد شاكر – الناشر: دار الحديث – القاهرة – الطبعة الأولى 1416 هـ –1995م.

19- مطالع المسرات بجلاء دلائل الخيرات. المؤلف: محمد المهدي الفاسي. الناشر: المكتبة العصرية للطباعة والنشر – مصر – 2005.

20- ولله الأسماء الحسنى فادعوه بها. جمع وترتيب: أحمد عبد الجواد – قراءة: عبد الحليم محمود – الناشر: مكتبة الكليات الأزهرية – الأزهر – القاهرة – 1985.

www.ingramcontent.com/pod-product-compliance
Lightning Source LLC
Chambersburg PA
CBHW080327030726
47593CB00010B/2919